Research Reports ESPRIT

Project 300 · REQUEST · Vol. 1

Edited in cooperation with
the Commission of the European Communities

M. Kersken   F. Saglietti (Eds.)

Software Fault Tolerance

Achievement and Assessment Strategies

 Springer-Verlag

Berlin Heidelberg New York London Paris
Tokyo Hong Kong Barcelona Budapest

Editors

Manfred Kersken
Francesca Saglietti
Gesellschaft für Reaktorsicherheit (GRS) mbH
Forschungsgelände, W-8046 Garching, FRG

ESPRIT Project 300 "Reliability and Quality of European Software Technology (REQUEST)" belongs to the Subprogramme "Software Technology" of ESPRIT, the European Strategic Programme for Research and Development in Information Technology supported by the Commission of the European Communities.

Project 300 aims at progress in quantification of software quality and reliability, thus enabling their specification, prediction, measurement, and assurance. The areas of work include: identification and validation of metrics for the "quality" concept, and construction of a quantitative model for its prediction; development of metrics and models for reliability prediction, both for software systems in general and for domains requiring ultra-high reliability; and investigation of the impact of using formal methods on reliability prediction and demonstration. The commitment to work in metric and model validation has led to an emphasis on the topic of collection of software project data.

CR Subject Classification (1991): D.1, D.2.0 − 1, D.4.5, C.4, B.4.5, K.6.4, J.7

ISBN 3-540-55212-X Springer-Verlag Berlin Heidelberg New York
ISBN 0-387-55212-X Springer-Verlag New York Berlin Heidelberg

Publication No. EUR 13538 EN of the
Commission of the European Communities,
Scientific and Technical Communication Unit,
Directorate-General Telecommunications, Information Industries and Innovation,
Luxembourg

LEGAL NOTICE
Neither the Commission of the European Communities nor any person acting on behalf of the Commission is responsible for the use which might be made of the following information.

Typesetting: Camera ready by author
Printing and Binding: Weihert-Druck GmbH, Darmstadt
45/3140 – 543210 – Printed on acid-free paper

Foreword

The first ESPRIT programme contained several ambitious projects, of which REQUEST, with its wide brief covering all issues of assessment of quality and reliability of software process and product, was one. Within REQUEST, the research described in this volume, concerning those special problems of software that is required to have extremely high reliability, was particularly difficult and ambitious.

The problems of software reliability are essentially twofold. On the one hand there is a concern with methods for *achieving* adequate reliability, on the other hand there is a need to *evaluate* what has actually been achieved in a particular case. Naturally, far more effort has been spent over the years on the former problem; indeed, there is a sense in which all of conventional software engineering can be seen as a response to this problem. However, it is becoming clearer than ever that we can only claim to have a truly scientific approach, and so justify the description software *engineering*, when we are able to measure the attributes of process and product.

It is still common to find software development methods recommended to users on purely anecdotal grounds. This is not good enough. Rational choices between rival approaches can only be made on the basis of quantified costs and benefits.

Even more worrying is the tendency to argue that a software product can be depended upon merely because it has been developed by honest men using such anecdotal 'good practice'.

These concerns become extremely serious when we are dealing with software that will play a safety-critical role - that, in the worst case, can kill many people if it fails. Here it seems clear that special techniques are required, over and above those used in ordinary best practice, *and we need objective evidence of their efficacy.* Perhaps even more important in cases like this, we need to know that the actual software product is sufficiently dependable *by evaluating its reliability.* It is to these crucial issues concerning the evaluation of process and product for very high reliability that the work in this volume is addressed.

The difficulties here are immense. Consider, as an example, the analogy that is sometimes drawn between hardware *redundancy* and software *diversity.* In the hardware case it is often claimed that is possible to build a system of arbitrarily high reliability from components of arbitrary unreliability. Of course, such an assertion rests upon the assumption of independence of random component failures, but this may sometimes be quite plausible. In the case of failures arising from software faults (or indeed from hardware design faults) in a design-diverse system, such an assumption is simply false, and the theoretical modelling problems become very hard.

Issues of diversity, of version dependence, of adjudication between the outputs of different versions are the subject matter of the volume. This is new work at the frontiers of our current understanding. As Manfred Kersken says in the Introduction, this is not intended for students; rather it is a description of some significant new work which has advanced our understanding in this difficult, but vitally important area of computer science.

I was involved with the REQUEST project as a reviewer for almost five years. This was a very enjoyable time, involving interesting discussions and not a little argument. Now that I have had a chance to see all the results collected together, I can only say that it confirms my original view that this should be read by anyone with a professional interest in safety-critical and fault-tolerant computing.

Bev Littlewood
Centre for Software Reliability
City University
London

Acknowledgement

The software fault-tolerance group of the REQUEST project would like to thank the Commission of the European Communities for supporting its work. These thanks go especially to the CEC Project Officers of DG XIII, Pierre-Yves Cunin, Jack Metthey and Jean-Jacques Lauture who have accompanied the project with their most helpful administrative and professional advice.

We also would like to thank our project reviewers

Professor Bev Littlewood, The City University, London
Harry Sneed, SES GmbH, Neubiberg
Robert Troy, Verilog, Toulouse
Sinclair Stockman, British Telecom, Martlesham Heath

who have always taken a great interest in our work and contributed actively to the success of the project. Their ideas and proposals as well as their constructive criticism were always highly appreciated by our group.

The good quality of research and development work in projects like REQUEST is always dependent on discussions and exchange of experience among colleagues. We cannot name here the numerous colleagues within the REQUEST project who contributed with fruitful discussions, ideas and proposals to our work, but we would like to express here many thanks to all of them. We are also grateful to our man at the wheel G. Hugh Browton, STC. We know that it was not always easy to navigate such a heavy ship through the reefs, but we always felt safe and fairly treated.

We gratefully acknowledge the publication of parts of this book by the following publishers:

IEE & British Computer Society:

F. Saglietti: Software Diversity Metrics Quantifying Dissimilarity in the Input Partition. In: IEE Software Engineering Journal, January 1990, Vol.5, No.1

IEEE Computer Society Press:

F. Saglietti: Location of Checkpoints in Fault-Tolerant Software. In: Proc. of the 5th Jerusalem Conf. on Information Technology (JCIT-5), Jerusalem (IL), October 1990

Elsevier / North-Holland:

F. Saglietti: A Theoretical Evaluation of the Acceptance Test as a Means to Achieve Software Fault-Tolerance. In: Proc. of the IFIP/IFAC/EWICS Conf. on Hardware and Software for Real-Time Process Control, Warsaw (PL), May/ June 1988

Pergamon Press:

F. Saglietti, W. Ehrenberger: Software Diversity - Some Considerations about its Benefits and its Limitations. In: Proc. of the 5th IFAC Workshop on Safety of Computer Control Systems (SAFECOMP 86), Sarlat (F), 1986

F. Saglietti: Strategies for the Achievement and Assessment of Software Fault-Tolerance. In: Proc. of the 11th IFAC World Congress, Tallinn (USSR), August 1990

Springer-Verlag:

F. Saglietti, M. Kersken: Quantitative Assessment of Fault-Tolerant Software Architecture. In: Proc. of the 3rd Int. GI/ ITG/ GMA Conf. on Fault-Tolerant Computing Systems, Informatik-Fachberichte, Band-Nr. 147, F. Belli, W. Görke (Hrsg.), Bremerhaven (D), September 1987

F. Saglietti: The Impact of Voter Granularity in Fault-Tolerant Software on System Reliability and Availability. In: Proc. of the 4th International GI/ ITG/ GMA Conf. on Fault-Tolerant Computing Systems, Informatik-Fachberichte, Band-Nr. 214, W. Görke, H. Sörensen (Hrsg.), Baden-Baden (D), September 1989

F. Saglietti: The Impact of Forced Diversity on the Failure Behaviour of Multi-Version Software. In: Proc. of the GI & VDI/VDE-GMA Conf. "Prozeßrechensysteme '91", Informatik-Fachberichte, Band-Nr. 269, G. Hommel (Hrsg.), Berlin (D), February 1991

Finally, our thanks go to Helga Moosmang for the careful preparation of the manuscript.

Garching, November 1991   M. Kersken, F. Saglietti

Table of Contents

Chapter 4

The Impact of Forced Diversity on the Failure Behaviour of Multiversion Software

Francesca Saglietti

Chapter 5

Functional Diversity

Paola Burlando, Laura Gianetto, Maria Teresa Mainini

Chapter 6

**Estimation of Failure Correlation in Diverse Software Systems
with Dependent Components**
Francesca Saglietti

Chapter 7

**Measurement of Diversity Degree by Quantification of Dissimilarity
in the Input Partition**
Francesca Saglietti

Chapter 8

Comparison of Mnemonics for Software Diversity Assessment
Michael Martin Burke, David Nicholas Wall

Chapter 9

The FRIL Model Approach for Software Diversity Assessment
Michael Martin Burke, David Nicholas Wall

Chapter 10

Reliability Evaluation
Maria Teresa Mainini

Chapter 11

The Impact of Voter Granularity in Fault-Tolerant Software on System Reliability and Availability
Francesca Saglietti

Chapter 12

A Theoretical Evaluation of the Acceptance Test in Recovery Block Programming
Francesca Saglietti

Chapter 13

Location of Checkpoints by Considering Information Reduction
Francesca Saglietti

Chapter 14

Conclusions
Manfred Kersken

Contributors

Michael Martin Burke, SEMA Group Scientific Division,
Dorchester, United Kingdom

Paola Burlando, Esacontrol Bailey,
Genova, Italy

Wolfgang Ehrenberger, Gesellschaft für Reaktorsicherheit (GRS) mbH,
Garching, Germany

Laura Gianetto, Esacontrol Bailey,
Genova, Italy

Manfred Kersken, Gesellschaft für Reaktorsicherheit (GRS) mbH,
Garching, Germany

Maria Teresa Mainini, Esacontrol Bailey,
Genova, Italy

Francesca Saglietti, Gesellschaft für Reaktorsicherheit (GRS) mbH,
Garching, Germany

David Nicholas Wall, AEA Technology,
Winfrith, United Kingdom

Chapter 1

Introduction

Manfred Kersken

The increasing contribution of software to the overall project costs in information technology caused a strong demand from industry to control the development, validation and maintenance of software.

Software is also increasingly introduced into safety related systems. The computational power of systems including software, as against purely hardwired systems, allows a more accurate determination of process variables and functions. In many cases this results in the possibility of smoother control of process which reduces the stress on the plant under control, thus increasing its reliability. On the other hand, there is a need to qualify the system component software. The qualification of software is recognized as a difficult task, especially for software which has to fulfill high reliability requirements. Therefore improved methods and techniques to aid in the establishment and assessment of highly reliable software systems is required not only by the industry but also by assessors, licensors and regulatory bodies.

For controlling the process of establishing and assessing a software product in terms of quality and reliability to be achieved, measurable features of the product itself and measures related to the production process need to be identified. The measures are incorporated into models describing the behaviour of interesting parameters during specific phases of the software life cycle.

One problem is that observations during the production process may correlate only weakly with properties of the final product. For example there may be no unique relationship between error finding and removal during structured walk-throughs or design inspections and the reliability of the final software product in terms of its probability to perform correctly (according to its specification) during a given period of time.

Another problem arises from the fact that observations during production are often performed in a very unstable environment, e.g. during an informal debugging phase where the number of testers is changing together with their skill, altering test strategies and so forth. Improvement calls for tools that assist in achieving more persistent production and verification phases in the software life cycle and thus will allow a "smoother" input stream to the models coming, due to a more stable production and verification environment.

To tackle the problems of quantitative assessment of software quality and reliability it was felt that common efforts within Europe are necessary. Therefore the REQUEST project was established, running under the European Strategic Programme for Research and Development in Information Technology ESPRIT. Main objectives of REQUEST were

- to investigate reliability and quality in terms of both close control of the development process and measurement of the software product,

    - to provide techniques and tools that will assist in assurance and management procedures both pre- and post-production.

The sub-projects within REQUEST were concerned with

    - data collection and storage in order to obtain sound data for model validation,

    - quality measurement, modelling and prediction in order to establish a Constructive Quality Modelling System COQUAMO,

    - reliability measurement, modelling and prediction with the aims of

        - extending the applicability of models to more phases of the software life cycle,

        - improving and adapting existing models,

        - tackling the specific problems of software systems used in areas where high reliability requirements are stated.

This book covers especially the latter topic.

One of the basic principles to establish highly reliable software (besides fault-avoidance and fault-removal) is fault-tolerance. In software fault-tolerance dissimilar or diverse versions of programs are developed which solve the same specified problem in different ways. The outputs of the dissimilar versions are adjudicated according to some strategy which serves for failure detection. As a reaction the whole system may mask the failed output and continue its operation either as normal or in a controlled degraded manner. Crucial failures of such a fault-tolerant system are those of the adjudication mechanism as well as common failures of the single versions.

The work of the software fault-tolerance and diversity group within the REQUEST project was focussed on these specific aspects of fault-tolerant software systems.

Two methods for reducing failure dependence among dissimilar versions, i.e. forced diversity and functional diversity, were investigated.

Another focal point was the measurement of failure dependence among diverse versions. A set of practical methods including statistical inference from past failure data, static and dynamic analysis techniques, physical comparison of machine code and mnemonics as well as an expert system approach were proposed to meet this goal.

Furthermore, a software fault-tolerance model was developed which enables the evaluation of diverse software systems via Markovian chains, including the ability of handling common failure probabilities.

Specific important features of adjudication mechanisms have been considered with respect to their impact on reliability achievement. A strategy has been developed for the optimal location of checkpoints, determining the intermediate stages of program execution where the states of diverse programs are compared.

From these very specific topics which have been dealt with, it can be seen that this book is not meant to be an educational textbook for students. Its objective is rather to present the results of the research work of the

REQUEST fault-tolerance and diversity group to interested colleagues working in the area of computer fault-tolerance. It also aims to provide developers with guidelines for the construction of fault-tolerant computer systems.

Assessors and licensors of systems with high reliability requirements will find advice in identifying crucial areas in the development process of diverse software systems and in the software products themselves. This includes proposals for the quantitative measurement of safety attributes by observation of product characteristics and behaviour.

Chapter 2

Overview

Maria Teresa Mainini, Francesca Saglietti, David Nicholas Wall

2.1   The Concept of Software Fault-Tolerance

For safety-critical applications requiring the use of ultrahigh reliable computers, special techniques have to be adopted in order to develop and assess particularly reliable programs. So far, the existing constructive methods to avoid errors during the programming phase as well as the analytical methods to remove them during the testing phase have proved to be useful, but unfortunately insufficient to ensure the required degree of correctness.

Therefore, some additional measures have to be taken in order to permit the system to tolerate those errors, which could be neither avoided nor detected during development. This can be achieved by introducing redundancy into the system, so that it may survive or at least be safely shut down in spite of the occurrence of single component failures.

Of course, the concept of redundancy by reproducing perfect copies of the same item can only be effective with respect to failures caused by physical constraints such as the wear-out process in hardware.

Due to the logical nature of most programming errors, software redundancy will, on the contrary, achieve fault-tolerance only if it includes logically different alternative solutions intended to produce the same specified result: this is the fundamental concept of software diversity.

This strategy generally consists of a number of different versions written on the basis of the same specification, and of a decision mechanism - the so-called adjudicator - capable of determining, at each predefined checkpoint, the one among the alternate results to be accepted as correct. If this cannot be done, the adjudication mechanism will raise an alarm (s. Fig. 2.1).

In any case, when compared with the average behaviour of a single version, this architecture allows a remarkable reliability improvement by identifying the occurrence of sporadic component failures, possibly at the cost of a decreased system availability.

Thus, the undetectable failure probability reduces to the case of wrong adjudication, which may be due to an intrinsic error of the decision mechanism or to the occurrence of common failures in the diverse components.

This abstract configuration allows several realistic implementations, essentially differing in the order of subjecting the alternate results to the adjudicator. In this sense, the two basic structures are those resulting in a system output after having analyzed the diverse components

-   in parallel or
-   in series,

as described in detail in the following.

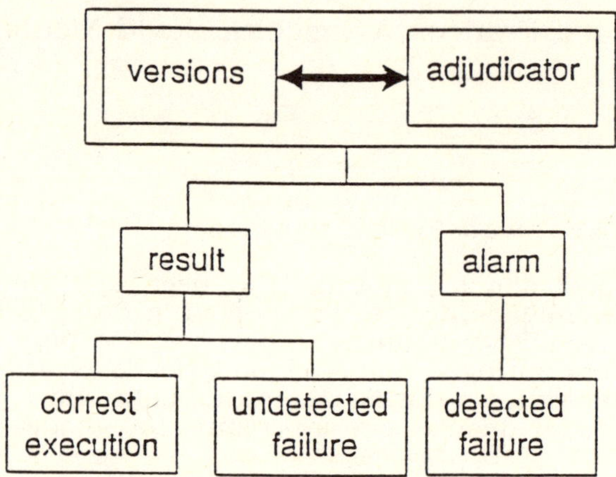

Fig. 2.1.   General structure of software diversity

N-Version Programming

The N-Version programming technique (abbreviated NVP) consists of N diverse programs executed in parallel and of a voter examining the N outputs and determining, if possible, a consensus value on the basis of a predefined majority, as shown in Fig. 2.2.

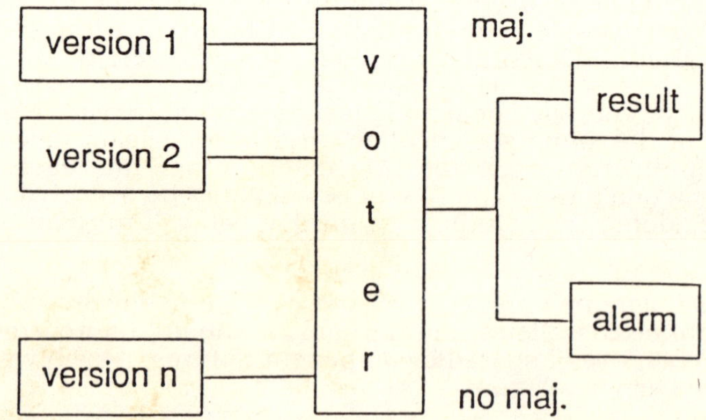

Fig. 2.2.   N-Version programming architecture

In this case, the undetectable system failure is due to the critical case of a majority of identically wrong results, whereas no existing majority will result in system unavailability.

Recovery Block Programming

The alternative method of adjudicating on the diverse results in a linear order is called Recovery Block programming (in the following RBP). The outputs are separately subjected in a predefined sequence to an acceptance test, which will check them for reasonableness until one of them is accepted, as illustrated in Fig. 2.3.

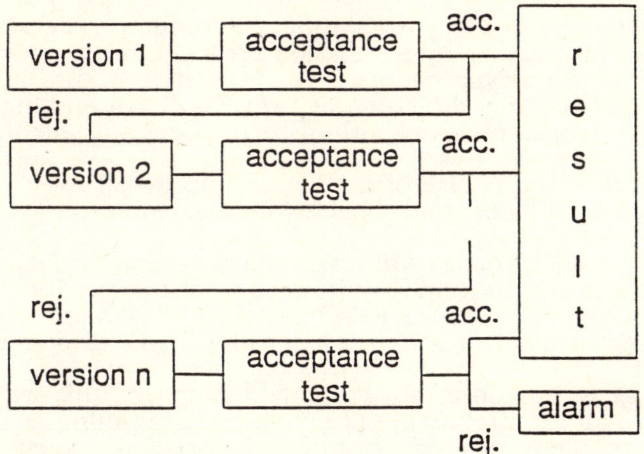

Fig. 2.3.   Recovery Block programming architecture

Here the crucial situation causing an undetected system failure is the acceptance of a wrong result, while the rejection of each alternative will lead to an alarm state.

These are in short the two fundamental software fault-tolerant architectures giving rise by their variation and combination to any other state-of-the-art configuration.

As already remarked, the crucial error causes may be subdivided into two groups:

-   errors affecting the diverse components

and

-   errors affecting the adjudicator.

Both error sources are analyzed in the following chapters, to identify the most important conclusions resulted from theoretical research and their links to real-world experimental observations.

2.2   Failure Dependence

2.2.1   The Problem of Failure Dependence

The question revealing as crucial for the achievement and assessment of software fault-tolerance concerns the failure dependence of diverse components.

Originally software diversity was modelled according to the already established theory for physical items; in other words, redundant products developed independently were assumed to show an independent failure behaviour, as their failure occurrence was represented by a random process without common error sources.

Soon, however, this assumption was rejected by both theoretical considerations (s. [ECK85]) and experimental data (s. [KNI86]).

In fact, it was easily recognized that the randomly developed diverse versions are linked together by a common error source represented by the identical input profile. Experiments have proved that the inputs are not equally failure-prone: the difficulty of correct data-handling will rather depend on the varying complexity within the problem specification.

This implies that the choice of a common input will have a remarkable impact on the probability of similar behaviour of the alternates.

In particular, the common failure probability cannot be estimated as simply as for hardware redundancy by means of the product of the single failure probabilities; for software this has to be additionally weighted by a factor describing the amount of dependence among the diverse programs.

Unfortunately, so far no accurate model estimating this weighting parameter is known, as the probability of similar programming errors is mainly due either to problem misunderstanding because of specification ambiguities or to thinking traps caused by unknown or unquantifiable human factors (s. [GRA88]).

In order to be able to reduce, as much as possible, this source of unreliability during development as well as to permit its estimation during validation, we have nonetheless identified several aspects which we regard as responsible or representative for the dependence degree and which will be presented in the next section.

It has to be pointed out that even an unknown degree of dependence may be suitably handled during the testing phase, assuming the common failure probability of diverse versions to be lower than the probability of at least one program performing correctly.

In fact, in addition to fault-tolerance, diversity also offers the possibility of an economic testing strategy, the so-called back-to-back test, which consists of the automatic comparison of diverse outputs.

Due to the low effort required, this test may be realistically carried out to a considerable length, being passed as long as there is agreement between the observed results. The main restriction of this testing technique is its inability to detect common failures resulting in identically wrong outputs.

With respect to the experimental data of Knight and Leveson (see [KNI86]) comparing 27 programs developed at the universities of Virginia and California-Irvine, these critical failures are shown in chapter 3 to be less than the detectable ones. Theoretical argumentations (also in chapter 3) imply that this condition should be expected to be fulfilled in general.

In this case a sufficiently long back-to-back testing phase without disagreement would permit to bound, with affordable effort, the rate of undetectable failures by the specific reliability requirements of the application considered.

2.2.2   Reduction of Failure Dependence

This section is devoted to methods to reduce failure dependence during the development process.

2.2.2.1   Forced Diversity

Diversity experiments performed so far (s. [BAR85], [BAR87], [KEL83], [KNI86]) have shown that common error occurrence is not only strongly affected by the specific characteristics of the underlying problem to be solved, but also by the techniques adopted to solve it. Therefore, beside the common bugs exclusively caused by the intrinsic difficulties of the task requested, we have in general to expect a number of similar errors generated and enabled to persist by commonalities in the development process. The latter may be due to process similarities resulting in identical failure-proneness, as ambiguities in the common specification, inaccuracies of a common numerical approach, inadequacies of the common programming language, difficulties in data handling because of unsuitable common data structures, unexhaustiveness of common testing strategies, etc.

Although we cannot reduce the problem complexity determined by the task to be performed by the system, we may try nonetheless to decrease the common failure probability with respect to this second error class; to obtain this reduction, we will extend the redundancy concept from the original mere product diversity to the more general process diversity, ensuring dissimilarity of the development methodologies, e.g. with regard to aspects as:

- specification language
- implementation language
- algorithms
- data structures
- tools
- personnel
- testing methods.

In this case those errors, which are preferably produced or remain undetected as a result of a particular methodology rather than of another one, will tend to affect different alternates and thus will be possibly tolerated by the redundant architecture. The success of this "forced diversity" highly depends, among other factors, on the adjudication mechanism: in [LIT87] Littlewood and Miller prove that the expected reliability of an inhomogeneous NVP-system requiring at least one correct version out of N is higher than that achieved by conventional, unforced diversity. In case of a voter requiring a (n+1)-out-of-(2n+1)-majority, however, the analogous result does not necessarily hold.

These theoretical results are confirmed in chapter 4 by means of the experimental data published in [KEL83] for both the cases of 1-out-of-2 and 2-out-of-3 systems. In fact, forcing the use of 3 different specification languages to develop 18 programs at UCLA only improved the average system reliability with respect to the former majority, not to the latter one. Moreover, even a positive impact of diversified methodologies may be too low to justify the additional effort required by them.

Thus the primary difficulty for the efficient use of this technique consists of identifying those error classes expected to essentially affect the programming process in question, in order to force effective dissimilarity with respect to the really responsible process phases.

2.2.2.2 Functional Diversity

The problem of masking software errors appears to be successfully solved by the extension of the fault tolerance technique from hardware to software. However, as already described in 2.2.1 , due to the basic difference between the nature of hardware and software faults, some important drawbacks exist. In conclusion, the limitations highlighted have created an obstacle to the adoption of normal diversity as an industrial solution for ultra reliable systems, because, in addition to a high cost of implementation, it cannot guarantee a sufficient certainty of having achieved the required reliability and/or safety level.

A promising answer to the problems posed by normal diversity is represented by functional diversity. Functional diversity is a methodology consisting of developing N different implementations of the same requirement specification where each implementation uses a different input set and different algorithms to compute the same required output. With respect to normal diversity, the basic difference consists in the fact that in functional diversity, the N teams begin to work separately immediately, having, as only common point, the requirement specification, which can be expressed as each team generating a different software specification. The modelling of the problem and the input data are different. These characteristics should grant a higher diversity degree and then avoid, at least to a certain extent, the drawbacks caused by dependency.

Due to the relevance of the potential improvements implied by the adoption of functional diversity with respect to normal diversity, a deep study of this methodology was undertaken. The major results are presented in chapter 5.

2.2.3 Measurement of Failure Dependence

Once the development of the versions is concluded, the crucial problem in assessing the system reliability is the quantification of the dependence degree correlating their failure behaviour. As already mentioned, this is still an open question, which may be approached from different sides by modelling more aspects possibly related to the occurrence of common errors.

2.2.3.1 Measurement by Statistical Inference from Past Failure Data

An estimation of failure dependence based on failure history of diverse versions is suggested in chapter 6. Here the failure process of a two-fold system is assumed to follow a bivariate exponential distribution with common failure rate λ_{12} and rates λ_1 resp. λ_2 for failures occurring only in the first resp. only in the second alternative.

The correlation coefficient $C_{12} = \lambda_{12}/(\lambda_1+\lambda_2+\lambda_{12})$ representing the pro-bability of common failure under the condition of an arbitrary failure occurrence, can then be evaluated as the quotient of common and arbitrary past failure observations; in fact, this quotient will not considerably vary throughout the testing and correction phase, assuming errors detected to have comparable contributions to the total failure rate.

Apart from this questionable assumption, the method requires a sufficiently high number of data related to system history, in order to achieve an acceptable estimation accuracy.

2.2.3.2 Measurement by Static Analysis

In case of insufficient failure observations available, we may compare the products with regard to their static features. An approach in this direction has been proposed in chapter 6, by comparing for each input x the corresponding control flow paths $P_1(x)$ and $P_2(x)$ in two diverse versions P_1 and P_2. To each path $P_i(x)$ we can associate a complexity metric $Z(P_i(x))$, $i \in \{1,2\}$, expected to represent its failure proneness. The lower of both path measures, i.e. $\min(Z(P_1(x)), Z(P_2(x)))$, maximizes the probability of x causing a common failure, whereas the higher one, i.e. $\max(Z(P_1(x)), Z(P_2(x)))$, models the minimal probability of an arbitrary failure resulting by handling x.

The correlation C_{12} mentioned above can then be conservatively approximated as the quotient of these both failure probabilities (min/max) averaged with respect to the operational input profile.

The main draw-back of this technique is the problematic question about the choice of a suitable complexity metric permitting to express our degree of confidence in the correctness of control flow paths.

On the other hand, this approach reflects the fact that similar design errors may result in similar wrong control decisions; analogously, common errors in different decision flows will probably affect non-identical input subsets, so that this will increase their detectability during an extensive testing phase.

This last statement is also valid for the program data flow: in case of dissimilar data processing, analogous programming errors are expected to propagate in different directions, thus increasing the probability of being found by the adjudicator.

2.2.3.3 Measurement by Dynamic Analysis

This was the underlying idea of a further method described in chapter 7 and based on the comparison of input partitions induced by diverse programs.

With respect to a predefined equivalence relation on the control and data flows, each program implies a subdivision of the input set into disjoint subsets of data, which are "commonly handled" by the program, as their execution will activate equivalent transformations.

Relative to design errors affecting all of such an input class, the efficiency of a redundant system can then be evaluated by comparing the alternative input partitions: similar subsets are interpreted as the result of similar reasoning during the program development, thus implying higher proneness to common faults.

Dependent on the equivalence relation considered, it may be very difficult to recognize or even quantify the degree of the partition difference by means of a static analysis. Therefore, the approach presented in chapter 7 suggests to make use of the dynamic program behaviour to obtain a graphical representation of the diversity achieved.

This can be easily done during a random testing phase by executing all alternates with the same inputs and by taking gradually into account the equivalence class coverage achieved. Tools for the automatic determination of structural coverage already exist, giving for example the percentage of segments, branches or paths having already been verified during a testing phase. The deviation of the resulting coverage curves may then be interpreted as a measure of partition dissimilarity.

2.2.3.4 A Pattern Matching Approach

This approach to measurement of failure dependence concentrates on determining the diversity of two programs as a starting point for a measure of failure dependence. Currently only the first stage of the process has been developed, i. e. the evaluation of program diversity. The move from this to having a measure of failure dependence has not been attempted. This second step is not trivial as, although diversity should contribute toward reduced failure dependence, the need to produce new code will lead to an increased number of failures, some of which could contribute to increased failure dependence.

This approach to assessing diversity relies on the fact that, in producing a working computer program regardless of high level language used, the implementation passes through a stage where it exists as assembler level mnemonics. The approach essentially takes the mnemonics of the two versions of the software and applies pattern matching techniques to them to determine how similar they are.

The actual matching process involves placing the two sets of mnemonics in a pair of circular buffers and performing the matching process as one set of mnemonics is stepped past the other. The patterns can be compared by taking single mnemonics or in pairs, threes up to groups of five.

The number of matches for each position can then be plotted as a histogram. The form of the histogram gives information on the similarity of the two software versions.

For example, if the same software is placed in both buffers, then one would see a very large peak at position one. The number of matches at other positions would arise from random matches and can be regarded as a noise component, although there is a clear exception to this when pieces of code are repeated through the software. These repeats will produce subsidiary peaks on the histogram.

The initial work showed great promise being able to identify similar and different software versions. This exercise was restricted to very small programs and was only successful once areas of common code, essentially input and output coding, were removed by hand. The extension to larger programs proved much less encouraging, for single mnemonic matching the noise level was found to be high. This observation led to the introduction of the mechanism for matching groups of mnemonics, which considerably improved the results, but they remained far from satisfactory in terms of the procedures ability to identify commonality and diversity.

The causes of the failure of the method based on such simple matching procedures are easy to identify from an examination of any piece of code. The program structure can be broken down into blocks, e.g. at a coarse level of sub-routines and procedures. Within these large blocks there are many further sub-units down to single lines of code, whose order of execution does not alter the outcome of the program, but whose order makes a great difference to the result obtained from the diversity analysis.

Should it be possible to do some pre-analysis of the programs, whose diversity is to be assessed, to identify the major elements of the coding, then the method could still prove helpful. The blocks of code with identical functionality could be compared to ascertain diversity rather than attempt a global comparison. This approach would appear to be possible and would be quite consistent with the construction of code that contains checkpoints as the location of the checkpoints would appear to introduce natural divisions in the code that could be used for comparison purposes. It is however concluded that much more sophisticated pattern matching techniques can accommodate effects of line juxtaposition and the like if the method is to be successful.

This approach is presented in more detail in chapter 8.

2.2.3.5 An Expert System Approach

The development of an expert system approach to measure diversity, like the use of pattern matching, is only one of the two steps required to obtain a measure of failure dependence. The approach adopted to making this first step however could, it is believed, be extended to help make the second step from a diversity assessment to producing a measure of failure dependence.

The basis of much judgement on the level of redundancy and diversity in many areas of engineering rests upon experience. The common nature of engineering systems means that this experience is quite wide-spread and believed to be well understood. However in some areas of engineering the experience and knowledge base is rather narrow, in these cases attempts have been made to encapsulate the experience and knowledge that is available in a formal structure through an expert system. In such a system the attributes, features thought to be important are identified and then weighted according to their importance in a formal logic structure. This formal structure can then be used to evaluate the property in question of the new system from its attributes. In the case of engineering systems there is often a sufficient number of examples available to validate the system.

The attempt has been made to use a similar expert system approach to produce a means of assessing software diversity. The reasons for the choice of this method are limited experience and knowledge base. Further, because the rules that arise from the experience and knowledge base and that are to be captured are uncertain, it was chosen to use the fuzzy support logic language FRIL to construct the expert system. This language has the property that it contains as part of its fundamental structure uncertainty. In place of a simple true or false logic it works on measures for the support for a statement and against a statement being true expressed in terms of a support pair.

As a very much simplified example of this property one might take the statement "motor vehicles with large engines go quickly". Experience shows this is generally true, there is a definite degree of support for this, but there is also definite support for this not being true, e.g. large haulage vehicles have large engines and are slow. The support pair would then be expressed as (X, Y) where X would be the fractional support for the statement being true and 1-Y being the fractional support for the statement being false, the fraction Y-X being the uncertainty. The ability of the language to deal with uncertainty has one further advantage in that it allows the situations when the information about the system or systems in question is incomplete to be treated.

The software diversity tool gathers the attributes contributing to diversity at the lowest level; this might be information such as: programming language, computer, cost of production, size of the software. These attributes are formed into a hierarchical structure with information being fed in at the lowest level only. This low level information is then combined to build up support for higher level attributes such as process and product diversity. The combinatorial structure providing the necessary weighting of importance of the attributes such support for, against and the uncertainty for the software being diverse emerges at the highest level.

The resulting tool has been set up to run on a PC and provided with a simple menu-driven user interface. The validation of the basic structure has been undertaken in terms of checking for logical consistence. However validation against real data remains to be undertaken as does the step from producing a support pair for software diversity and timing it into a statement about common mode failure of the software versions which is of ultimate interest. It is noted that these last steps are difficult because of the very limited amount of data that is available to provide an effective validation/calibration of the system. Until such data becomes available two roles for the tool are foreseen.

In the first role the system should be examined by those having competence in the area of software diversity to ensure that the results the tool produces are consistent with expert opinion. This will give the expert knowledge embodied in the system a broader base of opinion and not be restricted to that of those directly involved in the development of the tool.

The second use is for application to practical problems, the first class being the use of the tool to produce a measure of the diversity of software versions that are already in existence. The availability of a reproducible standard rather than a mechanism subject to the vagaries of daily variation in human opinion being of value. Second, the tool can be used to explore the best means of producing diverse software versions for a given application.

The concept of the FRIL model and its subsequent implementation as a tool are described in chapter 9. The tool runs on a PC with expanded memory and can be made available through its joint developers CAP Scientific and Winfrith Technology Centre with the agreement of FRIL systems.

2.2.3.6 Measurement of Functional Diversity

The basic point, permitting a substantial degree of diversity to be achieved among the N versions of a functionally diverse architecture, are the different input sets. Of course this epidermic feeling must be consolidated by a deeper investigation on the nature of the approaches; it is important that the difference of the input sets is not overwritten and invalidated by a transformation mapping the original, different inputs into data common to multiple versions on which the same algorithms are applied. The effectiveness of the architecture lies in its correct and not only formal methodology application that must be checked and controlled.

To identify if the differentiation among the N versions really exists, it is necessary to model each version so that the specific features contributing to the achievement of functional diversity can be outlined. The modelling approach followed is based on the so called "functional semantics". A semantic model is applied to the process models underlying the N versions composing a system. Based on the identification of functional semantics, it will be possible to define metrics that, taking into account commonalities and differences of their semantic aspects, will permit to measure the degree of functional diversity achieved.

The functional semantics of a process model is then represented by the meanings of its functions and of the objects, or domains, on which the functions operate.

To evaluate the diversity degree of the process model, using their functional semantics, it is necessary to evaluate the degree of diversity of their functional semantics. In this evaluation, a particularly crucial role is played by the semantic domains. In fact, it can be demonstrated that if the process models use different domains, they cannot use the same functions.

The basic approach in the definition of functional diversity metrics relies on the classification of the domains on the basis of the number of different process models using them. It is clear that if a high percentage of domains is used by more process models, the diversity degree of the system will not be satisfactory, whilst if the common domains are very few the process models will not have many commonalities.

Following this approach, a number of different metrics can be defined. Each of them measures a different aspect of diversity degree impact on the more relevant system features; the features that have been considered are:

- EFFECTIVENESS of the system w. r. t. the planned redundancy,

- INDEPENDENCE of the versions composing the system with respect to each other,

- REDUNDANCY of the versions,

- GLOBAL REDUNDANCY of the system.

In section 5.9 a description of the methods adopted to model the process models represented by the different versions composing a functionally diverse system is given. In section 5.12 some metrics are proposed, permitting to evaluate the diversity degree of versions and systems.

2.3   Evaluation of Reliability of Fault Tolerant Software

2.3.1   General Considerations

Fault tolerant software architectures have been mainly designed to achieve better system figures from the point of view of correct system behaviour. A particular relevance is obviously given to system reliability. It is then necessary to have a mean to evaluate the actual reliability level achieved.

Usually reliability evaluations are achieved by means of models, which use the behavioural and/or structural characteristics of the system as parameters for the evaluation.

The traditional fault tolerant architecture models, having been designed for hardware components, are not portable to software, due to the different nature of errors: in fact, they must not handle random errors due to breakage or aging of components, but design errors. On the other hand, many computer scientists have dealt with software reliability modelling on the basis of two different approaches: a topological one, aiming to predict reliability considering the program architecture, or a black-box one considering a program as a source of errors having a certain rate that can be calculated as a function of the observed error distributions. Hardly any of these models takes into account redundancy and its implications on system reliability. Scott's model (see [SCO84] and [SCO84a]) is the only one meeting these requirements. The approach explained in chapter 10 is inspired by it. The main differences consist in the formalism used (Markovian chains) and in the capability of dealing with common error probabilities.

2.3.2 Model Application to Functionally Diverse Software

An attempt to apply the markovian model to functionally diverse software has been made. In this case the model predicts the reliability of the system on the basis of its specifications. The three factors influencing its reliability are: the reliability of the versions, the commonalities among them and the architecture type. The reliability of the versions may be estimated on the basis of their complexity and of an error rate per line derived from previous experiences. The commonalities among the versions are evaluated using their semantics and particularly identifying those parts using the same semantic domains. These parts are identified as "common parts". The modelling approach is based on the assumption that an error which occurred in a common part affects all the versions in the same way, whilst an error occurring in a non common part is specific of the version and thus will not imply a similar erroneous behaviour in another version. This conservative assumption permits to easily evaluate the conditional probabilities used in the markovian model of the specific architecture. In section 5.14 the approach followed and the results achieved are described.

2.4 Adjudication Mechanisms

Beside the still unsolved problem of failure dependence, a further decisive question regards the choice of a suitable adjudication procedure determining one out of possibly more diverging outputs resulting from the single versions. In fact, even within the two major categories of mechanisms intended to fulfill this task - voting systems for NVP and acceptance tests for RBP - there is still a wide range of features to be selected in order to determine the most suitable fault-tolerant configuration for the particular application considered. Many of these aspects can have opposite consequences on the reliability achievement, so that the optimal solution has to be determined by maximizing the overall positive impact of these drivers on the resulting fault-tolerance.

2.4.1 Voting Systems

The essential characteristic of a voter is the majority required to accept a consensus value and which has to be determined on the basis of the underlying reliability targets and redundancy costs.

A particular feature hereby is its granularity, i.e. the level at which the output is adjudicated (s. [KEL86], [TSO87]). In fact, in case of a result of complex type, a majority may be necessary at high level, comparing the output vectors as a whole, or it may be sufficient to find an agreement at a lower level, adjudicating each vector component separately. In case of multi-level complexity, this question includes many intermediate possibilities. Obviously, a higher-level majority is more demanding than a lower-level one and thus will result in more reliable, but less available consensus values. According to the safety requirements of the specific application with respect to single output variables, an optimizing strategy has been developed in chapter 11 to support the choice of the most suitable level of voting granularity.

2.4.2   Acceptance Tests

A test of acceptance is generally defined to check a condition expected to be met by successful program execution; in particular, it is not intended to guarantee complete result correctness and thus includes a wide scope of possible comprehensiveness levels, ranging from a cursory check for anomalous states in the program to a completely exhaustive output verification. In order to cope with the problem of classifying this large variety of adjudicators bearing the same name, they were characterized in chapter 12 by introducing the concept of "coarseness" resp. "fineness" to measure their exhaustiveness.

The effectiveness of an acceptance test obviously will highly depend on this quantifiable parameter, although aiming at too high comprehensiveness may lead to large and complex test programs and therefore to high costs and design fault proneness. On the other hand, keeping the acceptance test simple, so that its run-time overheads are reasonable and the test itself is reliable will probably cause cursoriness. In order to permit a rational selection of the suitable check for a given application, the test behaviour may be optimized by modelling its error detection capability and required costs with respect to its filtering coarseness and design correctness.

2.4.3   Location of Checkpoints

A fundamental question in applying software redundancy concerns the level of modular decomposition at which it should be applied, i.e. how large a recovery block or the piece of code between two successive comparisons should be (see [STR85]). In fact, the code size between checkpoints can be determinant for the effectiveness and the cost of the fault-tolerant strategy. Checking the intermediate results after small pieces of code obviously implies lower error latency, but also higher execution time overhead. Moreover, decision points limit design diversity, as their definition requires the agreement of alternate versions at a higher level of detail, increasing their expected failure dependence. On the other hand, a large modular decomposition ensures higher version independence and lower execution time overheads, but may result in a cursory test incapable of localizing the occurring errors.

The optimal solution will vary for each specific case, depending on the loss of information involved by the modular computations: the more the information contained in the inputs is reduced by their transformation, the better it will be to insert additional checkpoints to support the identification of incorrect intermediate values (at the cost, however, of time and failure dependence). A strategy to evaluate the effectiveness of checkpointing in order to optimize it, is presented in chapter 13.

2.5   Conclusion

In spite of the higher effort required by software redundancy, it is presently considered as a major strategy to achieve ultra-high reliability. In fact, recent experiments (e.g. those reported in [SHI88]) have shown that a number of errors tolerated by diversity could not be detected by the conventional testing techniques.

The intention of this chapter was to provide an overview on all the aspects we identified as possibly restricting software fault tolerance; in particular, the scope of this work includes the indication of a number of new parameters defined and studied within a topic, which so far still represents an open question.

Many of the drivers investigated may have opposite consequences on the final system reliability. The major trade-offs were reported, referring to the specific models optimizing them.

The effects described are considered as mainly responsible for the system failure behaviour and may thus serve as guidelines during the development of fault-tolerant architectures.

References

[BAR85] M. Barnes, P. Bishop, B. Bjarland, G. Dahll, D. Esp, P. Humphreys, Y. Lahti, S. Yoshimura, A. Ball, O. Hatlevold: PODS (the Project on Diverse Software). OECD Halden Reactor Project, HRP-323, 1985

[BAR87] M. Barnes, P. Bishop, B. Bjarland, G. Dahll, D. Esp, Y. Lahti, H. Välisuo, P. Humphreys: Software Testing and Evaluation Methods (the STEM Project). OECD Halden Reactor Project, HWR-210, 1987

[ECK85] D.E. Eckhardt, L.D. Lee: A Theoretical Basis for the Analysis of Multiversion Software Subject to Coincident Errors. IEEE Transactions on Software Engineering, Vol. SE-11, No. 12, 1985

[GRA88] T. Grams: Thinking Traps in Programming - A Systematic Collection of Examples. Proc. of the IFAC Symposium SAFECOMP '88, Fulda, F.R.G., 1988

[KEL83] J.P.J. Kelly, A. Avizienis: A Specification-Oriented Multi-Version Software Experiment. 13th Int. Symposium on Fault-Tolerant Computing, Milano, Italy, 1983

[KEL86] J.P.J. Kelly, A. Avizienis, B.T. Ulery, B.J. Swain, R.T. Lyu, A. Tai, K.S. Tso: Multi-Version Software Development. Proc. of the IFAC Workshop SAFECOMP '86, Sarlat, France, 1986

[KNI86] J.C. Knight, N.G. Leveson: An Experimental Evalution of the Assumption of Independence in Multiversion Programming. IEEE Transactions on Software Engineering, Vol. SE-12, No. 1, 1986

[LIT87] B. Littlewood, D.R. Miller: A Conceptual Model of Multi-Version Software. Procs. of FTCS-17, IEEE 1987

[SCO84] R.K. Scott, J.W. Gault, D.F. McAllister, J. Wiggs: Experimental Validation of Six Fault Tolerant Software Reliability Models. IEEE 1984

[SCO84a] R.K. Scott, J.W. Gault, D.F. McAllister, J. Wiggs: Investigating Version Dependence in Fault Tolerant Software. IEEE 1984

[SHI88] T.J. Shimeall, N.G. Leveson: An Empirical Exploration of Five Software Fault Detection Methods. Proc. of the IFAC Symposium SAFECOMP '88, Fulda, FRG, 1988

[STR85] L. Strigini, A. Avizienis: Software Fault-Tolerance and Design Diversity: Past Experience and Future Evolution. Proc. of the IFAC Workshop SAFECOMP '85, Como, Italy, 1985

[TSO87] K.S. Tso, A. Avizienis: Community Error Recovery in N-Version Software: A Design Study with Experimentation. Proc. of FTCS-17, IEEE 1987

Considerations on Software Diversity on the Basis of Experimental and Theoretical Work

Francesca Saglietti, Wolfgang Ehrenberger

3.1 The Different Failure Sets of a Two-fold Diverse System

Diversity has been proposed as a method of achieving software fault-tolerance. Several versions of a program are written on the basis of the same specification and executed in parallel. Most of the past considerations about reliability improvement through multiversion programming depended on the assumption that independently developed programs would also fail independently. Recent work, however, has presented convincing arguments both in an experimental [KNI86] and a theoretical [ECK85] approach leading to the conclusion that the independence assumption does not hold in the general case. Therefore an analysis of reliability of diverse programming has to include the effect of dependent programming errors.

In the following we consider the economically interesting case of only two software versions S_1 and S_2, that may be regarded as two mappings f_1, f_2: $A \to B$ with the same input space A and output space B. The specification on which the two programs are based can be represented by a mapping f: $A \to B$, which defines the correct output data $f(x) \in B$ for each $x \in A$. If the programs are not error-free, two non-empty subsets F_1, $F_2 \subset A$ exist, consisting of exactly all input data, for which the respective program performs incorrect results, i.e.:

$$(1) \qquad F_i = \{x \in A \mid f_i(x) \neq f(x)\}, \; i \in \{1,2\}.$$

A diverse system can be designed in such a way that it does not fail in an uncontrolled manner as long as at least one of both programs performs correctly. Then the crucial input subset, which can lead to failure, is represented by the intersection of the above failure sets:

$$(2) \qquad F_{12} := F_1 \cap F_2 = \{x \in A \mid f_1(x) \neq f(x) \wedge f_2(x) \neq f(x)\}.$$

If we consider the possibility that an element $x \in F_{12}$ could be mapped by both versions on the same wrong output element $f_1(x) = f_2(x)$, we can further represent F_{12} as the union of the two disjoint subsets:

$$(3) \qquad F_{12} = F_{12}^{\neq} \cup F_{12}^{=},$$

where

$$(4) \qquad F_{12}^{\neq} = \{x \in F_{12} \mid f_1(x) \neq f_2(x)\}$$

and

(5) $F_{12}^{=} = \{ x \in F_{12} \mid f_1(x) = f_2(x) \}.$

The above considerations can be illustrated by Fig.3.1.

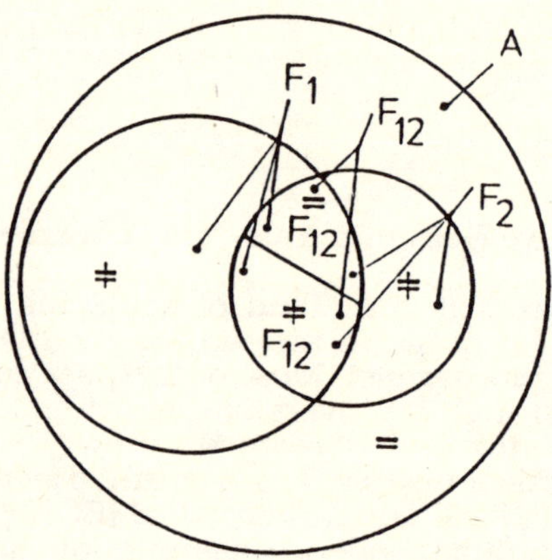

Fig. 3.1.   Sets of different failure types of a two-fold diverse software system

Interpreting the input data selection in future real operation as a process which selects the input data randomly according to a known operational demand profile Q, we can define the probabilities of selecting input data from each of the above subsets:

(6a) $p_i = Q(F_i), i \in \{1,2\}$

(7a) $p_{12}^{\neq} = Q(F_{12}^{\neq})$

(8a) $p_{12}^{=} = Q(F_{12}^{=}).$

In the case of real-time software we can similarly regard the time-dependent input data process as a random process modelled by the following variables:

(6b) T_i = time until the occurrence of an input from F_i, $i \in \{1,2\}$.

(7b) $T_{12}^{\neq}$ = time until the occurrence of an input from $F_{12}^{\neq}$.

(8b) $T_{12}^{=}$ = time until the occurrence of an input from $F_{12}^{=}$.

These variables are assumed to be exponentially distributed with the rates

$\lambda_1+\lambda_{12}$, $\lambda_2+\lambda_{12}$, $\lambda_{12}^{\neq}$ and $\lambda_{12}^{=}$ respectively, where $\lambda_{12}= \lambda_{12}^{\neq} + \lambda_{12}^{=}$.

An important advantage of the diverse situation is given by the possibility to estimate the "size" of the set

$$(9) \qquad A^{\neq} := (F_1 \cup F_2) \setminus F_{12}^{=} ,$$

through an automatic test, which only verifies the agreement or disagreement of the output data. Of course the effort taken by such a test is minimal compared with the cost of a test which requires at each step the manual or independent determination of the exact result.

If we could assume that in practical cases the subset $F_{12}^{=}$ would be small compared with the set $A^{\neq}$, i.e.

$$(10a) \qquad Q(F_{12}^{=}) < Q(A^{\neq})$$

or

$$(10b) \qquad \lambda_{12}^{=} < \lambda_1 + \lambda_2 + \lambda_{12}^{\neq},$$

we could rely with a certain confidence level on an automatic test, which, according to its low cost, could be performed to any possibly desired accuracy.

In this case, after having performed

(a) n test runs,

or

(b) a test of duration t_0,

without lack of agreement of the output data, we can bound the probability of selecting input data from

$A^{\neq}$ by $Q_f^{\neq}$ (or alternatively the rate $\lambda_1+ \lambda_2+ \lambda_{12}^{\neq}$ by $\lambda_f^{\neq}$)

at a given confidence level α:

$$(11a) \qquad P\,(Q(A^{\neq}) \leq Q_f^{\neq}) \geq \alpha$$

or

$$(11b) \qquad P\,(\lambda_1+ \lambda_2+ \lambda_{12}^{\neq} \leq \lambda_f^{\neq}) \geq \alpha,$$

applying as in [EHR83] the following formulae:

$$(12a) \qquad Q_f^{\neq} = 1 - \sqrt[n]{1-\alpha}$$

or

$$(12b) \qquad \lambda_f^{\neq} = \frac{-\ln(1-\alpha)}{t_0}$$

Conversely, if one would like to verify some given number for $Q_f^{\neq}$ or $\lambda_f^{\neq}$, we have to execute a test with

$$(13a) \qquad n = \frac{\ln(1-\alpha)}{\ln(1-Q_f^{\neq})} \quad \text{runs}$$

or of

$$(13b) \qquad t_0 = \frac{-\ln(1-\alpha)}{\lambda_f^{\neq}} \quad \text{duration.}$$

Together with the assumptions (10a), alternatively (10b), these considerations also imply a lower bound for the probability P_a, respectively $P_a(t)$ that both programs perform correctly (to the time t):

$$(14a) \qquad P_a = 1 - Q(A^{\neq}) - Q(F_{12}^{=}) > 1 - 2\,Q(A^{\neq}) \geq 1 - 2 \cdot Q_f^{\neq}$$

$$(14b) \qquad P_a(t) = e^{-(\lambda_1+\lambda_2+\lambda_{12})t} > e^{-2(\lambda_1+\lambda_2+\lambda_{12}^{\neq})t} \geq (e^{-\lambda_f^{\neq}t})2.$$

Now the question is, whether the above assumption is a realistic one or whether it represents an unacceptable restriction to the general case.

3.2　Experimental Approach

As described in [KNI86], at the universities of Virginia and California Irvine 27 versions of a program were developed independently from the same specification and then subjected to one million test cases. The major goal of this experiment was a statistically rigorous test of independence: The null hypothesis of independence of programming errors and subsequent execution failures was rejected with a confidence level of 0.99.

In the above notation the experimental results for each pair of programs are:

$$(15) \qquad n_i = \text{number of failures of } S_i, \; i \in \{1,2\}$$

$$(16) \qquad n_{12} = \text{number of failures of both } S_1 \text{ and } S_2,$$

so that we can approximate the failure probabilities by

$$(17) \qquad p_i \approx n_i \cdot 10^{-6}, \; i \in \{1,2\}$$

$$(18) \qquad p_{12} := p_{12}^{=} + p_{12}^{\neq} \approx n_{12} \cdot 10^{-6}$$

From these assumptions we can easily derive:

$$(19) \qquad Q(A^{\neq}) \geq Q(F_1 \backslash F_{12}) + Q(F_2 \backslash F_{12}) \approx (n_1+n_2 - 2 \cdot n_{12}) \cdot 10^{-6}$$

$$(20) \qquad Q(F_{12}^{=}) \leq Q(F_{12}) \approx n_{12} \cdot 10^{-6}.$$

In particular, if $n_{12} < n_1 + n_2 - 2 \cdot n_{12}$, we can consider the basic assumption (10a) as met.

The following tables 3.1, 3.2 and 3.3 give the results of the experiment of Knight and Leveson; see [KNI86] for details. In total 162 pairs of diverse versions have been considered. 153 of them reported failures.

Table 3.1. Version failure data (from [KNI86])

Version	Failures	Version	Failures
1	2	15	0
2	0	16	62
3	2297	17	269
4	0	18	115
5	0	19	264
6	1149	20	936
7	71	21	92
8	323	22	9656
9	53	23	80
10	0	24	260
11	554	25	97
12	427	26	883
13	4	27	0
14	1368		

Table 3.2. Correlated failures between UVA and UCI (from [KNI86])

		UVA Versions							
		1	2	3	4	5	6	7	8	9
	10	0	0	0	0	0	0	0	0	0
	11	0	0	58	0	0	2	1	58	0
	12	0	0	1	0	0	0	71	1	0
	13	0	0	0	0	0	0	0	0	0
	14	0	0	28	0	0	3	71	26	0
	15	0	0	0	0	0	0	0	0	0
	16	0	0	0	0	0	1	0	0	0
	17	2	0	95	0	0	0	1	29	0
UCI	18	0	0	2	0	0	1	0	0	0
Versions	19	0	0	1	0	0	0	0	1	0
	20	0	0	325	0	0	3	2	323	0
	21	0	0	0	0	0	0	0	0	0
	22	0	0	52	0	0	15	0	36	2
	23	0	0	72	0	0	0	0	71	0
	24	0	0	0	0	0	0	0	0	0
	25	0	0	94	0	0	0	1	94	0
	26	0	0	115	0	0	5	0	110	0
	27	0	0	0	0	0	0	0	0	0

Table 3.3. Occurrences of multiple failures in the experiment of Knight and Leveson
(from [KNI86])

Number	Probability	Occurrences
2	0.00055100	551
3	0.00034300	343
4	0.00024200	242
5	0.00007300	73
6	0.00003200	32
7	0.00001200	12
8	0.00000200	2

For these numbers the pairs of data $(n_{12}, n_1+n_2-2n_{12})$ are shown in figure 3.2.

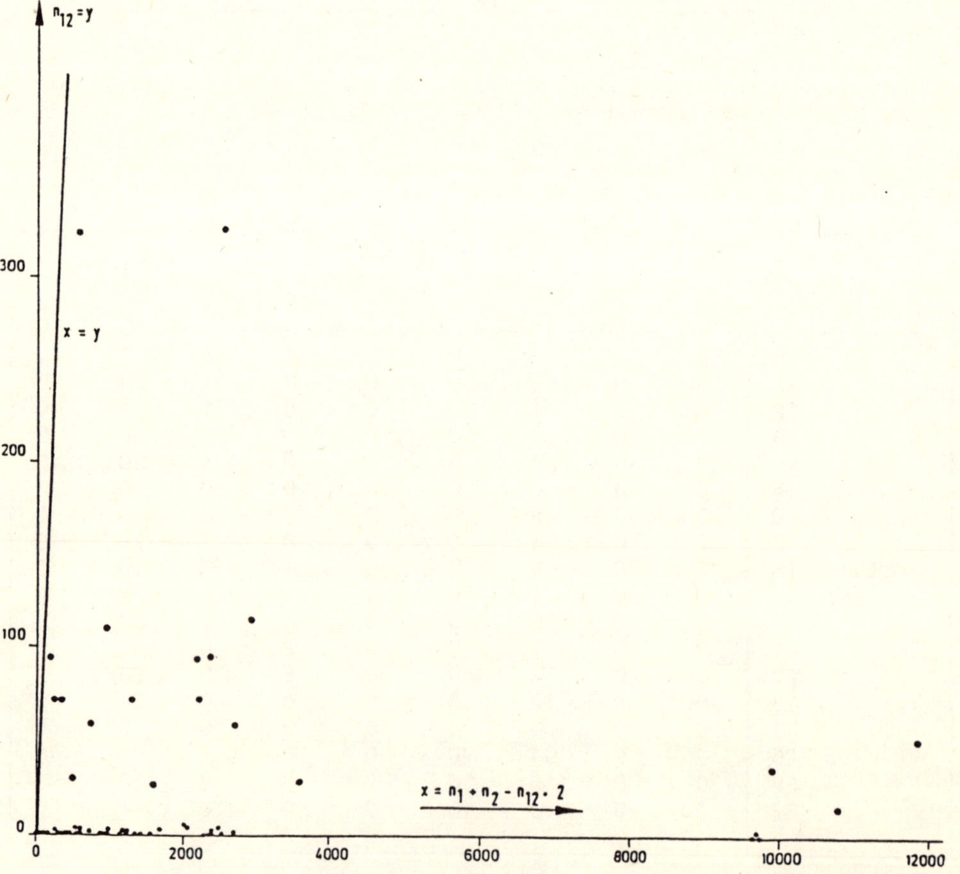

Fig. 3.2.   Common failures versus single failures in the experiment of Knight and Leveson

All points lie below the line x=y, thus supporting the assumption that failures in single versions of a diverse system are more probable than common failures of both versions. So (10a) can be considered as being fulfilled. A more detailed analysis shows: The arithmetic mean of the quotient $Y = n_{12}/(n_1 + n_2 - 2n_{12})$ is :

(21) $E(Y) = 0.013$,

with the variance

(22) $V(Y) = 0.004$.

Using Tchebychev's inequation

(23) $P(|Y-E(Y)| < k \cdot \sqrt{V}) \geq 1 - 1/k^2$

we obtain:

(24) $1/Y > 3.3$

for $1 - 1/k^2 = 0.95$, i.e. $k = 4.47$.

This means: With a confidence level of 95% it is to be expected that a single failure is at least 3.3 times more frequent than a common failure.

3.3 Theoretical Approach

A theoretical analysis of coincident errors is presented in [ECK85]. The model proposed there is based on the following considerations. The intensity function

(25) $\Theta : A \rightarrow [0,1]$

estimates for each $x \in A$ the proportion $\Theta(x) \in [0,1]$ of a large number of programs resulting in failure when executing on x. This mapping represents the varying difficulty in handling the single data correctly and thus the probability that a version S, chosen at random, will fail on a particular input.

In other words, Θ exactly defines the mathematical expectation of the score function V(x) of S given by:

(26) $V(x) = \begin{cases} 1 & \text{if S gives an incorrect output when executing x} \\ 0 & \text{if S gives a correct output when executing x} \end{cases}$

Thus

(27) $E[V(x)] = \Theta(x), \forall x \in A$

With the above notation, if we randomly choose two programs S_1 and S_2 with score functions $V_1(x)$ and $V_2(x)$ to a given specification, the probability that they will fail is:

(28) $Q(F_i) = \int V_i(x) \, dQ, \ i \in \{1,2\}$

with the expected value

$$(29) \qquad E[Q(F_i)] = E[\int V_i(x)\, dQ] = \int \Theta(x)\, dQ.$$

(Integrals are to be taken over the whole input space).
Moreover, we have

$$(30) \qquad Q(F_{12}) = \int V_1(x)\cdot V_2(x)\, dQ,$$

so that the mean common failure probability is given by

$$(31) \qquad E[Q(F_{12})] = E[\int V_1(x)\cdot V_2(x)\, dQ] = \int \Theta(x)^2 dQ,$$

owing to the fact that S_1 and S_2 have been independently chosen among a conceptual population of programs, which could have possibly been written.

In applications of software redundancy, Eckhardt and Lee [ECK85] expect the intensity function to be bounded by a relatively small value. In their examples the worst case presents 0.6 as the upper bound of Θ. This assumption is confirmed by the experiment of Knight-Leveson. Table 3.3 shows the occurrences of multiple failures. Thinking of the one million test cases being representative for the whole input space, we can estimate an upper bound of the intensity function considering the worst case of an input x causing 8 failures out of 27 programs. Thus we can apply the statistical theory of confidence intervals for the binomial distribution as in [STÖ70]:

$$(32) \qquad P(\,\Theta(x) \le g\,) \ge 0.95 \;\; \text{with}$$

$$(33) \qquad g = \frac{9 \cdot F_{18,38}(0,95)}{19 + 9\cdot F_{18,38}(0,95)} = 0.47$$

In our case condition (10a) is a very crucial one. It is expected to be satisfied if

$$(34) \qquad E\,[Q(F_{\overline{12}})] < E\,[Q(A^{\neq})].$$

This is always fulfilled, if

$$(35) \qquad E[Q(F_{12})] < E[Q(F_1 \backslash F_{12})] + E[Q(F_2 \backslash F_{12})],$$

which is a much weaker condition than above. Considering that

$$(36) \qquad E[Q(F_1 \backslash F_{12})] + E[Q(F_2 \backslash F_{12})] = 2\cdot E[Q(F_i)] - 2\cdot E[Q(F_{12})], \; i \in \{1,2\}$$

we can take formulae (29) and (31), obtaining

$$(37) \qquad \int \Theta(x)^2 dQ < 2\int (\Theta(x) - \Theta(x)^2)\, dQ,$$

which is equivalent to

$$(38) \quad 3\int \Theta(x)^2 dQ \quad < \quad 2\int \Theta(x) dQ.$$

As long as we can estimate the intensity function Θ to be below the value 2/3, as expected by Eckhardt and Lee for the general case, we can take the basic requirement to be fulfilled.

3.4 Additional Requirements

Of course all previous considerations were conservative in the sense that both the experimental and the theoretical approaches analyzed the total intersection F_{12} of two failure subsets, whereas to our intentions the only knowledge of the subset of F_{12} with identical wrong outputs would suffice to estimate the reliability of the system in case of ultra-high reliability requirements. So we should consider the probability that, given that two programs fail on an input x, they also produce exactly the same output. This possibility obviously depends at a great extent upon the range of values forming the output set B. We will clearly have two extremely different situations in case of B simply consisting of two boolean elements:

$$(39) \quad B = \{0,1\}$$

or if B ranges over n-tuples of real numbers out of a large interval:

$$(40) \quad B \;]-x,x[^n \; \text{with large x and n}.$$

Such aspects must certainly be regarded as important when deciding on automatic testing.

Besides, we should always require from diverse programs the use of different solution techniques (for example, distinct algorithms for numerical approximation) as often as possible. In this case the unavoidable common failures, which are due to the human limits in treating a particularly difficult input, wouldn't be surely eliminated, but they would probably have different effects on the final result, thus allowing the fault to be detected.

3.5   Comparison between Single and Diverse Use of Programs

In cases where failures occur, automatic testing is not sufficient. In such situations it is quite important to make sure whether diversity really brings an advantage when compared with a single program's execution. With the help of reliability models such as Littlewood's and Verrall's described in [LIT73], one can make a prediction of the failure rate $\lambda(t_0)$ of a single program, which has been tested and corrected for a period of duration t_0, so that leaving the test phase, the product in question is believed to have the probability of no failure in [0,t]:

$$(41) \quad R(t) = \exp(-\lambda(t_0)t).$$

The cost C_1 spent up to this point consists of the development cost C_S of the program S plus the cost of testing, which is proportional to the test time t_0 with proportionality constant σ_1, plus the cost C_T for test bed procurement:

$$(42) \quad C_1 = C_S + t_0 \cdot \sigma_1 + C_T.$$

Assuming both versions of a diverse system having equal development cost and the same prediction function of their failure rate, we can thus estimate the cost C_2 after a manual test phase of the same duration t_0 by:

$$(43) \qquad C_2 = 2 \cdot C_S + t_0 \cdot \sigma_2 + C_T,$$

where σ_2 is usually expected to be larger than σ_1, including corrections of both variants, although the simultaneous verification of the results is surely cheaper than the double work:

$$(44) \qquad \sigma_1 < \sigma_2 < 2 \cdot \sigma_1$$

Formulae (42) and (43) show that the additional effort required by diversity is given by:

$$(45) \qquad C_2 - C_1 = C_S + t_0 \ (\sigma_2 - \sigma_1).$$

If we had chosen the single version, the cost difference to the diverse system could have been spent to increase the test time t_0 by an additional duration

$$(46) \qquad \hat{t}_0 = \frac{C_S + t_0 \ (\sigma_2 - \sigma_1)}{\sigma_1} \ .$$

So finally we could expect the probability of no failure:

$$(47) \qquad \hat{R}(t) = \exp(-\lambda(t_0 + \hat{t}_0) \ t).$$

The probability of correct performance of the parallel application of two programs is computed interpreting the failure occurrence as a combination of three independent Poisson processes with failure rates λ_1, λ_2 and λ_{12} referring to the same times as in (6b) - (8b). They represent the randomness of the single and the common failures.

Defining T_1 and T_2 as in (6b) to be the random variables given by the time between failures of S_1 and S_2, it is easily seen that they are exponentially distributed with rates $\lambda_1 + \lambda_{12}$ and $\lambda_2 + \lambda_{12}$ respectively, so that (T_1, T_2) has a bivariate exponential distribution. As mentioned before, we assume here $\lambda_1 = \lambda_2$ and calculate the probability of correct performance of at least one version until time t:

$$
\begin{aligned}
(48) \quad R_{one}(t) \ &= \ 1 - P\{T_1 \le t, T_2 \le t\} = \\
&= \ P\{T_1 > t, T_2 > t\} + P\{T_1 > t, T_2 \le t\} + P\{T_1 \le t, T_2 > t\} = \\
&= \ \exp(-(\lambda_1 + \lambda_2 + \lambda_{12})t) + \exp(-(\lambda_1 + \lambda_{12})t) \cdot (1 - \exp(-\lambda_2 t)) \\
&\quad + (1 - \exp(-\lambda_1 t)) \cdot \exp(-(\lambda_2 + \lambda_{12})t) = \\
&= \ \exp(-\lambda_{12} t) \cdot (\exp(-\lambda_1 t) + \exp(-\lambda_2 t) - \exp(-(\lambda_1 + \lambda_2)t)) = \\
&= \ \exp(-\lambda_{12} t) \cdot (2 \cdot \exp(-\lambda_1 t) - \exp(-2\lambda_1 t))
\end{aligned}
$$

With $R_1(t) = \exp \ (-(\lambda_1 + \lambda_{12})t)$ being the probability of correct performance of each single version, this yields

$$(49) \qquad \frac{R_{one}(t)}{R_1(t)} = 2 - \exp(-\lambda_1 t) \leq 2 - \exp(-(\lambda_1 + \lambda_{12})t) = 2 - R_1(t)$$

Therefore, the reliability of the combined system is bounded by:

$$(50) \qquad R_{one}(t) \leq (2 - R_1(t)) \cdot R_1(t),$$

whereas the single program, once tested for the same total cost, had achieved the value given in (47):

$$(51) \qquad \hat{R}(t) = \exp((-\lambda(t_0 + \hat{t_0}) + \lambda(t_0)) \ t) \cdot R(t);$$

so, if it is probable to expect:

$$(52) \qquad \exp((-\lambda(t_0 + \hat{t_0}) + \lambda(t_0)) \ t) \geq 2 - \exp(-\lambda(t_0) \ t),$$

it will be reasonable to decide against diversity.

3.6 Conclusion

Software diversity can still be considered as an attractive method to ensure safe operation of programs. Due to economic reasons a system of two diverse programs is particularly important. Since independence of programming errors may not be taken for granted, the probability of common failures is by far larger than assumed earlier.

This chapter, however, has shown that for realistic applications the probability of failures that are not in common is expected to be larger than the probability of common failures. The considerations have been based both on experimental results and theoretical investigations.

So from the single failure probability conclusions can be made upon the common failure probability. This makes back to back testing attractive. Software diversity is therefore an interesting means of achieving safe software systems that consist of programs, which are so large that deterministic verification methods cannot be applied.

Some cost considerations lead to a comparison between single and two-fold diverse systems with respect to the effort required in each case. In particular, the probability of correct performance of at least one version of a diverse system consisting of two equally reliable programs can be bounded by a quadratic expression of the single reliabilities.

Dependent upon this formula as well as upon the expected failure rate after a testing phase of a given length, one can thus decide on using diversity or on investing more effort in testing a single version.

References

[ECK85] D.E. Eckhardt, L.D. Lee: A Theoretical Basis for the Analysis of Multiversion Software Subject to Coincident Errors. IEEE Trans. on Software Engineering, Vol. SE-11, No. 12, December 1985

[EHR83] W.D. Ehrenberger, B. Krzykacz: Probabilistic Testing. Proc. of the EWICS meeting in Graz, (V. Haase ed.), Springer Verlag, April 1983

[KNI86] J. C. Knight, N. G. Leveson: An Experimental Evaluation of the Assumption of Independence in Multi-version Programming. IEEE Trans. on Software Engineering, Vol. SE-12, No. 1, January 1986

[STÖ70] H. Störmer: Mathematische Theorie der Zuverlässigkeit. Oldenbourg-Verlag, München, 1970

[LIT73] B. Littlewood, J.L. Verrall: A Bayesian Reliability Growth Model for Computer Software. Journal of the Royal Statistical Society, Series C, Appl. Stat., Vol. 22, No. 3, pp. 332-346, 1973

Chapter 4

The Impact of Forced Diversity
on the Failure Behaviour
of Multiversion Software

Francesca Saglietti

4.1   Introduction

The principal means to achieve software fault-tolerance is certainly represented by the use of diversity, where the "independent" (in the sense of separate) development of more versions aiming to provide the same service is
intended to randomly distribute the unavoidable errors onto the diverse
programs, thus permitting them to be detected and tolerated by the output
comparison of a voter.

Unfortunately, we know by theoretical and experimental investigations
that the randomness of the error occurrence is strongly affected by the specific characteristics of the underlying problem to be solved and of the techniques adopted to solve it, so that in general we have to expect a number of
common bugs caused by some intrinsic difficulties in the problem solution,
but also generated and enabled to persist by the commonalities in the development processes.

This obviously leads to a dependent failure behaviour of parallel versions
with increasing probabilities of simultaneous failures.

On the other hand, fault-tolerance would be best achieved by forcing the
errors occurring in each program to affect disjoint input subsets, thus
yielding the best possible failure behaviour, even much better than the
originally desired independence.

As the problem complexity is essentially determined by the task to be
performed by the system, we may try to decrease the common failure probability by extending the original mere product diversity to the more general
concept of process diversity, ensuring dissimilarity of the development
methodologies, e.g. with respect to aspects as:

- specification language
- implementation language
- algorithms
- data structures
- tools
- personnel
- testing methods.

In this case some particular classes of errors will be preferably produced
or remain undetected as a result of a particular process rather than of another one, and even coincident errors will probably have different effects on
the final result, allowing their detection.

The intention of this chapter is to study the failure behaviour improvement expected by the additional diversity introduced into the fault-tolerant system by dissimilar methodologies, in particular with respect to the majority and the granularity of the voter.

The second section summarizes the already known theoretical results of Littlewood and Miller, which will be successively analyzed and confirmed by use of calculations performed on the basis of published experimental results.

Section 4.3 proposes an extension of the existing theory taking also into account the granularity of the voter, which will allow the interpretation of further experimental data.

4.2   Common Failure Behaviour of Forced and Unforced Diverse Systems with respect to the Voter Majority

4.2.1   Theoretical Results of Littlewood and Miller

In [LIT87] Littlewood and Miller propose a generalization of the work presented by Eckhardt and Lee in [ECK85].

The key measure in the original work was represented by the intensity function $\Theta(x)$ indicating the probability that a program, which is randomly chosen out of a population of versions intended to satisfy the same set of requirements, will fail for a particular input x. Because of the differing difficulty in processing different inputs, Eckhardt and Lee came to the convincing conclusion that the random variable Θ will generally take different values for different randomly chosen inputs x, and on this basis they proved the failure dependence of parallel versions.

This concept was extended by Littlewood and Miller, considering for each available development methodology the corresponding set of programs to be produced on the basis of a given specification. Within each particular methodology the situation is exactly the one previously described, so that we may distinguish for the different development techniques A, B, C, ... considered the corresponding random variables Θ_A, Θ_B, Θ_C, ... representing the failure intensity within each method.

The following main result of Littlewood and Miller is essentially based on the indifference assumption between the various methodologies considered, supposing that a multi-version system developed within a methodology A can be expected to be as good as one resulting by means of another technique B.

This assumption is obviously very idealistic and in practical cases not to be realistically verified; in praxis it may only represent a statement about our subjective indifference, which is mainly based on lack of knowledge; anyway, applying the mathematical conclusions we should always be conscious of the difference between the required indifference and the mere ignorance mostly replacing it.

In case of a 1-out-of-2 system, succeeding when at least one of both component versions succeeds, this theory results in the following rule:

If one is indifferent between a randomly chosen AA system and a randomly chosen BB system, it would be recommendable to build instead a randomly chosen AB system.

Littlewood and Miller generalize this result for an arbitrary 1-out-of-n system failing if none of the n versions provides the correct output; the analogous assumption requires indifference between designs which involve merely permutations of methodologies. They show then that the best design is the one which uses all the available methodological diversity and spreads it as evenly as possible among versions.

Of course, these results simply refer to the average system behaviour both concerning the program space and the input space. Nonetheless, being as usually ignorant about the detailed conditions of the situation considered, the above implicit average inequalities can usefully assist in decision making in terms of providing advice and rules for design choice.

In [LIT87a] the same authors extend these concepts in an even wider sense, in that they allow more levels of decision. This means that each overall methodology can be interpreted as the final result of more design decisions related to different development aspects.

Assuming the single design choices to be independent in the sense that they will not influence each other, it can again be proved that the more diverse methodologies are preferable, i.e. the ones introducing dissimilarity at a higher number of levels.

Of course, all the reported results following from the summarized theories are not particularly surprising, basically confirming our intuitive expectations.

The more astonishing is the fact that the above statements about 1-out-of-2 systems (resp. 1-out-of-n systems) do not analogously hold for configurations with 2-out-of-3 (resp. (n+1)-out-of-(2n+1)) majority.

In fact, for these architectures Littlewood and Miller show in [LIT87] that diverse design may be worse than homogeneous design, thus coming to the surprising conclusion that forced diversity may not be the most desirable strategy.

4.2.2   Experimental Results of Kelly and Avizienis

This section is devoted to the data analysis of an experiment on forced diversity described in [KEL83] by Kelly and Avizienis. It is our intention to propose an interpretation of the results in the light of the theoretical considerations previously presented. The experiment considered was performed at UCLA, where 18 programs were produced on the basis of a specification written in one of the following 3 different specification languages:

-   the formal language OBJ (7 versions)

-   the program design language PDL (5 versions)

-   the natural language English (6 versions).

A test consisting of 100 input transactions was developed to uncover as many bugs as possible. The outputs were classified as

-   good points including correct outputs and cosmetic errors

-   detected points representing wrong results rejected by the respective self-checking mechanism with which the program was instrumented

- undetected points determined by incorrect outputs which were not identified as failures by the corresponding error indicator mentioned above.

This distinction allows two possible interpretations of failure occurrence:

a) the system is considered to fail only when it cannot identify an erroneous output

or

b) the system fails each time it does not correctly provide the service requested.

Thus the first definition concerns primarily the output reliability, whereas the second one requires additionally system availability. With respect to these measures we can now look at the failure behaviour within program classes with the same specification language, obtaining table 4.1.

Table 4.1. Stand alone test data, mainly from [KEL83]

Stand Alone Test Data						average failure probability	
Version	OK Points	Cosmetic Errors	Good (OK+Cos)	Detected Errors	Undetected Errors	a	b
OBJ1	73	0	73	2	25		
OBJ2	71	18	89	8	3		
OBJ3	67	11	78	4	18		
OBJ4	69	3	72	8	20	23.6	27.7
OBJ5	67	12	79	0	21		
OBJ6	46	0	46	0	54		
OBJ7	52	17	69	7	24		
PDL1	59	2	61	1	38		
PDL2	54	2	56	32	12		
PDL3	95	0	95	4	1	15.8	24.2
PDL4	45	28	73	0	27		
PDL5	94	0	94	5	1		
ENG1	74	12	86	0	14		
ENG2	67	27	94	0	6		
ENG3	97	1	98	0	2	22.7	28.3
ENG4	30	5	35	25	40		
ENG5	55	6	61	0	39		
ENG6	53	3	56	9	35		

In spite of a slight difference in favour of the PDL class, we will regard the deviations on the whole as negligible and assume in the following methodology indifference, in order to permit a first evaluation about the applicability of the theoretical results in real situations.

On the basis of the data published in [KEL83] and regarding the behaviour of triplets of homogeneous type OOO, PPP, EEE and of diverse type OPE, we can calculate average values for the common failure behaviour of two- and three-fold redundant systems with respect to 1-out-of-2 resp. 2-out-of-3 votes, obtaining the following tables 4.2 and 4.3.

Table 4.2. Failure probability of 1-out-of-2 systems

	OO	PP	EE	OP OE PE
a	10,5%	2,3%	6,9%	5,5%
a	average: 6,6% >			5,5%
b	13,3%	6,6%	9,7%	9,6%
b	average: 9,9% >			9,6%

Table 4.3. Failure probability of 2-out-of-3 systems

	OOO	PPP	EEE	OPE
a	17,5%	4,7%	17,2%	13,2%
a	average: 13,1% <			13,2%
b	23,6%	15%	23%	20,8%
b	average: 20,5% <			20,8%

These figures fulfill the relations stated in subsection 4.2.1, thus confirming the theoretical results of Littlewood and Miller: achievement of behaviour improvement by forcing diversity is expected in case of two-fold systems, but not in case of three-fold systems.

In this particular situation, however, even the positive influence exerted by two diverse methodologies is too low to justify the additional effort required for producing the same specification in two languages.

The reason for this lack of profitableness lies in the distribution of related errors shown in tables 4.4 a), b), c) for three different error types, where

- related errors are errors "related by symptoms", including both identical-cause errors and distinct-cause errors that produce acceptably similar symptoms

- specification errors are errors made at the specification phase of software development, including language inadequacies

- implementation errors are errors caused by a misinterpretation of the specification, rather than a mistake in the specification

- logic errors are errors caused by any other intrinsic inability to correctly develop a version.

Tables 4.4 a), b), c).   Related errors from [KEL83]

a)

Related Specification Errors		
Error appears in		
OBJ	PDL	ENG
1,4,5,7		
		4,5,6
		4,5,6
		2,4
		6

b)

Related Implementation Errors		
Error appears in		
OBJ	PDL	ENG
2	1,2,3,4,5	
	1,4	
1,2,5	4	1
4	4	1
	2,4	5
3	1	6
	1	4
6		
	2	

c)

Related Logic Errors		
Error appears in		
OBJ	PDL	ENG
1		
3		5
7		
	1	
	1	
		4
		4

The first of the three tables shows that there are only related specification errors within methodology classes. This means that diversity of specification language was successful in preventing forced diverse systems from being affected by common specification faults.

Also most of the related logic errors appearing in table 4.4 c) are class-specific, concerning (apart from one exception) only single programs.

Thus the real cause for the high common failure probability of (both forced and unforced) diverse systems is represented by the high number of related implementation errors illustrated in table 4.4 b) and spreading over all language classes.

In fact, as reported in [KEL83], many programmers were unable to understand the specifications relying, instead, on the examples and on their intuition, so that many misunderstandings could have been prevented by giving more examples. This special case clearly shows that methodology diversity may be successful, but obviously only with regard to the particular type of errors concerning the diversified development stage. Thus, before expecting too much from forcing diversity at a given level, we should rather accurately consider the different error classes which are likely to affect the final problem solution, investing at the most promising stage the additional effort required by introducing different development techniques.

In particular, if the requirements strongly depend on complex numerical computations, diversity should be introduced at algorithm level, whereas in case of lack of specification understandability, common implementation errors could be reduced by providing different clarifying examples.

4.3   Common Failure Behaviour of Forced and Unforced Diverse Systems with Respect to the Voter Granularity

4.3.1   Theoretical Results

In case of outputs of complex data type, the consensus determined by the voter may be at basic type level, adjudicating separately each output variable, or at complex type level, considering all output variables as a single result that is either correct or incorrect.

For example, if the system is supposed to produce a pair of results (A,B) and the parallel versions actually produce the outputs (A,B), (A,X) and (Y,B), where $A \neq Y$ and $B \neq X$, then a 2-out-of-3 voter at component level would find each time two identical correct results and an incorrect one: (A,A,Y) and (B,X,B). Thus in this case a consensus value (A,B) exists, consisting of both components A and B identified as majority at the basic type level. By treating the output as a single result, on the contrary, the system has no consensus despite the fact that there is a majority on each of the output values.

The voter characteristic determining which output components to be jointly adjudicated is called its granularity. Thus voting systems with coarser granularity will grant a higher system reliability, but under some circumstances they may be too unforgiving, possibly excluding the contribution of essentially correct versions with some wrong unimportant details.

On the other hand, adjudication mechanisms with finer granularity will increase the system availability, but if the components are intended to be semantically connected, e.g. by forming a bit pattern, then making a decision on each output variable separately may create a nonsensical display.

Apart from these impacts of granularity on reliability and availability aspects, which are beyond the scope of this paper, we intend to study in this context the influence of granularity on the common failure behaviour of successfully forced diverse systems.

To simplify the problem representation we consider the case of a specification S defining an output o consisting of two components o_1 and o_2, each of which can be interpreted as being specified by a part S_1 resp. S_2 of S, according to Fig. 4.1.

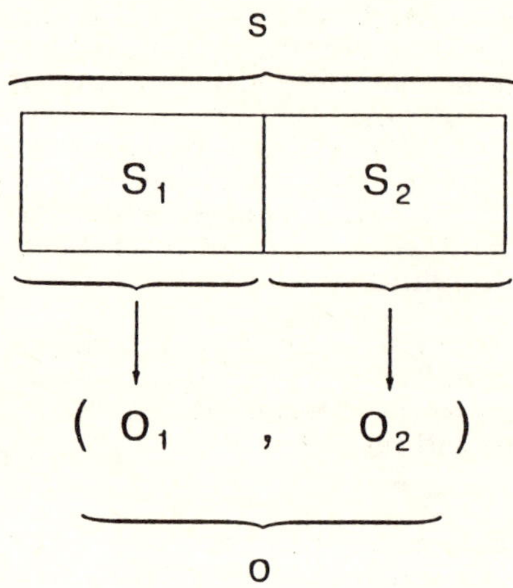

Fig. 4.1.   Specification decomposition

The output variables may depend from one another in the sense that the calculation of o_2 may make use of values already obtained to determine o_1 (In the extreme case, both components might be identically defined and evaluated). Here we will, on the contrary, assume an independent decomposition, in that the development of the software specified by S_1 will not influence the development of the one specified by S_2.

Introducing analogous random variables to the ones adopted in section 2 with

Θ_A indicating the intensity function of S w.r.t. methodology A,

Θ_B indicating the intensity function of S w.r.t. methodology B,

Θ_{A1} indicating the intensity function of S_1 w.r.t. methodology A,

Θ_{B1} indicating the intensity function of S_1 w.r.t. methodology B,

Θ_{A2} indicating the intensity function of S_2 w.r.t. methodology A,

Θ_{B2} indicating the intensity function of S_2 w.r.t. methodology B,

the development independence assumption yields then the following expressions:

$$\Theta_A = \Theta_{A1} + \Theta_{A2} - \Theta_{A1} \cdot \Theta_{A2}$$

and

$$\Theta_B = \Theta_{B1} + \Theta_{B2} - \Theta_{B1} \cdot \Theta_{B2}$$

The impacts of forced diversity on common failure probability will be represented for coarse and fine granularities by:

$$C \quad := \quad \Theta_A^2 - \Theta_A \cdot \Theta_B$$

$$C_1 \quad := \quad \Theta_{A1}^2 - \Theta_{A1} \cdot \Theta_{B1}$$

$$C_2 \quad := \quad \Theta_{A2}^2 - \Theta_{A2} \cdot \Theta_{B2}$$

In case of indifference we expect according to the theoretical results of Littlewood and Miller reported in section 4.2.1 an improvement by forcing diversity:

$$E[C] \geq 0$$
$$E[C_1] \geq 0$$
$$E[C_2] \geq 0$$

The following results hold for the particular case where each methodology will produce failures in a different component, (as expected for highly reliable versions, if diversity has been successfully forced), e.g. without restricting generality:

$$\Theta_{A1} \equiv 0 \, , \, \Theta_{B2} \equiv 0$$

This yields:

$$C \quad = \Theta_A^2 - \Theta_A \cdot \Theta_B \leq \Theta_A^2 = \Theta_{A2}^2$$

$$C_1 \quad = \Theta_{A1}^2 - \Theta_{A1} \cdot \Theta_{B1} = 0$$

$$C_2 \quad = \Theta_{A2}^2 - \Theta_{A2} \cdot \Theta_{B2} = \Theta_{A2}^2$$

In particular:

$$C \geq 0 \Rightarrow C_1, C_2 \geq 0$$

This means that in case of successful forced diversity separating failure occurrence of each version into disjoint output domains, if this actually improves the common failure behaviour (as expected) w.r.t. coarse granularity, it will do the same also w.r.t. fine granularity.

The other direction however, does not always hold: comparison by a voter with fine granularity may show an improvement achieved by diversifying methodologies, which cannot be recognized by use of coarser granularity, i.e. it is possible that:

$$C_1, C_2 \geq 0 \quad , \text{but } C \leq 0,$$

even if only methodology-dependent single faults may be assumed within each component. An intuitive explanation for this theoretical result can be found by observing the example presented in the next section.

4.3.2 Experimental Results of PODS and STEM

In this subsection we intend to analyze some data obtained by the PODS experiment in the light of the theoretical considerations previously presented.

The PODS project (s. [BAR85]) developed 3 programs named CERL, HRP, VTT after the corresponding programming teams.

Diversity was enforced in a number of areas:

- Halden and VTT used the formal specification language X, while CERL specifications were in free format.

- CERL and VTT used a high level language, FORTRAN, while Halden programmed in Nord assembler.

- Finally, CERL was constrained to use a 5th order polynomial as the main algorithm, while Halden and VTT had to use a table look-up algorithm, incorporating interpolation routines.

The diversity forced among the programming teams is summarized in Table 4.5.

Table 4.5. Summary of diversity among the programming teams

TEAM	PROGRAMMING LANGUAGE	MAIN ALGORITHM	SPECIFICATION LANGUAGE
CERL	Fortran	Polynomial	Free format
Halden	Assembler	Table	Formal (X)
VTT	Fortran	Table	Formal (X)

We can identify different degrees of forced diversity:

- HRP and VTT have been diversified with respect to the implementation language (one aspect).

- CERL and VTT have been diversified with respect to the specification language and the main algorithm (2 aspects).

- Finally, CERL and HRP have been diversified with respect to all aspects: specification and implementation languages and main algorithms (3 aspects).

The different degrees of forced diversity are summarized in Fig. 4.2.

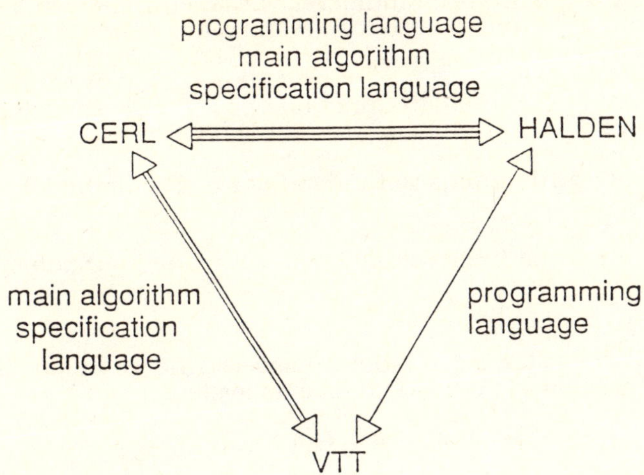

Fig. 4.2. Degrees of forced diversity

The results of a test consisting of 65.000 runs after a previous acceptance test of the three programs are shown in Table 4.6.

Table 4.6. PODS results with post-acceptance programs (from [BAR87])

number of faults detected in program:

golden	test		C	H	V	CH	CV	HV	CHV	ANY
ANY			1152	32428	388	1134	0	108	0	32726
DL		<	0	0	33	0	0	0	0	33
DL		>	0	50	87	0	0	50	0	87
OS	0	1	0	0	0	0	0	0	0	0
OS	1	0	0	0	0	0	0	0	0	0
LS	0	1	0	28	28	0	0	28	0	28
LS	1	0	0	0	0	0	0	0	0	0
CB	0	1	0	0	0	0	0	0	0	0
CB	1	0	32	0	0	0	0	0	0	32
AL	0	1	0	0	0	0	0	0	0	0
AL	1	0	26	0	0	0	0	0	0	26
ST	0	1	0	0	0	0	0	0	0	0
ST	1	0	17	0	0	0	0	0	0	17
TA	0	1	0	0	0	0	0	0	0	0
TA	1	0	0	0	0	0	0	0	0	0
TF0	0	1	0	0	0	0	0	0	0	0
TF0	1	0	0	0	0	0	0	0	0	0
TF2	0	1	1115	0	0	0	0	0	0	1115
TF2	1	0	0	0	0	0	0	0	0	0
TF4	0	1	0	0	0	0	0	0	0	0
TF4	1	0	0	0	0	0	0	0	0	0
TF5	0	1	0	0	240	0	0	0	0	240
TF5	1	0	0	32388	0	0	0	0	0	32388

We can observe that the HRP program has a very high failure probability, which is not particularly due to the language aspect distinguishing it from the other programs, but merely to a specification ambiguity. Before the testing phase we would have been indifferent between the diversified aspects and thus, according to the theoretical results of section 4.2 and to the following notation:

Θ_C indicating the intensity function w.r.t. the methodology used by CERL,

Θ_H indicating the intensity function w.r.t. the methodology used by HRP,

Θ_V indicating the intensity function w.r.t. the methodology used by VTT,

we would expect the following relations between the common failure probabilities of the three possible two-fold diverse systems:

$$E[\Theta_C \cdot \Theta_H] \leq E[\Theta_C \cdot \Theta_V] \leq E[\Theta_H \cdot \Theta_V]$$

The calculations performed for the experimental data, however, yield for the common failure probabilities P_{CH}, P_{CV}, P_{HV}:

$$P_{CH} = 0.0175$$
$$P_{CV} = 0$$
$$P_{HV} = 0.0017$$

This means that one of both expected relations is not fulfilled.

If we look at the results with respect to a finer granularity, we may distinguish two components consisting of the following output variables:

    1.   {DL,LS,TF5}

and

    2.   {CB,AL,ST,TF2}.

The remaining output variables will be neglected in the following, as they were always correct in the test results.

In this case we obtain for the common failure probabilities P_1 and P_2 of the respective components:

$$P_{1CH} = 0 \qquad P_{2CH} = 0$$
$$P_{1CV} = 0 \qquad P_{2CV} = 0$$
$$P_{1HV} = 0.0017 \qquad P_{2HV} = 0$$

We see that here the expected relations are fulfilled, confirming the theoretical considerations of the previous sub-section.

The intuitive explanation expressing in words the context represented by the formulae in section 4.3.1 is given in the following.

In spite of diverse methodologies successfully preventing both versions from containing errors in the same output component, their common failure probability might be nonetheless astonishingly high with respect to a coarse voter, if inputs simultaneously cause failures in different components (as for the pair CH).

The finer voter, on the other hand, only considers common failures occurring in the same component, which obviously represent only a sub-set of the previous ones.

4.4 Conclusion

This chapter presented a study on two specific characteristics of the adjudicator in a diverse system - its majority and its granularity - in the light of the improvement expected to be achieved by forcing dissimilarity during development.

Known and original theoretical results were confirmed and explained by means of real-world examples.

On the whole from the observations analyzed it can be concluded that forced diversity may be an extremely powerful technique; its main restriction is represented by its strict relation to specific error classes, possibly resulting in an unjustified effort, if the fault categories chosen to be tolerated later show to be only partly representative for the application considered.

References

[BAR85] M. Barnes, P.G. Bishop, B. Bjarland, G. Dahll, D. Esp, P. Humphreys, Y. Lahti, S. Yoshimura, A. Ball, O. Hatlevold: PODS (the Project on Diverse Software). OECD Halden Reactor Project, HRP-323, June 1985

[BAR87] M. Barnes, P. Bishop, B. Bjarland, G. Dahll, D. Esp, Y. Lahti, H. Välisuo: P. Humphreys Software Testing and Evaluation Methods (the STEM Project). OECD Halden Reactor Project, HWR-210, May 1987

[ECK85] D.E. Eckhard, L.D. Lee: A Theoretical Basis for the Analysis of Multiversion Software Subject to Coincident Errors. IEEE Trans. on Software Engineering, Vol SE-11, No.12, Dec 1985

[KEL83] J.P.J. Kelly, A. Avizienis: A Specification-Oriented Multi-Version Software Experiment. 13th Int. Symposium an Fault-Tolerant Computing, Milano, Italy, 1983

[LIT87] B. Littlewood, D.R. Miller: A Conceptual Model of Multi-Version Software. Digest of 17th Annual Symposium on Fault Tolerant Computing (FTCS-17), Pittsburgh, July 1987

[LIT87a] B. Littlewood, D.R. Miller: A Conceptual Model of the Effect of Diverse Methodologies on Coincident Failures in Multi-Version Software. 3rd International GI/ITG/GMA Conference on Fault-Tolerant Computing Systems, Bremerhaven 1987

Appendix

Derivation of figures in 4.2.2, table 4.2 and table 4.3.

From [KEL83] we obtain the original data for the triplets OOO, PPP, EEE and OPE with respect to each of the following failure types (regardless of the order of the three outputs):

	OOO	PPP	EEE	OPE
V_1: (G,G,G)	48.7%	44.8%	41.0%	44.5%
V_2: (G,G,D)	3.7%	12.8%	8.3%	6.4%
V_3: (G,G,U)	24.1%	27.4%	27.7%	28.3%
V_4: (G,D,D)	1.4%	0.8%	1.6%	1.7%
V_5: (G,D,U)	4.0%	8.8%	4.0%	5.0%
V_6: (G,U,U)	7.5%	1.8%	10.3%	8.3%
V_7: (G,U*,U*)	2.5%	1.2%	4.1%	1.8%
V_8: (D,D,D)	0.1%	0.0%	0.0%	0.3%
V_9: (D,D,U)	0.6%	0.7%	0.2%	0.6%
V_{10}:(D,U,U)	0.3%	0.6%	1.1%	1.3%
V_{11}:(D,U*,U*)	0.2%	0.0%	0.0%	0.1%
V_{12}:(U,U,U)	4.9%	0.1%	1.0%	1.3%
V_{13}:(U,U*,U*)	1.4%	0.0%	0.4%	0.3%
V_{14}:(U*,U*,U*)	0.7%	1.0%	0.3%	0.1%

where G represents a good point, D represents a detected error, U represents an undetected error that does not appear in one of the other two versions, while U* is an undetected error that is related to both or all three versions.

Table 4.3 easily results from these informations by adding the corresponding percentage values according to both error interpretations defined as a) resp. b), i.e.:

a) cases where at least 2 versions cannot detect an error:

$$V_6 + V_7 + V_{10} + V_{11} + V_{12} + V_{13} + V_{14}$$

b) cases where at least 2 versions cannot provide the correct answer:

$$V_4 + V_5 + V_6 + V_7 + V_8 + V_9 + V_{10} + V_{11} + V_{12} + V_{13} + V_{14}$$

Table 4.2, on the other hand, has been established by averaging the given data about triplets to represent homogeneous resp. inhomogeneous pairs.

For each pair OO, PP, EE the required estimations have been provided on the basis of the corresponding triplet OOO, PPP, EEE, taking into account the three possible pairs resulting from the triplet, e.g. (G,G,G) yields three good pairs (G,G), whereas (G,D,U) yields three pairs (G,D), (D,U) and (G,U).

Similarly, for the inhomogeneous pairs OP, OE, PE we obtain an average value by considering the inhomogeneous triplet OPE as including information on all of them.

On the whole we obtain for

a) cases where both versions cannot detect an error:

$$(V_6 + V_7 + V_{10} + V_{11})/3 + V_{12} + V_{13} + V_{14}$$

b) cases where both versions cannot provide the correct answer:

$$(V_4 + V_5 + V_6 + V_7)/3 + V_8 + V_9 + V_{10} + V_{11} + V_{12} + V_{13} + V_{14}$$

Chapter 5

Functional Diversity

Paola Burlando, Laura Gianetto, Maria Teresa Mainini

5.1 Introduction

The limitations posed by fault tolerance applied to software have stimulated the study of different solutions permitting to overcome such problems; functional diversity seems to be one of the most promising ideas in this field. The study of this methodology and of its implications on the development process and the final product constitutes the preliminary step to a deeper study of its impact on the global software system reliability.

For this purpose, it is necessary to assess functional diversity not only at a merely qualitative level, but in a quantitative way. This implies that metrics characterizing the functional diversity level and the system reliability achieved must be found out. The problem of efficient and meaningful metrics can be solved only if a convenient modelling of the methodology is realised.

The choice of a satisfactory modelling approach requires the examination of different possibilities. The semantic point of view appears as the one fitting the problem in the most exhaustive and comprehensive way.

The semantic modelling relies on the identifications of crucial entities able to encapsulate the semantics of the different versions: the so called semantic domains and functions. Intuitively it is clear that many common semantic entities in the versions imply a low diversity degree and a high probability of common errors among the versions. In order to quantify this intuitive concept, a study was undertaken. The first result was an abstract definition of degree of functional diversity which finds in several purposed metrics well-grounded and realistic instances. The second one was a method to evaluate the reliability of functionally diverse systems through an error analysis based on the architectural characteristics and the complexity and commonalities of the specifications of the different versions composing the systems.

In order to use the theoretical results, it was necessary to find out methods to identify the semantic entities inside specifications, to outline their common parts and to evaluate their correctness. To achieve these goals, a new specification language was proposed which supports these activities by means of particular constructs emphasizing the functional semantic aspects of the specification.

5.2 Limitations of Normal Diversity

The problem of masking software errors appears successfully solved by the extension of the fault tolerance technique from hardware to software.

However, due to the basic difference between the nature of hardware and software faults, some important drawbacks exist. Firstly, the N versions of software are developed starting from a common specification that is a possible source of common faults. In fact, while errors introduced in the development process can be virtually tolerated by the use of multiple versions, the errors contained in the specification are reflected in all the versions. These errors are particularly subtle and difficult to detect.

Secondly, experimental results have shown that the probability of common errors in the N versions should not be neglected. These common errors are not due to an erroneous specification, but have been justified with a common proneness of all the programmers to perform the same errors; typical examples can be the bad management of boundary conditions or limiting cases. Such limitations, being innate in the human brain attitude, are difficult to overcome.

These limitations may create an obstacle to the adoption of normal diversity as an industrial solution for ultra reliable systems, because, in addition to a high cost of implementation, it cannot guarantee a sufficient certainty of having achieved the required reliability and/or safety level. The need of alternative approaches appears urgent due to both the increasing number of critical applications realised by computerized systems and the need of a methodology in which one can be confident.

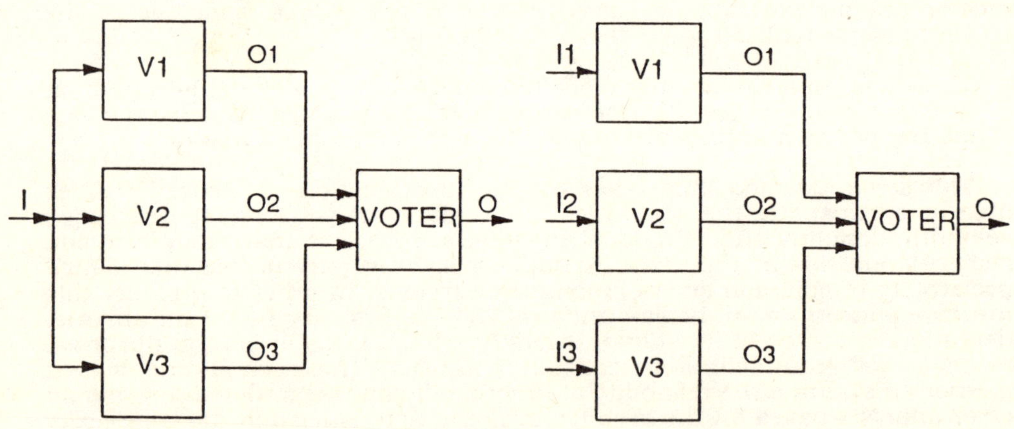

Fig. 5.1.   Normal diversity (left) vs. functional diversity (right)

5.3 Description of Functional Diversity Methodology

A promising answer to the problems posed by normal diversity is represented by functional diversity. Functional diversity is a methodology consisting of developing N different implementations of the same requirement specification where each implementation uses a different input set and a different algorithm to compute the same required output. The basic difference between the two methodologies lies in the diversity starting point. In normal diversity, the N teams begin to work separately only after the specification has been written, then they use the same or a similar approach, the same modelling of the process, the same data types; the differences among them lie only in the implementation techniques and in the details of the algorithms. In functional diversity, the N teams begin to work separately immediately, having, as only common point, the system requirements; the approaches to the problem and the input data are different. Figure 5.1 shows the schema of the two methodologies.

5.4 Advantages of Functional with Respect to Normal Diversity

For its structural characteristics, functional diversity successfully overcomes the limitations of normal diversity.

A single specification is a potential source of common errors. In the case of functional diversity, each version corresponds to a different specification. As a side effect, multiple specifications which are integrated within a process model can be mutually checked by a back-to-back test underlining their discrepancies and divergences with respect to the system requirements. Concerning the problem of common faults due to the attitude of programmers to make similar errors, it is to note that, also if no methodology can change the human brain mechanisms, the probability that these errors lead to common failures is considerably lower. In fact, if the modelling approaches to the same physical problem are different, boundary conditions, limiting cases, etc. will not be the same and especially they will not happen in the same process state. For instance, a version could fail when a certain process configuration exists, whilst another one could fail in a different configuration, but, very unlikely, in the one unsuccessfully treated by the first version, due to the basic differences of the two versions.

Besides these two points, it is also to note that functional diversity is a potential stimulus to develop a more integral diversity, including: basic software, hardware configuration and interfaces with the process. When implementing different specifications, the designers, in choosing the best environment for the development of their own version, will probably (and certainly more probably than in the case of normal diversity) select different computing machines, process interfaces, operating systems, languages, utilities and development tools. These further elements of diversity will ensure a wider protection against potential sources of common faults due to errors in part of the system outside the versions (errors in the compilers, in the operating system, in the hardware, etc.), but will also ensure a higher protection against common errors due to the use of the same development environment (errors due to typical structures of the language or in the interfaces with the operating system, etc.).

5.5 Disadvantages of Functional Diversity

The positive characteristics of functional diversity must not induce to think of having found the panacea to all the problems of software reliability; some drawbacks exist that must be considered carefully before adopting this solution.

The first problem is its applicability. The basic requirement to apply functional diversity is that the problem can be approached from different points of view, meaning that different modelling of the process can be pursued.

The second problem is the outputs comparability. This problem must be carefully considered; in fact, the versions, due to their diversity, could deliver outputs that, even if they are of the same nature, have not the same value when compared by the voter. The differences, due to a different model of the process, are substantially due to two factors: different response time of the models, different precision and/or granularity of the calculations. This problem could be overcome, in some cases, by the adoption of sophisticated decision algorithms taking into account the process and the modelling characteristics. But it is necessary to be very careful in choosing this solution because it increases the size and then the criticality of the voter that is not a replicated piece of code. Thus, generally speaking, the problem of outputs comparability could be a further limitation to the application fields of functional diversity.

5.6 Application Fields

To schematize the ideal application fields of functional diversity is not easy. Economic considerations lead to think that only in cases of very critical systems the major costs implied by functional diversity can be justified. The characteristics of the methodology itself appear to fit best to physical rather than purely informatics problems. The underlined problems of output comparability suggest to focus on applications where the outputs can have only well defined values, permitting to avoid the spread of solutions on a large range.

A possible candidate could be a system whose function consists in detecting a particular situation, for instance a protection system. Such a system usually is critical for safety and its malfunction has serious consequences in terms of human lives and economic losses; then the use of an expensive technology is widely justified. The problem of detecting a situation can usually be approached from different points of view; for instance, starting from the causes (top-down) or from the consequences (bottom-up). The problem of output comparability is less crucial because the number of states to be identified is not large (alarm, prealarm, normal, etc.) and, anyway, the eventual different response times could be overcome by a safety policy that privileges the most conservative version.

As an example, a typical problem that could be solved using functional diversity is presented. This example is not inspired by a real application, so it must be considered only as a formal, theoretical exercise whose aim is to better explain the methodology and to clarify the points that could have been obscure in the foregoing pages.

The problem is to reduce the high number of mortal accidents happening in motorway tunnels due to vehicle queues in tunnels that cannot be perceived by the cars that are entering there. The objective of the protection system is to detect the existence of a queue and to set a proper signal warning the arriving drivers about the dangerous situation.

The criticality of the application is high enough to justify a redundant system and its characteristics fit the ideal profile: a physical problem, different approaches to model it, a single, digital output to be delivered, an applicable safety policy.

The first approach is top-down: it detects the anomalous situation controlling its causes i.e. a too high number of vehicles staying in the tunnel with respect to the external traffic conditions. Then the first version will use, as input sensors, magnetic coils giving a signalization whenever crossed by the ingoing or the outgoing vehicles and an indication of the traffic conditions given by an external agent, e.g. an operator. The computation consists of:

- counting the cars simultaneously present under the tunnel

- elaborating this number to obtain an external traffic sensitive number

- dispatching the information of the alarm situation to the output actuators when the number exceedes a predefined threshold

- dispatching the information of the restored normal situation to the output actuators when the number is lower than a safety threshold.

The second approach is bottom-up: it detects the anomalous situation controlling one of its typical effects, i.e. a too high percentage of carbon monoxide in the air inside the tunnel, taking into account also the atmospheric situation (pressure, wind speed, etc.) according to a thermodynamic model of the phenomenon. The second version will use, as input sensors, chemical transducers measuring the gases percentage in various tunnel sections and environmental transducers measuring all the atmospheric variables that can influence the distribution of gases inside the tunnel. The computation consists of:

- modelling the physical phenomenon, to find, given the present values of the environmental variables, the acceptable carbon monoxide percentages in the tunnel sections,

- dispatching the information of the alarm situation to the output actuators when a statistical function of the percentages exceeds a predefined threshold,

- dispatching the information of the restored normal situation to the output actuators when a statistical function of the percentages is lower than a safety threshold.

The two versions pursue the same objective starting from different points of view and using different input sets, so it is clear that commonalities among them will be unlikely; besides this, the different computation complexity will suggest to use different hardware and basic software. It is also clear that the response time of the two models will be different: the first approach, being based on the count of cars, will respond more quickly than the second one, because a longer time interval will be necessary before the gases percentage becomes higher than the threshold. Anyway, a safety policy can easily be applied providing the alarm delivery as soon as at least one of the two versions detects an anomalous situation.

5.7   Choice of the Modelling Approach for Functional Diversity

The basic point, permitting to achieve a substantial diversity among the approaches, are the different input sets; in fact, data are always an image of the modelling adopted and their difference is, at least, a qualitative guarantee of diversity. Of course this epidermic feeling must be consolidated by a deeper investigation on the nature of the approaches; it is important that the difference of the input sets is not overwritten and invalidated by a transformation mapping the original, different inputs into data common to multiple versions on which the same algorithms are applied. Figure 5.2 presents the ideal functional diversity compared with an apparent functional diversity.

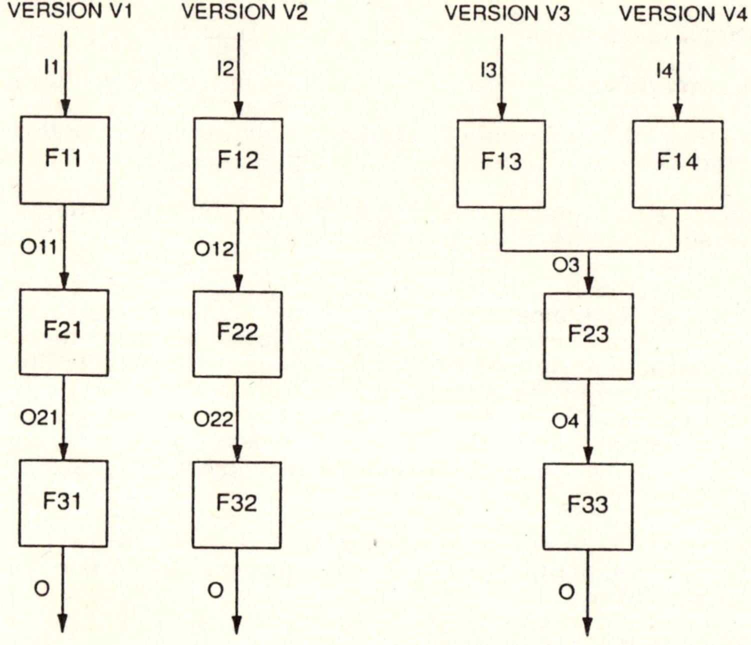

Fig. 5.2.   Ideal (left) vs. apparent (right) functional diversity

As the figure shows, in the case of ideal functional diversity, the elaborations F11, F12, F21, F22, etc. applied to the inputs I1 and I2 in the 2 versions V1 and V2 are respectively different and so are the intermediate outputs O11, O12, O21, O22, etc.; in the case of apparent functional diversity, the elaborations F13 and F14 applied to the inputs I3 and I4 generate the same intermediate outputs O3, the following elaborations F23 and F33 are common to the two versions and so are the intermediate outputs O4.

This example shows that, while functional diversity is potentially a good answer to the problems posed by normal diversity, its effectiveness lies in its correct and not only formal application that must be checked and controlled.

To identify if the differentiation among the N version really exists it is necessary to model each version so that the specific features contributing to the achievement of functional diversity can be outlined.

A process model corresponds to each version. This model can be seen as a free object of study in its own right without any implied meaning or as an object with its own meaning. The second one appears to be the best way to model functional diversity, because only through the analysis of the model meaning, the functional characteristics can be completely identified.

Considering that these models are implemented on computer through programs, in the following the semantic study, that is the approach taken in computer science to outline the meaning of a program, will be analyzed.

After a presentation of the classical semantic approach, an abstraction will be made to define a semantics useful for the characterization of functional diversity.

Applying this semantic modelling to the process models that underlay the N versions composing a system based on functional diversity, it will be possible to define metrics that, taking into account commonalities and differences of their semantic aspects, will permit to measure the degree of functional diversity achieved.

5.8 Classical Semantic Approach

The idea of giving a semantics for programming languages originates in the first reports about ALGOL 60, edited by NAUR (1960, 1963). These reports are very important, because they show the need to give a rigorous methodology of programming language description. After this intuitive idea, the most important definitions of programming language semantics are due to McCarthy, Landin and Strachey in the sixties. McCarthy defined the basis of a mathematical theory of computation, whose formalism allows to use conditional expressions to specify recursively defined functions on arbitrary sets. Landin described the so-called "SECD machine" as a mean of defining the meaning of the evaluation of lambda calculus expressions and he expanded this machine to give a "compiler/interpreter" semantics for ALGOL 60. Strachey introduced the general method of defining mathematical semantics as a set of recursively defined functions from syntactic domains to semantic domains. In conclusion, in the seventies, an algebraic approach to semantics was defined by Scott in his theory on computation (see [STO77]) which is the basis of the mathematical semantics of the most important programming languages.

The goal of using formal methods to communicate understanding about programming languages has certainly not been the only motivation behind the   efforts in formal semantics. Initially, the objective was to give a sufficiently precise description to construct correct compilers. Nowadays, the emphasis is more on a description sufficiently precise for programmers to make rigorous statements about the behaviour of the programs they write, and for language designers to design programming languages with simpler formal descriptions.

For this reason, there are many different approaches to semantics. In fact, just as a language can be described at several abstraction levels, so the semantic descriptions are provided at various abstraction levels suited for the particular purpose for which a formal definition is required.

Two of the main methods, which have been developed for giving semantic description of programming languages, are the operational semantics and the denotational semantics. In these methods, which will be presented in the following, the meaning is given in terms of transformations of syntactic objects into their semantic interpretations. More precisely, in operational semantics the meaning is given by the interpretation of the results on the basis of derivation rules, whilst in denotational semantics the meaning is given by the interpretation of the language constructs.

To describe these techniques of semantic definition in a more concrete form, the definition of an exemplifying language, called ASTE, is presented. ASTE's syntax is defined by the following grammar:

```
<program>       ::=   PBEGIN <statement> ENDP

<statement>   ::=   <assignment>
                    |   <sequence>
                    |   <while-loop>
                    |   <cond-choise>
                    |   <read>
                    |   <write>

<assignment>  ::=   <identifier> := <expression>

<sequence>     ::=   BEGIN <statement> ; <statement> END

<while-loop>  ::=   WHILE <bool-exp> DO <statement>

<cond-choise>::=   IF <bool-exp> THEN <statement>
                                  ELSE <statement>

<read>          ::=   READ <identifier>

<write>         ::=   WRITE <identifier>
```

5.8.1 Operational Semantics

An operational model of a programming language is given by:

1. definition of an "abstract machine", which has a "state", probably with
   several components, and a certain set of primitive instructions

and

2. definition of the machine by specifying how the components of the
   state are changed by each of the instructions.

Then the semantics of a programming language is defined in terms of a
state transformation

```
            sem-op
  S ----------> S
```

In the given operational definition, the state transitions, rather than
producing a single new state, produce a sequence of states representing all
the intermediate states produced during the computation. The most
important characteristic of operational semantics is that the sequence of
intermediate states is explicitly given by the definition, even if the only
interesting state is the final one.

The operational definition of the language ASTE can be given in terms of
a transformation of a program text and a state vector (s,i,o). The state
vector represents the current state of the computation, where s is the
function STORE, which associates to any component x its value v, i is the
sequence of the inputs and o is the sequence of the outputs.

In the definition of the operational semantics of the language ASTE, the
following notations are used:

   - The transformation EVAL, which produces the value of an expression
depending on the current store of the state

```
                              eval
          <expression,s> -------> value
```

- The substitution of value in the state s[x/v], defined as

    s[x/v]{x}=v
    s[x/v]{y}=s(y) for all y ≠ x

which can be read as "change the x component of s to have the value v", leaving unvaried the state of all the other components.

- The conditional expression

```
                    A
                   ---
                    B
```

defined as "if the transformation A is true, then the transformation B is true"

- The char e defined as generic expression

- The char b defined as boolean expression

- The char x defined as generic identifier

- The chars c, c1 and c2 defined as generic statements.

The definition of the operational semantics of the language ASTE follows, covering all the syntactic categories of statements:

- **<assignment>**

```
                              eval
              <e,s> --------> v
        ------------------------------------------
                              sem-op
        <x:=e, (s,i,o)> --------> (s[x/v],i,o)
```


- **<sequence>**

```
                                 sem-op
              <c1, (s,i,o)> --------> (s',i',o')
        ----------------------------------------------------
                                 sem-op
        <BEGIN c1; c2 END, (s,i,o)> --------> <c2,(s',i',o')>
```

- <while-loop>

```
                              eval
                    <b,s> -------> true
      --------------------------------------------------------------
                    sem-op
    <WHILE b DO c, (s,i,o)>--------><BEGIN c ; WHILE b DO c END, (s,i,o)>



                              eval
                    <b,s> -------> false
        ----------------------------------------------------
                              sem-op
      <WHILE b DO c, (s,i,o)> -------->  (s,i,o)
```

- <cond-choice>

```
                              eval
                    <b,s> -------> true
      ------------------------------------------------------------
                              sem-op
      <IF b THEN c1 ELSE c2, (s,i,o)> --------> < c1, (s,i,o)>


                              eval
                    <b,s> -------> false
      ------------------------------------------------------------
                              sem-op
      <IF b THEN c1 ELSE c2, (s,i,o)> --------> < c2, (s,i,o)>
```

- <read>

```
                              sem-op
      <READ x,(s,v_i,o)> --------> (s[v/x],i,o)
```

- <write>

```
                              sem-op
      <WRITE x,(s,i,o)> --------> (s,i,o_s(x))
```

If P is a program, then a transformation (s,i,o) is associated to
$\langle P,(s{\sim},i{\sim},l)\rangle$, where s~ is the initial function store, undefined for every x, i~
is the input of the program, and l is the empty output. Then o can be
defined as the result of P corresponding to the initial value of i~.

<program>

$$\text{<PBEGIN c ENDP, (s~,i~,l)>} \xrightarrow{\text{sem-op}} \text{<c, (s~,i~,l)>}$$

<result>

$$\text{(s,i,o)} \xrightarrow{\text{sem-op}} \text{o}$$

5.8.2 Denotational Semantics

The approach taken in denotational semantics is to abstract from the operational point of view to consider the program as a function of some appropriate type. Analogously, at a lower level, the meaning of each syntactic construct is given not in terms of state transformations, but in terms of semantic functions.

The semantic functions map syntactic constructs in the program into abstract objects (numbers, truth values, functions etc.), elements of semantic domains. These functions are usually recursively defined, i.e. the value denoted by a construct is specified in terms of the values denoted by its syntactic subcomponents.

The denotational semantics of the ASTE language follows, given by the semantic domains and the semantic functions.

Semantic Domains

The semantic domains are the sets of the abstract objects manipulated by the constructs of the language.

- **<programs>**

```
A-prog  = [INPUT ---> OUTPUT]
```

- **<statements>**

```
A-stat  = [STORE x INPUT x OUTPUT ---> STORE x INPUT x OUTPUT]
```

- **<values>**

```
A-value = [STORE ---> VALUE]
```

- <booleans>

```
A-bool  = [STORE ---> BOOLEAN]
```

- <identifier>

```
A-ident = VAR
```

Semantic Functions

The semantic functions give the meaning of the syntactic constructs.

* MEANING OF THE EXPRESSIONS:

- <boolexp>

```
B : BOOLEXP -------- > A-bool = [STORE -------> BOOLEAN]
```

B is the function that, taken any boolean syntactic expression, gives its meaning as a function of the store.

- <valuexp>

```
T : VALUEXP -------- > A-value = [STORE -------> VALUE]
```

T is the function that, taken any generic syntactic expression, gives its meaning as a function of the store.

* MEANING OF THE VARIABLE:

- <ident>

```
V : IDENT -------> A-ident = VAR
```

V is the function that takes any identifier into the corresponding variable.

* MEANING OF THE STATEMENTS:

- <assignment>

The meaning of "assignment" is a function that, taken a variable, i.e. the meaning of an identifier, and the meaning of an expression, produces the meaning of the statement "assignment". This function associates the value of the expression to the variable in the corresponding store.

```
A(assignment) : A-ident x A-value  -------> A-stat

A(assignment)(V(x),T(e)) (s,i,o) = (s[T(e)(s)/V(x)],i,o).

 Sem-den (x:=e) (s,i,o) =

    = A(:=)  (V(x),T(e)) (s,i,o) =

    = (s[T(e)(s)/V(x)],i,o).
```

- <sequence>

The meaning of "sequence" is a function that, taken two statement meanings, produces the meaning of the statement "sequence". This function is the concatenation function of two statement meanings.

```
A(sequence)  : A-stat x A-stat -------> A-stat

A(sequence)(f,g) = f * g

 Sem-den (BEGIN c1 ; c2 END) (s,i,o) =

A(BEGIN ; END)(Sem-den(c1),Sem-den(c2))  (s,i,o) =

Sem-den(c1) * Sem-den(c2)  (s,i,o) =

Sem-den(c2) ( Sem-den(c1)(s,i,o) ).
```

- <while-loop>

The meaning of "while-loop" is a function that, taken the meaning of a boolean expression and the meaning of a statement, produces the meaning of the statement "while-loop". If the meaning of the boolean expression is true, the function gives the meaning of the statement concatenated with itself, else, if the meaning of the boolean expression is false, it produces the identity function of the state.

```
A(while-loop) : A-bool x A-stat -------> A-stat

A(while-loop) (B(b), f) = cond (B(b), f * A(while-loop), Id ).

 Sem-den(WHILE b DO c) (s,i,o) =

= A(while-loop) (B(b), Sem-den(c)) (s,i,o) =

=       cond (B(b), Sem-den(c) * Sem-den(WHILE b DO c), Id ) (s,i,o) =

=       cond (B(b)(s), Sem-den (WHILE b DO c) (Sem-den(c) (s,i,o)),
        (s,i,o)).
```

- <cond-choice>

The meaning of "cond-choice" is a function that, taken the meaning of a boolean expression and the meaning of two statements, produces the meaning of the statement "cond-choice". If the meaning of the boolean expression is true, this function produces the meaning of the first statement, else, if the meaning of the boolean expression is false, it produces the meaning of the second statement.

```
A(cond-choice) : A-bool x A-stat x A-stat -------> A-stat

A(cond-choice)(B(b), f , g ) = cond (B(b), f, g).

 Sem-den(IF b THEN c1 ELSE c2) (s,i,o) =

= A(IF_THEN_ELSE) (B(b), Sem-den(c1), Sem-den(c2)) (s,i,o) =

= cond (B(b)(s), Sem-den(c1) (s,i,o), Sem-den(c2) (s,i,o)).
```

- <read>

The meaning of "read" is a function that, taken a variable, i.e. the meaning of an identifier, produces the meaning of the statement "read". This function associates the value of the first element of the input sequence to the variable in the corresponding store.

```
A(read) : A-ident -------> A-stat

A(read) (V(x)) (s,v_i,o) = (s[T(v)(s)/V(x)],i,o).

 Sem-den (READ x) (s, v_i, o) =

= A(READ) (V(x)) (s,v_i,o) =

= (s[T(v)(s)/V(x)],i,o).
```

- <write>

The meaning of "write" is a function that, taken a variable, i.e. the meaning of an identifier, produces the meaning of the statement "write". This function includes the value of the variable, allocated in the store, into the output sequence.

```
A(write) : A-ident -------> A-stat

A(write) (V(x)) (s,i,o) = (s,i,o_s(V(x))).

 Sem-den (WRITE x) (s,i,o) =

= A(WRITE) (V(x)) (s,i,o) = (s,i,o_s(V(x))).
```

* MEANING OF PROGRAM:

- **<program>**

The meaning of a program is a function that takes an input into an output. Defining (s~,i~,l) to be the initial state, where s~ is the initial function store, undefined for every x, i~ is the input of the program, and l is the empty output, the meaning of a program is the output o of the state given by the meaning of the statement corresponding to the body of the program.

```
A(program) : INPUT -------> OUTPUT

A(PBEGIN c ENDP) (i~) =

      = outputpart (Sem-den(c) (s~,i~,l))

outputpart : STORE x INPUT x OUTPUT -------> OUTPUT

outputpart (s,i,o) = o
```

5.9 Functional Semantics

The semantic approach we are looking for should allow to completely identify the functional characteristics of the process model.

For this purpose the classical semantic approach exhibits positive and negative aspects.

First of all, the classical semantics are strictly related to the programming language, this is a too low level for our purpose. Besides this general limitation, the operational and the denotational semantics show their own positive and negative aspects. The denotational semantics does not allow to interpret the internal sequence of the program, whilst it properly maps the language constructs by means of semantic domains and functions. The operational semantics permits to identify the sequence of the program but only in a mechanical way.

Mixing the positive aspects of both the classical semantics, it is possible to define a new semantic approach having the following characteristics:

- a higher abstraction level,

- an identification and interpretation of all the functions used by the process model,

- an interpretation of all the objects composing the functions.

This leads to define FUNCTIONAL SEMANTICS as "a formalization that allows to identify all the interpretative concepts of the hypotheses and of the modelling principles adopted in a process modelling".

Let f be the function representing a process modelling; the corresponding FUNCTIONAL SEMANTICS is defined by:

$$FUN\_SEM\ (f) = (D\_f, I\_f)$$

where:

I_f is the set of the semantic functions, i.e. the set of the meanings of the formalization hypotheses and the modelling principles in f,

D_f is the set of the semantic domains, i.e. the set of the meanings of the objects on which I_f operates.

The semantic domains can be of input, output, intermediate.

With reference to the example described in 5.6, in the following the corresponding semantic domains and functions are identified.

- SEMANTIC DOMAINS

Ic : number of in_cars	(input domain)
Oc : number of out_cars	(input domain)
Pc : number of cars present in the tunnel	(inter. domain)
Tc : traffic conditions	(input domain)
Tv : threshold value of car	(input domain)
Sn : external traffic sensitive number of cars	(inter. domain)
O : output to the actuators	(output domain)

Then :

$$D = \{Ic, Oc, Pc, Tc, Tv, Sn, O\}$$

- SEMANTIC FUNCTIONS

Val : in_car number evaluation

Sen : external traffic sensitive number of cars evaluation

Res : output to the actuators evaluation

Then :

$$I = \{Val, Sen, Res\}$$

5.10 Semantic Modelling of Functional Diversity

Given an application relating to a process P for which the functional diversity methodology is used, it can be schematized as:

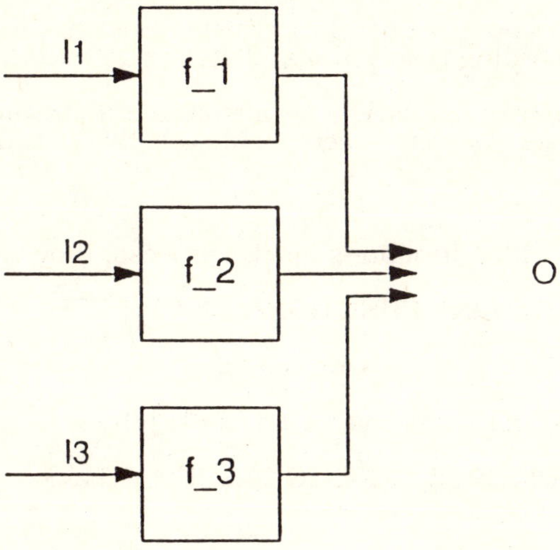

Fig. 5.3. Functional diversity methodology

where f_i is the function corresponding to the modelling i adopted for the process.

f_i can be seen as composed by some service functions Fs_i and a kernel function Fk_i.

Service functions for the modelling f_i are pre-elaboration or post-elaboration functions. These functions execute only the management of the input/output, but they are not strictly related to the modelling adopted.

The Kernel function Fk_i is the formalization of the model and it is typical of it.

For the purpose of functional diversity modelling, the only relevant part is the kernel function Fk_i that is the crucial part for the characterization of the model adopted.

For this reason, it is meaningful to consider only the FUNCTIONAL SEMANTICS associated to the kernel functions and to neglect the service functions.

Let Fk a kernel function, the corresponding FUNCTIONAL SEMANTICS is defined by:

$$FUN\_SEM \ (Fk) = (D, \ I)$$

Let Fk_i and Fk_j be two kernel functions for a process; they have different FUNCTIONAL SEMANTICS

if and only if

$$D\_i \cap D\_j = \text{dom\_out} \quad \text{and} \quad I\_i \cap I\_j = \varnothing$$

where dom_out is the output domain corresponding to the output common to the N versions according to functional diversity definition.

This definition permits to assess an absolute criterion to establish if the ideal functional diversity has been achieved by the different process modelling.

Given f_i and f_j modelling functions for the process, they are

IDEALLY FUNCTIONALLY DIVERSE

if and only if

the corresponding kernel functions Fk_i and Fk_j have

DIVERSE FUNCTIONAL SEMANTICS

These concepts are expressed by the following definition:

Definition 1

Two modelling functions f_i and f_j are IDEALLY FUNCTIONALLY DIVERSE if and only if

$$D\_i \cap D\_j = \text{dom\_out} \quad \text{and} \quad I\_i \cap I\_j = \varnothing$$

where (D_i,I_i) and (D_j,I_j) are the FUNCTIONAL SEMANTICS of the Kernel functions Fk_i and Fk_j associated to f_i and f_j.

The first condition imposes that a different modelling operates on different semantic objects, apart from the output domain dom_out; the second condition imposes that the formalization hypotheses and the modelling principles of the two functions are different.

A theorem, which will simplify the ideal functional diversity definition, follows:

Theorem 1

Given two Kernel functions Fk_i and Fk_j, let

$$\text{SEM\_FUN(Fk\_i)} = (D\_i, I\_i)$$

$$\text{SEM\_FUN(Fk\_j)} = (D\_j, I\_j)$$

be their functional semantics such that:

$$D\_i \cap D\_j = \text{dom\_out}$$

Then

$$I\_i \cap I\_j = \varnothing$$

Proof:

Assuming $\exists\, h \in I\_i \cap I\_j$, such that:

$$h : \text{dom\_h}_1 * \ldots * \text{dom\_h}_m \relbar\relbar\joinrel\rightarrow \text{dom\_h}_{m+1}$$

Then, for all k, k=1..m+1,

$$\text{dom\_h}_k \in D\_i \quad \text{and} \quad \text{dom\_h}_k \in D\_j$$

i.e.

$$\text{dom\_h}_k \in D\_i \cap D\_j$$

which implies:

$$(1) \qquad \text{dom\_h}_k = \text{dom\_out}.$$

This is absurd, because from the definition of the Kernel function it follows that dom_out cannot be the input domain of a semantic function; in fact dom_out is always and only an output domain, while in (1) dom_out is an input domain for h.

Theorem 1 is very important, because it allows to simplify the definition of IDEAL FUNCTIONAL DIVERSITY without reducing its strength.

Corollary 1

Two modelling functions f_i and f_j are IDEALLY FUNCTIONALLY DIVERSE if and only if

$$D\_i \cap D\_j = \text{dom\_out}$$

where D_i and D_j are the sets of the semantic domains of the Kernel functions Fk_i and Fk_j associated to f_i and f_j.

Extending this definition to n functions, it follows

Definition 2

n modelling functions $f\_1, \ldots, f\_n$ are IDEALLY FUNCTIONALLY DIVERSE if and only if

$$D\_i \cap D\_j = \text{dom\_out} \qquad \text{for } i,j=1..n,\ i \neq j$$

where $D\_1, \ldots, D\_n$ are the sets of the semantic domains of the Kernel functions Fk_1, ..., Fk_n associated to $f\_1, \ldots, f\_n$.

This definition allows to determine the ideal functional diversity taking into account only the sets of the semantic domains, i.e. the meanings of the objects considered by the Kernels of the modelling functions.

5.11 Functional Diversity Metrication

From definition 2, the metric of ideal functional diversity can be derived.

Definition 3

Let d be the metric of ideal functional diversity

$$d : D^n \longrightarrow 0,1$$

where D is the space of the semantic domains, such that:

$$d(D\_1,...,D\_n) = \begin{cases} 1 & \text{if } D\_i \cap D\_j = dom\_out \quad i,j=1..n, \ i \neq j \\ 0 & \text{otherwise} \end{cases}$$

Then n modelling functions f_1, ..., f_n are IDEALLY FUNCTIONALLY DIVERSE if and only if

$$d(D\_1, ...,D\_n) = 1$$

where D_1, ..., D_n are the sets of the semantic domains of the Kernel functions Fk_1, ..., Fk_n associated to f_1, ..., f_n.

Rather than defining a test permitting to decide if the ideal functional diversity is achieved or not, a more realistic and practical approach is to define a metric permitting to give a measure, ranging from 0 to 100%, of the functional diversity level of the system. In fact, metrics taking into account the content of the intersection of the sets of the semantic domains permit to define a functional diversity degree related to the metric chosen.

Definition 4

Let

$$\mu : D^n \longrightarrow [0..1]$$

be a metric taking into account the content of the intersection of the sets of the semantic domains.

Then the DEGREE OF FUNCTIONAL DIVERSITY of the n modelling functions related to μ is:

$$\mu (D\_1, ..., D\_n)$$

where D_1, ..., D_n are the sets of the semantic domains of the Kernel functions Fk_1, ..., Fk_n associated to f_1, ..., f_n.

5.12 Definition of Functional Diversity Metrics

Before introducing some metrics to evaluate the degree of functional diversity of n modelling functions, the assumptions made are presented.

- All the modelling functions are considered to be equivalent, i.e. no priority exists among the models. This assumption implies that the sets of semantic domains are considered to be equivalent.

- For each modelling the semantic domains are considered equivalent, i.e. they are not weighted on the basis of complexity of the semantic functions using them. This assumption represents an operative limitation, but it does not invalidate the significance of the metrics presented. Furthermore, it is possible to suppose to modify them introducing a corrective factor taking into account the weights of the semantic domains.

In the definition of the metrics to evaluate the degree of functional diversity, the following notations are used:

- n: the number of modelling functions of the process.

- D: the space of the sets of semantic domains.

- D_i: the set of semantic domains of the Kernel function associated to i-th modelling function excluding dom_out.

- CARD: D ----> POSITIVE INTEGER

is the function which, taken a set of semantic domains, produces the number of its elements.

$$INT_i : D^n ----> D \qquad i= 1..n$$

are n functions, where the i-th function, taken n sets, produces the set of semantic domains common exactly to i sets.

To describe the metrics evaluating the functional diversity degree in a more concrete form, an exemplifying case will be used. Let a process be modelled by the three modelling functions f_1, f_2 and f_3 and Fk_1, Fk_2 and Fk_3 be the corresponding Kernel functions, having D_1, D_2 and D_3 as semantic domain sets. The figure shows the relations existing among these three sets of semantic domains quantified by the following expressions.

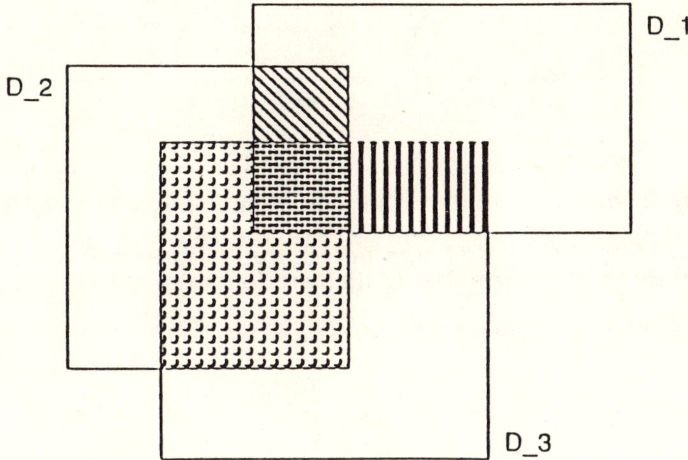

Fig. 5.4. Example of relations among semantic domains

$$CARD(D\_1) = 24$$

$$CARD(D\_2) = 20$$

$$CARD(D\_3) = 30$$

$$CARD(D\_1 \cap D\_2) = 3$$

$$CARD(D\_1 \cap D\_3) = 6$$

$$CARD(D\_2 \cap D\_3) = 12$$

$$CARD(D\_1 \cap D\_2 \cap D\_3) = 2$$

$$CARD(INT_1 (D\_1,D\_2,D\_3)) = 38$$

$$CARD(INT_2 (D\_1,D\_2,D\_3)) = 15$$

$$CARD(INT_3 (D\_1,D\_2,D\_3)) = 2$$

Metrics to evaluate the degree of functional diversity of modelling functions $f\_1,...,f\_n$ follow.

5.12.1 The EFF_WOR Metric

Definition 5

The EFF_WOR metric is defined as:

$$EFF\_WOR : D^n \longrightarrow [0..1]$$

$$EFF\_WOR (D\_1,...,D\_n) =$$

$$\min_{i=1..n} \left(\frac{CARD\left(D\_i \setminus \left(\bigcup_{\substack{j=1 \\ j \neq i}}^{n} (D\_i \cap D\_j)\right)\right)}{CARD(D\_i)} \right)$$

The EFF_WOR metric equates the functional diversity degree of n modelling functions to the minimum of the n ratios calculated for each version as the number of the domains not shared with any other modelling function divided by the total number of its own domains.

The value of EFF_WOR for the exemplifying case is:

$$EFF\_WOR(D\_1,D\_2,D\_3) = \min \left(\frac{7}{20}, \frac{17}{24}, \frac{14}{30} \right) = \frac{7}{20}$$

5.12.2 The IND_WOR and IND_AVE Metrics

Let

$$D\_ij = \min_{k=i,j} \left(\frac{CARD(D\_k \setminus (D\_i \cap D\_j))}{CARD(D\_k)} \right)$$

be the DISTANCE BETWEEN TWO SETS given by the minimum of the two ratios calculated for each version as the number of the domains not shared with the other one divided by the total number of its own domains.

and let

$$DM\_i = \frac{1}{n-1} \sum_{\substack{j=1 \\ j \neq i}}^{n} D\_ij$$

be the DISTANCE OF A SET FROM THE OTHERS given by the mean of the distances of the set from the other ones.

The mean values of the distances for the exemplifying case are:

$$DM\_1 = \frac{1}{2} \left(\frac{17}{20} + \frac{18}{24} \right) = \frac{32}{40}$$

$$DM\_2 = \frac{1}{2} \left(\frac{17}{20} + \frac{8}{20} \right) = \frac{25}{40}$$

$$DM\_3 = \frac{1}{2} \left(\frac{8}{20} + \frac{18}{24} \right) = \frac{23}{40}$$

Definition 6

The IND_WOR metric is defined as:

$$IND\_WOR : D^n \longrightarrow [0..1]$$

$$IND\_WOR (D\_1, \ldots, D\_n) = \min_{i=1..n} DM\_i$$

The IND_WOR metric equates the functional diversity degree of n modelling functions to the minimum of the distances of each set of the semantic domains from the other ones.

The value of IND_WOR for the exemplifying case is:

$$IND\_WOR (D\_1, D\_2, D\_3) = \min \left(\frac{32}{40}, \frac{25}{40}, \frac{23}{40} \right) = \frac{23}{40}$$

Definition 7

The IND_AVE metric is defined as:

$$\text{IND\_AVE} \quad : D^n \longrightarrow [0..1]$$

$$\text{IND\_AVE} \ (D\_1,\ldots,D\_n) \ = \ \frac{1}{n} \ \sum_{i=1}^{n} DM\_i$$

The IND_AVE metric equates the functional diversity degree of n modelling functions to the mean of the distances of the n sets of the semantic domains from the other ones.

The value of IND_AVE for the exemplifying case is:

$$\text{IND\_AVE} \ (D\_1,D\_2,D\_3) \ = \ \frac{1}{3} \ (\ \frac{32}{40} \ + \ \frac{25}{40} \ + \ \frac{23}{40} \ ) \ = \ \frac{2}{3}$$

5.12.3 The VER_WOR and VER_AVE Metrics

Let the REDUNDANCY OF A SEMANTIC DOMAIN be the value (n-j), where j is the number of the sets the domain belongs to. The maximum redundancy value, achieved when a domain belongs only to one set, is (n-1). Let the REDUNDANCY OF A SET OF SEMANTIC DOMAINS be the sum of the redundancy values of its semantic domains. The maximum redundancy value of a set is the product of the number of domains belonging to the set multiplied by (n-1).

Definition 8

The VER_WOR metric is defined as:

$$\text{VER\_WOR} \quad : D^n \longrightarrow [0..1]$$

$$\text{VER\_WOR}(D\_1,..,D\_n) \ = \ \min_{i=1..n} \ \left(\frac{\sum_{j=1}^{n} CARD(D\_i \cap INT_j \ (D\_1,..,D\_n))*(n-j)}{(n-1) \ * \ CARD(D\_i)} \right)$$

The VER_WOR metric equates the functional diversity degree of n modelling functions to the minimum of the n ratios calculated for each version as the redundancy value of the set divided by its maximum value.

The value of VER_WOR for the exemplifying case is:

$$
\text{VER\_WOR} \ (D\_1, D\_2, D\_3) \ = \ min \ (\ \frac{39}{48}, \ \frac{25}{40}, \ \frac{42}{60} \ ) \ = \ \frac{25}{40}
$$

Definition 9

The VER_AVE metric is defined as:

$$
\text{VER\_AVE} \ : \ D^n \longrightarrow [0..1]
$$

$$
\text{VER\_AVE}(D\_1, \ldots, D\_n) \ = \ \frac{\displaystyle\sum_{j=1}^{n} \text{CARD}(\text{INT}_j \ (D\_1, .., D\_n)) * (n-j)}{(n-1) \ * \ \text{CARD}(\ \bigcup\limits_{i=1}^{n} \ D\_i)}
$$

The VER_AVE metric equates the functional diversity degree of n modelling functions to the ratio of the sum of the redundancy values of the domains of all the modelling functions divided by the sum of the corresponding maximum redundancy values.

The value of VER_AVE for the exemplifying case is:

$$
\text{VER\_AVE} \ (D\_1, D\_2, D\_3) \ = \ \frac{38*2 + 15*1}{55*2} \ = \ \frac{91}{110}
$$

5.12.4 The GLO_REL Metric

Let the DIVERSITY LEVEL OF A SEMANTIC DOMAIN be the value (n+1-j), where j is the number of the sets the domain belongs to. The maximum diversity level value, achieved when a domain belongs only to one set, is n.

Let the DIVERSITY LEVEL OF A SET OF SEMANTIC DOMAINS be the sum of the diversity level values of its semantic domains. The maximum diversity level value of a set is the product of the number of domains belonging to the set multiplied by n.

Let NORM be the linear function defined for n>1 as:

$$\text{NORM} : [1/n..1] \longrightarrow [0..1]$$

$$\text{NORM}(X) = \frac{n * X - 1}{n - 1}$$

which linearly transforms a number in the range [1/n..1] into a number in the range [0..1].

Definition 10

The GLO_REL metric is defined as:

$$\text{GLO\_REL} : D^n \longrightarrow [0..1]$$

$$\text{GLO\_REL}(D\_1,..,D\_n) = \text{NORM}\left(\frac{\sum_{j=1}^{n} \text{CARD}(\text{INT}_j(D\_1,..,D\_n))*(n-j+1)}{n * \text{CARD}(\bigcup_{i=1}^{n} D\_i)}\right)$$

The GLO_REL metric equates the functional diversity degree of n modelling functions to the linear transformation NORM_1 of the ratio of the sum of the diversity level values of the domains of all the modelling functions divided by the sum of the corresponding maximum diversity level values.

The value of GLO_REL for the exemplifying case is:

$$\text{GLO\_REL}(D\_1,D\_2,D\_3) = \frac{3}{2}\left(\frac{38*3 + 15*2 + 2*1}{55*3}\right) - \frac{1}{2} = \frac{91}{110}$$

5.13 Classification of the Metrics

Generally, a metric applied to a defined object is meaningful with respect to the object attribute one intends to measure, and to the weight one intends to give to that attribute.

As an example, if a metric measuring the space occupied by a body is required, the volume could be appropriate, but, if the objective is to use this metric to determine the number of bodies one can store in a room, the pure volume metric could be improper and an "equivalent body volume" should be defined according to the body shape and to the storage policy adopted.

Starting from these considerations, all the metrics presented in the latter paragraph are classified according to the following parameters:

- SYSTEM ATTRIBUTE, that is the system characteristic which is mainly influencing the value of the metric; four possible characteristics have been considered:

- EFFECTIVENESS of the system w.r.t. the planned redundancy. This attribute could be important if a predefined ideal redundancy had been specified, corresponding to the number of versions implemented, and the difference with respect to that must be measured.

- INDEPENDENCE of the versions composing the system. Metrics based on this attribute could be used as a pure "diversity evaluator" not taking into account any application or architecture constraint.

- REDUNDANCY of the versions.

- GLOBAL REDUNDANCY of the system. Metrics based on these two last attributes could be useful to evaluate the actual redundancy level of the system; the difference between them lays in the point of view: one version with respect to all the other ones or the global system view.

- WEIGHT, that underlines if the metric takes into account the average characteristics of all the versions or the characteristic of the worst one.

- WORST CASE, that identifies the situation corresponding to the value 0 for the metric (for all the metrics the value 1 corresponds to the case of ideal functional diversity).

The results of the classification are presented in the following table:

Table 5.1. Metrics classification

METRICS	ATTRIBUTE	WEIGHT	WORST CASE
EFF_WOR	EFFECTIVENESS	WORST	ONE SEMANTIC DOMAIN SET IS INSIDE THE UNION OF THE OTHERS
IND_WOR	INDEPENDENCE	WORST	ONE SEMANTIC DOMAIN SET IS CONTAINED IN OR CONTAINS ANY OTHER
IND_AVE	INDEPENDENCE	AVERAGE	ALL THE DOMAIN SETS ARE IN A "MATRIOSKA"-LIKE CONFIGURATION
VER_WOR	VERSIONS REDUNDANCY	WORST	ONE SET OF SEMANTIC DOMAINS IS CONTAINED IN THE INTERSECTION OF THE OTHERS
VER_AVE	VERSIONS REDUNDANCY	AVERAGE	ALL THE MODELLING FUNCTIONS USE THE SAME SET OF DOMAINS
GLO_REL	GLOBAL REDUNDANCY	AVERAGE	ALL THE MODELLING FUNCTIONS USE THE SAME SET OF DOMAINS

5.14 Reliability Analysis for Functionally Diverse Systems

In conformity with the approach followed to model functional diversity based on a high level specification analysis, the system reliability will be evaluated more properly on the basis of the specification correctness rather than on the run time system behaviour.

Then the reliability of a functionally diverse system is evaluated in terms of absence of errors in its specification.

In this context, at a single version level, the reliability is intended as "the probability of the corresponding specification correctness".

At system level, the reliability is intended as "the probability of system specification correctness"; it will be evaluated taking into account:

- the correctness of each version specification,

- the specification commonalities in terms of common parts among the versions,

- the system architecture.

It clearly appears that the crucial part of reliability evaluation is the specification analysis that, for the above mentioned reasons, can be considered as static.

In the following, the most important features of this analysis will be outlined.

5.15 Static Specification Analysis

It is assumed that the specification is the representation used to describe the process modelling adopted and that it is written using a formal language allowing to identify the semantic entities (functions and domains) involved.

This "semantic" specification language will have its own constructs, so the objective of the specification analysis will be the evaluation of some relevant factors involving these constructs.

The factors that better characterize a specification, from the point of view of reliability analysis, are:

- complexity factor C that takes into account the different complexity of the language constructs used in the specification,

- maximum number of errors for complexity unit factor Kc; this factor represents the relationship between the specification complexity unit and the number of errors that can be produced by it.

5.16 Reliability Evaluation

In this paragraph it will be described how to use the specification analysis for each version and for system reliability evaluation.

5.16.1 One Version Reliability Evaluation

The evaluation of one version reliability is based on the following hypothesis:

HYPOTHESIS 1V: the occurrence of one error in the specification is independent from the occurrence of another error, that is:

$$P(e1/e2) = P(e1)$$

Under this hypothesis, the reliability evaluation consists of the following steps:

- identification of the different language specification constructs used in order to evaluate the complexity factor C of the specification,

- evaluation of the factor Kc, that is the maximum number of errors that can occur per complexity unit,

- calculation of the maximum number of errors Nc that can occur in the specification as:

$$Nc=C*Kc$$

- evaluation of the probability p of occurrence of one error by means of the failure analysis of similar systems already in operation.

So, the reliability of one version is the probability that the version is correct, that is:

$$R=P(\text{version is correct})=(1-p)^{Nc}$$

This expression is a consequence of the independence hypothesis.

5.16.2 System Reliability Evaluation

As already mentioned, in system reliability evaluation it is necessary to take into account:

- the correctness of each version specification,

- the specification commonalities,

- the system architecture.

In the following the last two points will be detailed.

The specification commonalities will be identified through the following steps:

- analysis of each version specification to identify its own semantic entities (semantic function and domains),

- identification of the semantic entities belonging to more than one version,

- identification, for each version specification, of the parts referring to the common semantic entities; these parts, in the following, will be referred to as "common parts",

- calculation of the maximum number of errors present in each part of the specifications (both common and not common ones).

For the system architecture, the markovian model described in chapter 10 will be used. The equations of this model require the evaluation of terms like:

$P(Ii{\neq}Ij/Ij)$ = PROBABILITY OF VERSION i PRODUCING AN INCORRECT RESULT DIFFERENT FROM THE ONE PRODUCED BY VERSION j GIVEN THAT VERSION j PRODUCES AN INCORRECT RESULT

$P(Ii{=}Ij/Ij)$ = PROBABILITY OF VERSION i PRODUCING THE SAME RESULT PRODUCED BY VERSION j, GIVEN THAT VERSION j PRODUCES AN INCORRECT RESULT

For the notation used in these expressions, see chapter 10. Before evaluating these terms, the notation used will be described.

Let Vi, Vj be the version specifications corresponding to versions i and j. Each version Vi will be considered as being constituted as:

$Vi = Vii \cup Vij$

where:

Vii is the part of the specification belonging only to the version i and not to j; the fact that Vii is correct will be expressed as C(Vii) and the fact that Vii is incorrect will be expressed as I(Vii).

Vij is the part of the specification belonging to both i and j; the fact that Vij is correct will be expressed as C(Vij) and the fact that Vij is incorrect will be expressed as I(Vij).

Figure 5.5 shows this situation.

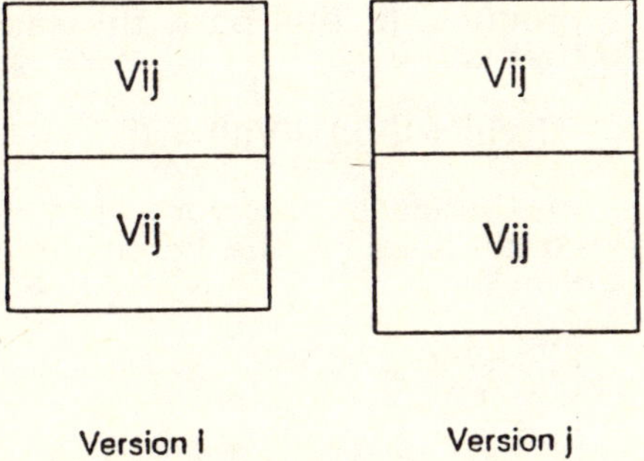

Fig. 5.5. Composition of versions Vi and Vj

The basic assumption to deal with such a general situation consists in considering that the common part of the two versions is totally identical and the not-common part is totally diverse. This implies that the behaviour of the two versions in the common part is exactly the same: if one fails, the other one does, too, producing the same erroneous output, and if one is correct, also the other one is. On the contrary, in the not common part, their behaviour is completely independent; this means that the behaviour of one does not provide any information about the behaviour of the other one.

In the case of multiple errors which occurred both in the common and in the not common part, the behaviour of the common part is assumed to be prevalent and then the outputs of the two versions are conservatively assumed to be equal, even if the presence of not common errors will probably modify the final outputs of the two versions.

These assumptions are, generally, conservative or, at least, realistic even if some implications (e.g. the correctness of the "common part" of a version implying the correctness of the "common part" of the other one) should be validated carefully.

In a more formal way, the following hypotheses can be stated:

HYPOTHESIS 1S: in the versions multiple errors can be present

HYPOTHESIS 2S: if V_j fails in V_{ij}, also V_i fails in V_{ij}, that is:

$$P(I(V_{ij})/I(V_{ji})) = 1$$

this implies that:

if V_j is correct in V_{ij}, also V_i is correct in V_{ij}, that is:

$$P(I(V_{ij})/C(V_{ji})) = 0$$

HYPOTHESIS 3S: if the two versions fail in the not-common part, they fail independently and they produce in this part different erroneous outputs, that is:

$$P(I(V_{ii})/I(V_{jj})) = P(I(V_{ii}))$$

and

$$P(I(V_{ii}) = I(V_{jj})/I(V_{jj}) \text{ and } I(V_{ii})) = 0$$

HYPOTHESIS 4S: if the two versions fail in the common part they produce, in this part, the same erroneous output, that is:

$$P(I(V_{ij}) = I(V_{ji})/I(V_{ji})) = 1$$

HYPOTHESIS 5S: in the case of errors, the versions outputs are conditioned by the behaviour of the common part, that is:

$$P(I(V_i)=I(V_j)/C(V_{ij})) = 0$$

and

$$P(I(V_i) \neq I(V_j)/I(V_{ij})) = 0$$

In the case of more than two versions, the situation is more complex. The case of three versions, shown in figure 5.4, will be considered for simplicity sake.

Let V_i, V_j, V_k be the corresponding specifications for a three versions system. Each version V_i will be considered as:

$$V_i = V_{ii} \cup V_{ij} \cup V_{ik} \cup V_{ijk}$$

where:

Vii is the part of the specification belonging only to version i and neither to j nor to k,

Vij is the part of the specification belonging both to i and j and not to k,

Vik is the part of the specification belonging only to i and k and not to j,

Vijk is the part of the specification common to the three versions.

The operators C(Vx) and I(Vx) will indicate respectively correctness and incorrectness of the set Vx.

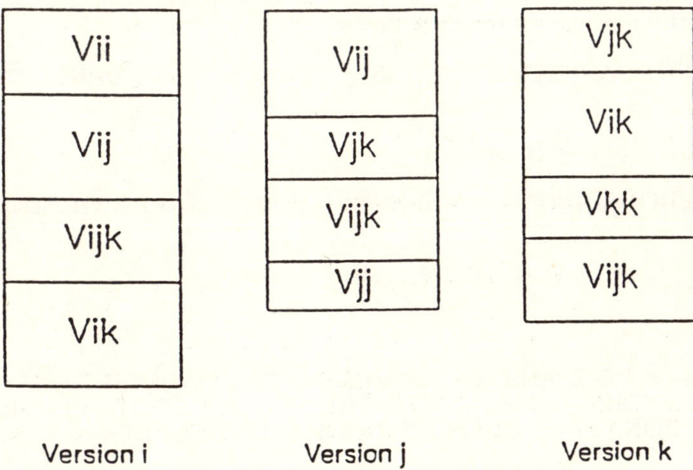

Fig. 5.6. Composition of versions Vi, Vj and Vk.

In the case of multiple errors, more possibilities must be considered. Again, it is possible to assume that the behaviour of the part common to all the versions is prevalent and then the presence of errors in Vijk implies that all the versions produce the same incorrect output.

In the case of a version having errors at most in two different parts common respectively to two other versions (e.g. if errors are present only in Vij and Vik and possibly in Vii, Vjj and Vkk), it can be assumed that the version fails producing an output equal either to one or to the other version (e.g. Ii=Ij and Ik≠Ii or Ii=Ik and Ij≠Ii), but it is impossible to state which versions produce the same output and which one produces a different one.

In the case of all the versions having errors in all the parts common to the other ones and correct in Vijk (e.g. if errors are present in Vij, Vik, Vjk and possibly in Vii, Vjj and Vkk, but not in Vijk), it can be assumed that two of the three versions produce the same incorrect output, whilst the other one produces a different output (e.g. Ii=Ij and Ik≠Ii or Ii=Ik and Ij≠Ii or Ij=Ik and Ii≠Ij) , but it is impossible to state which ones fail in the same way.

In a more formal way, and considering the general case of N versions, the hypothesis 5S must be generalized as follows:

HYPOTHESIS 5S1:   if k versions fail at least in a part common to all of them, they all produce the same erroneous output

HYPOTHESIS 5S2:   if k versions fail in parts common at most to m versions (m<k) round (k/m) different erroneous outputs will be produced and, at most, m versions will produce the same incorrect output.

In the following, the markovian model equations for a three version system will be calculated on the basis of these hypotheses.

In the equations besides Nc, maximum number of errors that can occur in one version specification, (referred to as Ni, Nj,...), the maximum number of errors that can occur in parts common to more specifications, (referred to as Nij, Nijk,...) will be considered.

The list of the equations terms follows:

P(Ci) = PROBABILITY OF VERSION i EXECUTING CORRECTLY =

$$= (1-p)^{Ni}$$

P(Ii) = PROBABILITY OF VERSION i EXECUTING INCORRECTLY =

$$= 1 - P(Ci) = 1 - (1-p)^{Ni}$$

P(Ii≠Ij/Ij) = PROBABILITY OF VERSION i PRODUCING AN INCORRECT RESULT DIFFERENT FROM THE ONE PRODUCED BY VERSION j GIVEN THAT VERSION j PRODUCES AN INCORRECT RESULT =

$$= \frac{P(C(Vij \cup Vijk)) * P(I(Vii \cup Vik)) * P(I(Vjj \cup Vjk))}{P(I(Vj))}$$

$$= \frac{(1-p)^{Nij} * [1-(1-p)^{Ni-Nij}] * [1-(1-p)^{Nj-Nij}]}{1 - (1-p)^{Nj}}$$

P(Ii=Ij/Ij) = PROBABILITY OF VERSION i PRODUCING THE SAME RESULT PRODUCED BY VERSION j, GIVEN THAT VERSION j PRODUCES AN INCORRECT RESULT =

$$= \frac{P(I(Vij \cup Vijk))}{P(I(Vj))}$$

$$= \frac{1 - (1-p)^{N_{ij}}}{1 - (1-p)^{N_j}}$$

$P(C_i/I_j)$ = PROBABILITY OF VERSION i EXECUTING CORRECTLY, GIVEN THAT VERSION j EXECUTES INCORRECTLY=

$$= \frac{P(C(V_{ij} \cup V_{ijk})) * P(I(V_{jj} \cup V_{jk})) * P(C(V_{ii} \cup V_{ik}))}{P(I(V_j))}$$

$$= \frac{(1-p)^{N_{ij}} * [1-(1-p)^{N_j-N_{ij}}] * (1-p)^{N_i-N_{ij}}}{1 - (1-p)^{N_j}} =$$

$$= \frac{(1-p)^{N_i} * [1 - (1-p)^{N_j-N_{ij}}]}{1 - (1-p)^{N_j}}$$

$P(I_i/C_j)$ = PROBABILITY OF VERSION i EXECUTING INCORRECTLY, GIVEN THAT VERSION j EXECUTES CORRECTLY =

$$= P(I(V_{ii} \cup V_{ik}))$$

$$= 1 - (1-p)^{N_i-N_{ij}}$$

$P(C_i/C_j)$ = PROBABILITY OF VERSION i EXECUTING CORRECTLY, GIVEN THAT VERSION j EXECUTES CORRECTLY =

$$= P(C(V_{ii} \cup V_{ik}))$$

$$= \frac{(1-p)^{N_i+N_j-N_{ij}}}{(1-p)^{N_j}} = (1-p)^{N_i-N_{ij}}$$

$P(Ik{\neq}Ii{\neq}Ij/Ii{\neq}Ij)$ = PROBABILITY OF VERSION k PRODUCING AN INCORRECT RESULT DIFFERENT FROM THE ONES PRODUCED BY VERSION i AND j GIVEN THAT BOTH VERSIONS i AND j PRODUCE 2 DIFFERENT INCORRECT RESULTS =

$$= \frac{P(Ik{\neq}Ii{\neq}Ij)}{P(Ii{\neq}Ij)}$$

$$= \frac{P(I(Vkk))*P(I(Vii))*P(I(Vjj))*P(C(Vij \cup Vik \cup Vjk \cup Vijk))}{P(C(Vij \cup Vijk))*P(I(Vii \cup Vik)) * P(I(Vjj \cup Vjk))} =$$

$$= \frac{[1-(1-p)^{Nk-Nik-Njk+Nijk}]*[1-(1-p)^{Ni-Nik-Nij+Nijk}]}{(1-p)^{Nij}*[1-(1-p)^{Ni-Nij}]*[1-(1-p)^{Nj-Nij}]} *$$

$$* \frac{[1-(1-p)^{Nj-Njk-Nij+Nijk}] * (1-p)^{Nij+Nik+Njk-2Nijk}}{1}$$

$P(Ck/Ii{\neq}Ij)$ = PROBABILITY OF VERSION k PRODUCING A CORRECT RESULT GIVEN THAT BOTH VERSIONS i AND j PRODUCE 2 DIFFERENT INCORRECT RESULTS =

$$= \frac{P(C(Vkk))*P(I(Vii))*P(I(Vjj))*P(C(Vij \cup Vik \cup Vjk \cup Vijk))}{P(C(Vij \cup Vijk))*P(I(Vii \cup Vik))*P(I(Vjj \cup Vjk))} =$$

$$= \frac{(1-p)^{Nk-Nik-Njk+Nijk}*[1-(1-p)^{Ni-Nik-Nij+Nijk}]}{(1-p)^{Nij} * [1-(1-p)^{Ni-Nij}]*[1-(1-p)^{Nj-Nij}]} *$$

$$* \frac{[1-(1-p)^{Nj-Nij-Njk+Nijk}]*(1-p)^{Nij+Nik+Njk-2Nijk}}{1} =$$

$$= \frac{(1-p)^{Nk-Nijk} * [1-(1-p)^{Ni-Nik-Nij+Nijk}]}{[1-(1-p)^{Ni-Nij}] * [1-(1-p)^{Nj-Nij}]} \ *$$

$$* \ \frac{[1-(1-p)^{Nj-Nij-Njk+Nijk}]}{1}$$

$P(Ik{\neq}Ii/Ii{=}Ij)$ = PROBABILITY OF VERSION k PRODUCING AN INCORRECT RESULT DIFFERENT FROM THE ONES PRODUCED BY VERSION i GIVEN THAT VERSIONS i AND j PRODUCES THE SAME INCORRECT RESULT =

$$= \frac{P(C(Vijk)) * P(I(Vij)) * P(I(Vkk \cup Vik \cup Vjk))}{P(I(Vij \cup Vijk))}$$

$$= \frac{(1-p)^{Nijk} * [1-(1-p)^{Nij-Nijk}] * [1-(1-p)^{Nk-Nijk}]}{1-(1-p)^{Nij}}$$

$P(Ik{=}Ii/Ii{=}Ij)$ = PROBABILITY OF VERSION k PRODUCING AN INCORRECT RESULT EQUAL TO THE ONES PRODUCED BY VERSION i GIVEN THAT VERSIONS i AND j PRODUCE THE SAME INCORRECT RESULT =

$$= \frac{P(I(Vijk))}{P(I(Vij \cup Vijk))}$$

$$= \frac{1-(1-p)^{Nijk}}{1-(1-p)^{Nij}}$$

$P(Ck/Ii{=}Ij)$ = PROBABILITY OF VERSION k PRODUCING A CORRECT RESULT GIVEN THAT BOTH VERSIONS i AND j PRODUCE THE SAME INCORRECT RESULT =

$$= \frac{P(C(Vijk) * P(I(Vij)) * P(C(Vkk \cup Vik \cup Vjk))}{P(I(Vij \cup Vijk))} =$$

$$= \frac{(1-p)^{Nijk} * [1-(1-p)^{Nij-Nijk}] * (1-p)^{Nk-Nijk}}{1 - (1-p)^{Nij}}$$

P(Ik≠Ii/IiCj) = PROBABILITY OF VERSION k PRODUCING AN INCORRECT RESULT DIFFERENT FROM THE ONE PRODUCED BY VERSION i GIVEN THAT VERSION i PRODUCES AN INCORRECT RESULT AND VERSION j PRODUCES A CORRECT RESULT =

$$= \frac{P(C(Vik))*P(I(Vii))*P(I(Vkk))}{P(I(Vii \cup Vik))}$$

$$= \frac{(1-p)^{Nik-Nijk}}{[1 - (1-p)^{Ni-Nij}]} *$$

$$* \frac{[1 - (1-p)^{Ni-Nik-Nij+Nijk}] * [1- (1-p)^{Nk-Nik-Njk+Nijk}]}{1}$$

P(Ik=Ii/IiCj) = PROBABILITY OF VERSION k PRODUCING AN INCORRECT RESULT EQUAL TO THE ONE PRODUCED BY VERSION i GIVEN THAT VERSION i PRODUCES AN INCORRECT RESULT AND VERSION j PRODUCES A CORRECT RESULT =

$$= \frac{P(I(Vik))}{P(I(Vii \cup Vijk))}$$

$$= \frac{1 - (1-p)^{Nik-Nijk}}{1 - (1-p)^{Ni-Nij}}$$

P(Ck/IiCj) = PROBABILITY OF VERSION k PRODUCING A CORRECT RESULT GIVEN THAT VERSION i PRODUCES AN INCORRECT RESULT AND VERSION j PRODUCES A CORRECT RESULT =

$$= \frac{P(C(Vik))*P(C(Vkk))*P(I(Vii))}{P(I(Vii \ U \ Vik))}$$

$$= \frac{(1-p)^{Nk-Nkj} * [1- (1-p)^{Ni-Nik-Nij+Nijk}]}{[1 - (1-p)^{Ni-Nij}]}$$

P(Ik/CiCj) = PROBABILITY OF VERSION k PRODUCING AN INCORRECT RESULT GIVEN THAT VERSIONS i AND j PRODUCE A CORRECT RESULT =

$$= P(I(Vkk))$$

$$= 1 - (1-p)^{Nk-Nik-Njk+Nijk}$$

P(Ck/CiCj) = PROBABILITY OF VERSION K PRODUCING A CORRECT RESULT GIVEN THAT VERSIONS i AND j PRODUCE A CORRECT RESULT =

$$= P(C(Vkk))$$

$$= (1-p)^{Nk-Nik-Njk+Nijk}$$

P(Ik=Ii/Ii≠Ij) = PROBABILITY OF VERSION k PRODUCING AN INCORRECT RESULT EQUAL TO THE ONE PRODUCED BY VERSION i GIVEN THAT BOTH VERSIONS i AND j PRODUCE 2 DIFFERENT INCORRECT RESULTS

P(Ik=Ij/Ii≠Ij) = PROBABILITY OF VERSION k PRODUCING AN INCORRECT RESULT EQUAL TO THE ONE PRODUCED BY VERSION j GIVEN THAT BOTH VERSIONS i AND j PRODUCE 2 DIFFERENT INCORRECT RESULTS

```
P(Ik=Ii/Ii≠Ij) + P(Ik=Ij/Ii≠Ij) =
```

$$= \frac{P(I(Vik))*P(C(Vij \cup Vjk \cup Vijk))*P(I(Vjj))}{P(C(Vij \cup Vijk))*P(I(Vii \cup Vik))*P(I(Vjj \cup Vjk))} +$$

$$+ \frac{P(I(Vjk))*P(C(Vij \cup Vijk \cup Vik))*P(I(Vii))}{P(C(Vij \cup Vijk))*P(Vii \cup Vik))*P(I(Vjj \cup Vjk))} +$$

$$+ \frac{P(I(Vik))*P(I(Vjk))*P(C(Vij \cup Vijk))}{P(C(Vij \cup Vijk))*P(I(Vii \cup Vik))*P(I(Vjj \cup Vjk))} =$$

$$= \frac{[1-(1-p)^{Nik-Nijk}] * (1-p)^{Nij+Njk-Nijk}}{(1-p)^{Nij} * [1-(1-p)^{Ni-Nij}]} *$$

$$* \frac{[1-(1-p)^{Nj-Nij-Njk+Nijk}]}{[1-(1-p)^{Nj-Nij}]} +$$

$$+ \frac{[1-(1-p)^{Njk-Nijk}] * (1-p)^{Nij+Nik-Nijk}}{(1-p)^{Nij} * [1-(1-p)^{Ni-Nij}]} *$$

$$+ \quad \frac{[1-(1-p)^{Ni-Nij-Nik+Nijk}]}{[1-(1-p)^{Nj-Nij}]} \quad +$$

$$+ \quad \frac{[1-(1-p)^{Nik-Nijk}] * [1-(1-p)^{Njk-Nijk}] * (1-p)^{Nij}}{(1-p)^{Nij} * [1-(1-p)^{Ni-Nij}] * [1-(1-p)^{Nj-Nij}]}$$

5.17 Semantic Specification Language

The approach followed to model functional diversity gives a strategic role to each system version specification; in fact, it is based on a high level specification analysis with the objective of identifying the semantic entities involved (semantic domains and functions) to evaluate the diversity degree.

It clearly appears that each specification should be written in such a way to constitute a "good" basis for functional diversity and reliability evaluation.

The guidelines contained in this chapter aim to define the characteristics of a language useful in supporting the outlining of semantic entities and the identification of commonalities among the version specifications.

5.17.1 Specification Language Characteristics for Functionally Diverse Systems

In this chapter the guidelines for the specification language are defined.

The specification language that should be used must satisfy some requirements that can be summarized in the following points:

- the language should allow to specify the process modelling corresponding to each version in terms of semantic entities (semantic domains and functions) and their relationships in a suitable detail for diversity and reliability evaluation.

- the language grammar should permit to outline the appropriate characteristics of each semantic entity.

The first step in the research of a specification language has been to study the most important existing specification languages.

None of them considers the semantic aspect involved in the specification of a system. For this reason the existing languages have formed only a starting point for our own semantic specification language definition.

The semantic entities declaration, on which it is based, is a feature derived from the specification languages based on the abstract data types.

Corresponding to abstract data types and their relationships are respectively semantic domains and semantic functions.

The most relevant extensions that have been made are:

- identification of keywords to be added to the domain attributes so that the semantic analysis should be simplified,

- identification of a limited subset of constructs to be used in the function description.

The language has been defined so that the specification assumes a particular format, that is it consists of a big declaration part where each item used is described and its semantics is outlined, whilst the functional part is constituted only by the relationships between the semantic entities.

In fact, also the expressions and the conditions have been described with their semantics in the declaration part.

For each item used in the specification (expressions, domains and functions) its semantics should be described.

The semantic items cannot change their semantics through the specification.

5.17.2 Guidelines for a Semantic Specification Language Definition

This paragraph contains the guidelines for the definition of a language for the "semantic specification".

The language should be structured so that the specification consists of two main blocks:

- the declaration block,

- the specification body.

5.17.2.1 Declaration Block

In this part of the specification, the semantic domains, functions and conditions that activate each function used in the specification body are identified.

SEMANTIC DOMAINS

The semantic domains are divided in abstract semantic domains and real semantic domains.

-abstract semantic domains:

These domains are empty structures used to specify the typology of the domains used by the different semantic functions.

There is only one abstract semantic domain for each typology.

For each of these domains the declaration structure has the following format:

has_name:

has_semantics:

is_used_by:

has_name: this field contains the name (identifier) of the abstract semantic domain, this is the name that is referred to in the structure of the semantic function using it

has_semantics: this field identifies the meaning of the domain, that is its semantics

is_used_by: this field contains a list of all the semantic functions using it

- real semantic domains:

These domains are the actual semantic domains involved in the version specification.

For each of the abstract semantic domains at least one real semantic domain must exist.

The only real semantic domains that have not the corresponding abstract semantic domains may be those with "has_attribute" field equal to constant.

The identified declaration structure for real semantic domains is:

has_name:

has_type:

has_semantics:

has_attribute:

is_created_by:

is_used_in:

has_name: this field contains the name (identifier) of the real semantic domain that is used in the occurrence of the function

has_type: this field contains the name of the corresponding abstract domain (not applicable for some constant domains: e.g. physical universal constant)

has_semantics: identifies its semantics

has_attribute: this field specifies if the domain is an input, output, intermediate or constant domain

is_created_by: this field identifies the semantic function creating it; not applicable for input and constant domains

is_used_in: this field contains the list of all the semantic functions using it. In the case that the semantic domain is used only within the scope of a function the corresponding symbol and the occurrence of the function must be specified as <function id.>=<symbol> with <function occurrence>

SEMANTIC FUNCTIONS

In the declaration block the semantic functions are described using the abstract semantic domains, whilst in their occurrence within the body of the specification they use the corresponding real semantic domain.

Each semantic function declaration structure is constituted as:

- declaration part

- expressions declaration

- expression condition declaration

- function body

- declaration part:

The identified declaration part structure for the semantic function is:

has_name:

has_semantics:

has_input:

has_intermediate:

has_output:

is_activated_by:

has_name:	this field contains the name (identifier) of the function
has_semantics:	identifies its semantics
has_input:	this field contains the list of the abstract semantic domains constituting the function input
has_intermediate:	this field contains the list of the intermediate abstract semantic domains that exist only within the scope of the function
has_output:	this field contains the list of all the abstract semantic domains constituting the function output
is_activated_by:	this part contains the list of all the conditions that in the body of the specification activate the function

- expression declaration:

This part contains the description of the expressions used by the function within its body.

For each expression the declaration format is:

has_name:

has_semantics:

is_activated_by:

has_structure:

has_name: name of the expression

has_semantics: the semantics of the expression

is_activated_by: the name of the condition that activates it

has_structure: the structure of the expression (e.g. (a+b)*c)

- expression condition declaration:

This part contains the description of the conditions used within the body of the function. The expression condition declaration format is:

has_name:

has_semantics:

has_structure:

has_input:

has_name: condition name

has_semantics: condition semantics

has_structure: condition structure (e.g. a<b))

has_input: identifies the name of the abstract domains used

- function body:

This part contains the logical flow for the function expressed in terms of   a set of sequence, iteration, selection constructs and expression names.

CONDITION DECLARATION

This part contains the description of the conditions used within the body of the specification.

The identified structure for the condition declaration is:

has_name:

has_semantics:

has_structure:

has_name: condition name

has_semantics: condition semantics

has_structure: condition structure

5.17.2.2 Specification Body

This is the body of the specification that is constituted of the logical flow
based on the three constructs: sequence, iteration, selection.

5.17.3 Specification Structure

In this section the structure of the specification is described.

```
SPECIFICATION

    <SDstart>

    - Domain Declaration

      - Function Declaration

      - F_condition Declaration

      - S_body Definition

    <SD_end>


    - DOMAIN DECLARATION

    <DD_start>
            <ADD_start>
                    --<*begin>
                    |                has_name:
                    |                has_semantics:
                    |                is_used_by:
                    --<*end>
            <ADD_end>


            <RDD_start>
                    --<*begin>
                    |                has_name:
                    |                has_semantics:
                    |                has_type:
                    |                has_attribute:
                    |                is_created_by:
                    :                is_used_in:
                    --<*end>
            <RDD_end>
    <DD_end>
```

- FUNCTION DECLARATION


```
<FD_start>
      --<*begin>
       |              <DP_start>
       :                           has_name:
       :                           has_semantics:
       :                           has_input:
       :                           has_intermediate:
       :                           has_output:
       :                           is_activated_by:
       :              <DP_end>
       |              <ED_start>
       |                    --<*begin>
       |                    |            has_name:
       :                    |            has_semantics:
       |                    |            is_activated_by:
       :                    |            has_structure:
       :                    --<*end>
       :              <ED_end>
       |              <ECD_start>
       |                    --<*begin>
       :                    |            has_name:
       :                    :            has_semantics:
       :                    |            has_structure:
       :                    |            activates:
       |                    --<*end>
       |              <FBD_start>
       |                           has_body:
       |              <FBD_end>
      --<*end>
<FD_end>
```


- F_CONDITION DECLARATION


```
<FCD_start>
      --<*begin>
       |            has_name:
       :            has_semantics:
       :            has_structure:
      --<*end>
<FCD_end>
```


- S_BODY DEFINITION


```
<SBD_start>
            has_body:
<SBD_end>
```

5.18 Semantic Specification Analysis Methodology

The practical problem to solve in order to apply the functional diversity theory is to define a methodology permitting: to identify the commonalities among the entities involved in the specifications, to classify the specification parts on the basis of the commonalities present in them and to define methods to evaluate the complexity of these parts.

5.18.1 Static Specification Analysis

The usage of a suitable language for the specification of functionally diverse systems as described in section 5.17 allows to structure a version specification in such a way to outline the semantic domains and functions and their relationships.

The specification is structured by means of four main blocks:

- domain declaration
- function declaration
- F_condition declaration
- specification body definition

The common entities among the specifications and the occurrence of each entity within the same specification can be outlined analysing the blocks.

In the following it will be explained how each block influences the evaluation of the factors that have to be used in functional diversity degree assessment and reliability evaluation.

5.18.1.1 Diversity Degree Assessment

In section 5.12 the metrics to evaluate the degree of functional diversity of n modelling functions have been analysed.

All these metrics are based on the common and not common semantic domains.

For this reason the first step in the specification analysis is the identification of the common and non common semantic domains.

The set of the semantic domains (common and not) will be derived from the declaration part of each specification.

The only semantic domains that have to be considered will be the real ones, in fact they represent the several occurrences within the specification of the abstract ones.

The result of the specification analysis will be:

SD(i,j)={real semantic domains belonging to version i and j}

SD(i,j,k)={real semantic domains belonging to i and j and k}

SD(i)={real semantic domains belonging only to the version i}

Performing all the required operations on these sets, it is possible to derive all the defined metrics.

5.18.1.2 Reliability Evaluation

As seen in section 5.16, concerning the correctness of each version specification the factors that must be evaluated are:

- the complexity factor C taking into account the different language constructs,

- the maximum number of errors that can occur per complexity unit: factor Kc,

- the probability p of occurrence of one error estimated by means of the failure analysis of similar systems already in operation.

Then the maximum number of errors Nc that can occur in the specification is calculated as:

Nc=CKc

So the reliability of one version is the probability that the version is correct, that is:

$R=P(\text{version is correct})=(1-p)^{Nc}$

The specification commonalities will be identified through the following steps:

- analysis of each version specification to identify its own semantic entities,

- identification of the semantic entities belonging to more than one version,

- identification, for each version specification, of the parts referring to the common semantic entities; these parts, in the following, will be referred to as "common parts",

- calculation of the maximum number of errors present in each part of the specifications (both common and not common ones).

For the system architecture, the markovian model (see chapter 10) will be used.

As seen in section 5.16, in the markovian model equations there are terms like Nc (maximum number of errors that can occur in one version specification), Nij (maximum number of error that can occur in parts common to more specifications), etc. that are to be evaluated.

In the following the specification analysis methodology to derive these terms and the assumptions made will be described. The hypotheses made are:

- the factor Kc will be 1,

- the probability of occurrence of one error p is derived from similar systems.

The first hypothesis implies that Nc=C, that is: the maximum number of errors that can occur in the specification or in a part of it is equal to the complexity of the specification or of that part.

The complexity of a specification (version) is influenced by the complexity of the semantic functions and the conditions constituting it.

The complexity of a semantic function F can be seen from two different points of view:

- the semantic one taken to define an "absolute complexity"

- the syntactical one taken to define a "structural complexity"

The "absolute complexity" of a semantic function is defined as "the proneness to errors due to its semantic and algorithmic complexity and the quantity of domains used".

Let CA(F) be the "absolute complexity"; it can be evaluated as:

$$CA(F)=C1*C2*C3$$

where:

C1 is a factor of semantic complexity that represents the intrinsic difficulty of the function F,

C2 is a factor that is influenced by the number of input, output and intermediate semantic domains used in F,

C3 is a factor taking into account the difficulty of the expressions and conditions contained in the function F.

Let CS(F) be the "structural complexity"; it can be evaluated as:

$$\sum_{i=1}^{3} pc_i * nc_i$$

where:

pc_i = weight of the construct i

nc_i = number of constructs of type i

The constructs are of three types (sequence, iteration and selection).

Let X be a real semantic domain used by a semantic function F, the complexity of F related to X: C(F/A) can be defined as:

$$C(F/X)=C_X*CA(F)/CS(F)$$

where:

C_X is the contribution of the domain X to the complexity of the function F and is evaluated as:

$$C_X = K_X * \left(\sum_{i=1}^{3} pc_{ix} * nc_{ix} \right)$$

where:

K_X is a factor representing the weight (importance) of the domain X

pc_{ix} = weight of the construct i in which X is involved

nc_{ix} = number of constructs of type i in which X is involved

Let SD be a set of real semantic domains used by a semantic function F
the complexity of the function is defined as:

$$C(F/SD) = \sum_{j=1}^{d} K_j * \left(\sum_{i=1}^{3} pc_{ij} * nc_{ij} \right) * \frac{CA(F)}{CS(F)}$$

where:

d=number of domains in SD

For the other elements of the specification body, F_conditions, it is
possible to evaluate the complexity as function of its criticality inside the
specification and of the construct types used in it.

Also in this case the complexity may be related to a set of domains
involved in it.

Let SD be a set of real semantic domains, CC(CI/SD), the complexity of
the F_conditions is evaluated as:

$$CC(CI/SD) = \sum_{i=1}^{d} KC_i * N_X$$

where:

- d is the number of domains in SD

- KC_i is the weight of the F_condition I

- N_X is the number of times the domain X is involved in I

The preceding definitions can be extended at version level considering
the complexity of the version due to a set of real semantic domains as:

$$C(VER/SD) = \sum_{i=1}^{f} C(F_i/SD) + \sum_{i=1}^{k} CC(C_i/SD)$$

where:

- f = number of semantic functions in the version

- k = number of F_conditions in the version

To evaluate the factors that are in the markovian model equations, the
version specifications have to be analysed following the steps:

- identification of the common and not common real semantic domains
  to obtain the sets of common and not common domains. This
  identification will be performed comparing the semantics of the
  domains

- identification of the semantic functions that use the real semantic domains

- specification analysis of each version to identify the constructs and the F_conditions of the specification in which the domains are involved

- evaluation of the complexity of each version related to the domain sets corresponding to the common parts as defined in the markovian model equations.

This procedure must be repeated for all the version specifications.

As a result, generally n different values for the common terms (Nij, Nijk etc.) will be obtained.

In order to be conservative, the value used in the terms of the markovian model equations will be the maximal one among them.

References

[AND84] T. Anderson: Can Design Faults be tolerated?. University of Newcastle upon Tyne Technical Report, 1984

[AVI84] A. Avizienis, J. Kelly: Fault Tolerance by Design Diversity: Concepts and Experiments. IEEE Computer, August 1984

[AVI85] A. Avizienis: The N-Version Approach to Fault Tolerant Software. IEEE Trans.on Software Engineering, Dec. 1985

[BIS85] P. Bishop, D. Esp, M. Barnes, et al.: Project on Diverse Software; An Experiment in Software Reliability. Proceedings of Safecomp '85, 1985, Pergamon Press

[DON76] J. Donahue: Complementary Definitions of Programming Language Semantics . Lecture Notes in Computer Science N. 42, 1976, Springer-Verlag

[ECK85] D.E. Eckhardt, L. D. Lee: A Theoretical Basis for the Analysis of Multiversion Software Subject to Coincident Errors. IEEE Transactions on Software Engineering, Dec. 1985

[FER82] E. Ferro: Appunti di istituzioni di analisi superiore: spazi metrici. Istituto di Matematica di Genova, 1982

[KEL86] J. Kelly, A. Avizienis, et al.: Multi-Version Software development. Proceedings of Safecomp '86, 1986, Pergamon Press

[KNI86] J. Knight, N. Leveson: An Experimental Evaluation of the Assumption of Independence in Multiversion Programming. IEEE Transactions in Software Engineering, Vol. SE-12, No 1, January 1986

[GNE79] B.V. Gnedenko: Teoria della probabilità. Editori Riuniti, 1979

[GUE81] I. Guessarian: Algebraic Semantics. Lecture Notes in Computer Science N. 99, 1981, Springer-Verlag

[OECD] The specification language X. OECD Halden Reactor Project Report

[RAN75] B. Randell: System Structure for Software Fault Tolerance. Proc. of the International Conference on Reliable Software, 1975

[SCO83] K. Scott: Experimental Validation of Six Fault Tolerant Software Reliability Models. IEEE 1983

[SCO84] K. Scott: Investigating Version Dependence in Fault Tolerant Software. IEEE 1984

[SHO83] M.L. Shooman: Software Engineering. Mc Graw Hill, 1983

[STO77] J. Stoy: Denotational Semantics : the Scott-Strachey approach to Programming Language Theory . MIT Press 1977

[TRE72] F. Trevisan: Appunti di osservazioni e misure. Istituto di Ingegneria Elettrotecnica di Genova, 1972

Appendix

GRAMMAR

1. SPECIFICATION

```
        +---------------+
---->| declaration 2 |---------->
        +---------------+
```

2. DECLARATION

```
      /---\
     / SD_ \      +-----------+        +-----------+
---\start/---->| dom_dec 3 |------->| fun_dec 4 |-----------|
     \___/        +-----------+        +-----------+           |
                                                               |
                                                               |
        -------------------------------------------------------|
     |
     |
     |                                                 /---\
     |   +---------------+        +----------+       / SD_ \
     |-->| F_cond_dec 5  |-------| S_body 6 |------\ end /---->
     |   +---------------+  ^     +----------+       \___/
     |                      |
     |______________________|
```

3 DOM_DEC

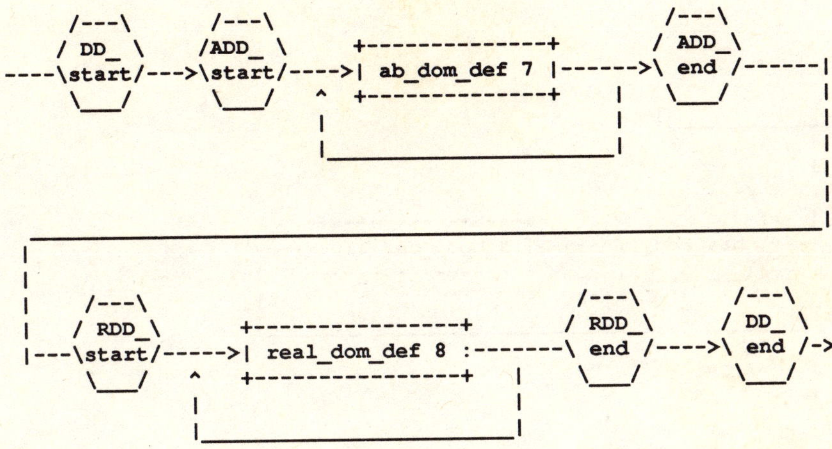

4 FUN_DEC

5 F_COND_DEC

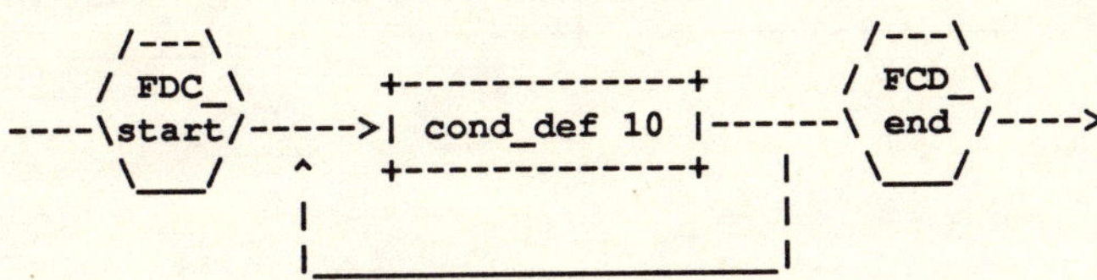

6 S_BODY

```
        /---\
       / SBD_\
    ----\start/--
        \___/  |
               |
               |
               |
    ___________|
   |
   |
   |       /--------\
   |      /          \          +----------------+
    ----\  has_body  /----->| S_body_def 11 :-----
         \          /          +----------------+   |
          \________/                                |
                                                    |
    ________________________________________________|
   |      /---\
   |     / SBD_\
   |--- \ end /----->
         \___/
```

7 AB_DOM_DEF

```
      /------\                                                    /----\
     /        \     +------------+     +------------+            /      \
  --\ *begin /-->| inv_stru 12 |--->| ab_stru 13 |--\ *end /-->
     \______/       +------------+     +------------+            \____/
```

8 RE_DOM_DEF

```
      /------\                                                    /------\
     /        \     +-------------+     +------------+           /        \
  ---\ *begin /--->| inv_stru 12 |--->| re_stru 14 |--\  *end  /--
     \______/        +-------------+     +------------+           \______/
```

9 FUN_DEF

```
        +----------+
  ----->| F_dec 18 |----->
        +----------+
```

10 COND_DEF

```
    /------\                                 /---------------\
   /        \        +---------------+      /                 \
---\ *begin /--->| inv_stru 12 |---\ has_structure : /------|
   \        /        +---------------+      \                 /      |
    \______/                                 \_______________/       |
                                                                     |
    ---------------------------------------------------------------- |
    |
    |                           /----\
    |        +----------+      /      \
    |---| text     |----\ *end /----->
    |        +----------+      \____/
```

11 S_BODY_DEF

```
                                          /----\
    +--------------------+               /      \
|->| function_occurrence |---\  ;      /----------->
|   +--------------------+      \      /
|                                \____/
|
|   /--\      /---\                              /---\
|  /    \    /     \    +----------------+      /     \
|-\ IF /--\  (  /-->| F_cond_name    |--\  )  /-|
|  \__/    \___/       +----------------+      \___/  |
|                                                     |
|    ------------------------------------------------:
|   |
|   |    +---------------------+
|   |---| function_occurrence |------------------:
|        +---------------------+                  |
|                                                 |
| |-----------------------------------------------:
| |  /--\    /--\
| | /    \  /    \  +-----------+  +-------------------+
| |-\ or /-\  ( /->|F_cond_name|->|function_occurrence|--|
| |^ \__/    \__/   +-----------+  +-------------------+|^|
| ||                                                   |||
| ||___________________________________________________|||
| |                                                    ||
| |                                                    ||
| |___________________________________________________||
|                                                     |
|                                                     |
|                                                     |
|                                                     |
| |---------------------------------------------------|
| |  /----------\                    /---\    /-\
| | /            \ +------------------+ /     \  /   \
| |-\ OTHERWISE /->|function_occurrence|-\ END /--\ ; /->
|    \__________/ +------------------+ \___/    \_/
|
:  /------\    /---\
: /        \  /     \ +-----------+  +-------------------+
:-\ WHILE /-\  (   /-|F_cond_name|->|function_occurrence|>
   \______/    \___/  +-----------+  +-------------------+
```

12 INV_STRU

```
     /----------\                      /-\   /--------------\
    /            \    +----------+     /   \ /                \
  -\ has_name : /-->|   name    |-\ . /---\ has_semantics: /--|
    \__________/     +----------+   \_/    \______________/   |
                                                              |
    ----------------------------------------------------------|
    |
    |
    |    +------+       /-\
    |    |      |      /   \
    |----| text |----\  .  /---->
         +------+     \_/
```

13 AB_STRU

```
        /--------------\                              /---\
       /                \    +---------------+       /     \
  ----\  is_used_by : /--->| function_name :----->\  .  /->
       \______________/     +---------------+       \___/
```

14 RE_STRU

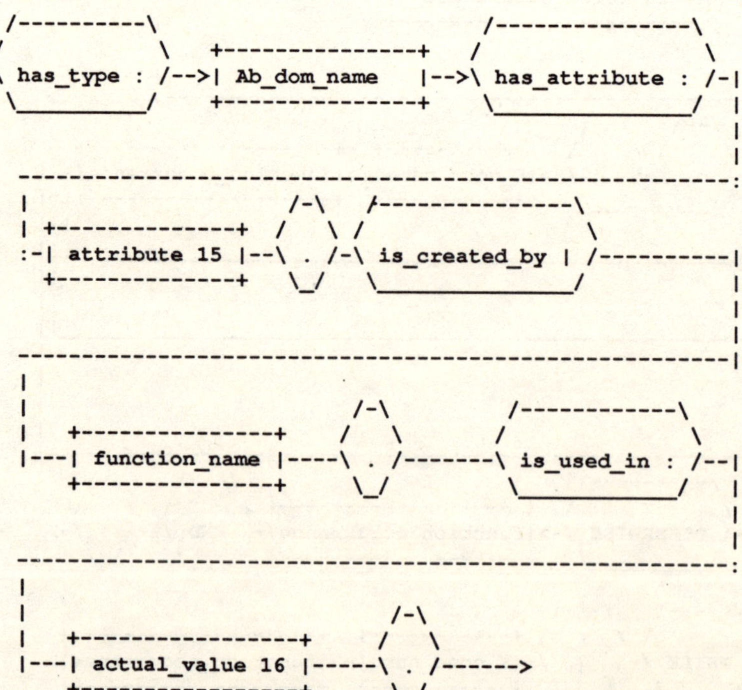

```
     /----------\                         /--------------\
    /            \    +---------------+   /                \
  -\ has_type : /-->| Ab_dom_name   |-->\ has_attribute : /-|
    \__________/     +---------------+    \______________/  |
                                                            |
       -----------------------------------------------------:
       |                   /-\  /--------------\
       | +--------------+ /   \/                \
      :-| attribute 15 |--\ . /-\ is_created_by | /----------|
        +--------------+   \_/  \______________/             |
                                                             |
       ------------------------------------------------------|
       |
       |                   /-\          /------------\
       | +--------------+ /   \        /              \
       |---| function_name |----\ . /-------\ is_used_in : /--|
           +--------------+     \_/         \__________/    |
                                                            |
       -----------------------------------------------------:
       |
       |                        /-\
       | +----------------+    /   \
       |---| actual_value 16 |-----\ . /------>
           +----------------+      \_/
```

15 ATTRIBUTE

```
              /-----\
             /       \
|---------\  input  /------->
|            \_____/
|
|            /-----------\
|           /             \
|---------\  intermediate /----->
|            \___________/
|
|            /------\
|           /        \
|---------\  output  /------>
|            \______/
|
|            /---------\
|           /           \
|---------\  constant  /----->
             \_______/
```

16 ACTUAL_VALUE

```
                         /-\                      /----\
      +--------+        /   \   +--------+       /      \
--->| id_ 76 |--->\ = /--->| id_ 76 |---\ WITH /-----------|
      +--------+        \_/      +--------+       \____/           |
                                                                  |
      ------------------------------------------------------------|
       |
       |
       |
       |      +--------------------+
       |-----| function_occurence |----->
              +--------------------+
```

17 FUNCTION_OCCURRENCE

```
                        /---\                         /-\
      +-----------------+   /     \   +-----------+   /   \
--| function_name |---\  ( /---| parameter |--\ ) /-
      +-----------------+   \___/      +-----------+   \_/
```

18 F_DEC

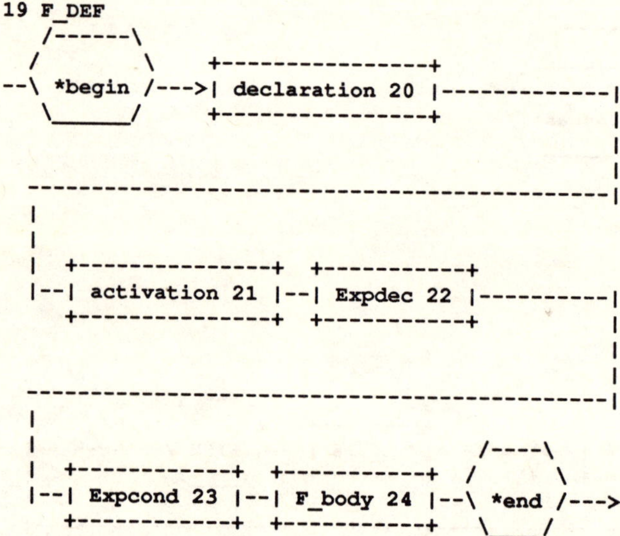

19 F_DEF

20 DECLARATION

```
   /-----\                              /----------\
  /  DP_  \    +--------------+        /            \
--\ start /---| inv_stru 12  |----\ has_input : /----|
  \_____/      +--------------+        \__________/    |
-----------------------------------------------------------|
  |
  |                          /-\
  |      +----------------+  / \
  |---| Ab_dom_name 25 |---\ . /--------------------|
  ^ +----------------+  | \_/                      |
     |                   |                          |
     |___________________|                          |

  |--------------------------------------------------|
  |    /-\    /----------------\
  |   / \  /                    \
  |--\ . /--\  has_intermediate: /--------------------|
     \_/    \__________________/                       |
  |--------------------------------------------------|
  |
  |
  |                             /-\
  |      +----------------+    / \
  |----| Ab_dom_name 25 :------\ . /--------------------|
  | ^ +----------------+  | ^ \_/                      |
  | |                     | |                          |
  | |_____________________| |                          |
  |                         |                          |
  |_________________________|                          |

  |_________________________________________________|
  |
  |  /-----------\              +----------------+    /-\
  | /             \             +----------------+   / \
--\ has_output: /----| Ab_dom_name 25|-----\ . /---|
   \___________/  ^ +----------------+ |  \_/     |
     |                 |                          |
     |_________________|                          |

  |_________________________________________________|
  |
  |
  |    /---\
  |   / DP_ \
  |---\ end /---->
      \___/
```

21 ACTIVATION

```
   /---------\
  /   is_     \   +--------------+      /--\
 -\activated_ /-|cond_name 26  |---\  /    \
  \   by:    /^  +--------------+  |  \  .  /-->
   \________/  |                   |   \__/
               |                   |
               |___________________|
```

22 EXPDEC

```
   /------\                         /---\
  /  ED_   \    +-----------+      /  ED_ \
 --\ start /---| E_def 27  |----\  end /----->
   \______/  ^  +-----------+  |   \___/
             |                 |
             |_________________|
```

23 EXPCOND

```
   /------\                         /---\
  /  ECD_  \    +-----------+      / ECD_\
 --\ start /---| E_cond 28|----\  end /----->
   \______/  ^  +-----------+  |   \___/
             |                 |
             |_________________|
```

24 F_BODY

```
   /------\       /----------\
  /  FBD_  \     /            \
 --\ start /---\  has_body:   /--------------|
   \______/     \____________/               |
                                             |
                                             |
                                             |
  |__________________________________________|
  |                      /---\
  | +-----------+       / FBD_\
  |--| F_body 29 |---\  end /------>
    +-----------+     \___/
```

25 AB_DOM_NAME

```
        +-------+
    ----| id 76 |---->
      ^  +-------+ |
      |           |
      |___________|
```

26 COND_NAME

```
        +-------+
    ----| id 76 |---->
      ^  +-------+ |
      |           |
      |___________|
```

27 E_DEF

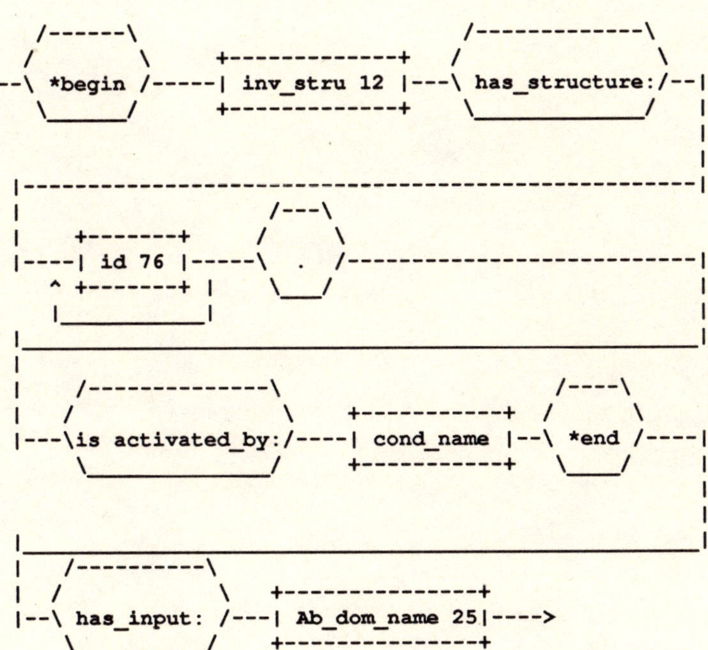

28 E_COND

```
      /------\                                      /-------------\
     /        \          +--------------+          /               \
  --\  *begin  /------| inv_stru 12 |---\ has_structure:/--|
     \________/          +--------------+          \_____________/   |
                                                                     |
                                                                     |
      |------------------------------------------------------------|
      |            +-------+         /---\                          |
      |            | id 76 |-----\     \                           |
      |----| id 76 |-----\  .  /--------------------------|
      ^    +-------+ |      \___/                          |
      |___________|                                       |
                                                          |
      |_________________________________________________|
      |      /----\                                       |
      |     /      \
      |---\  *end  /------>
          \____/
```

29 F_BODY_DEF

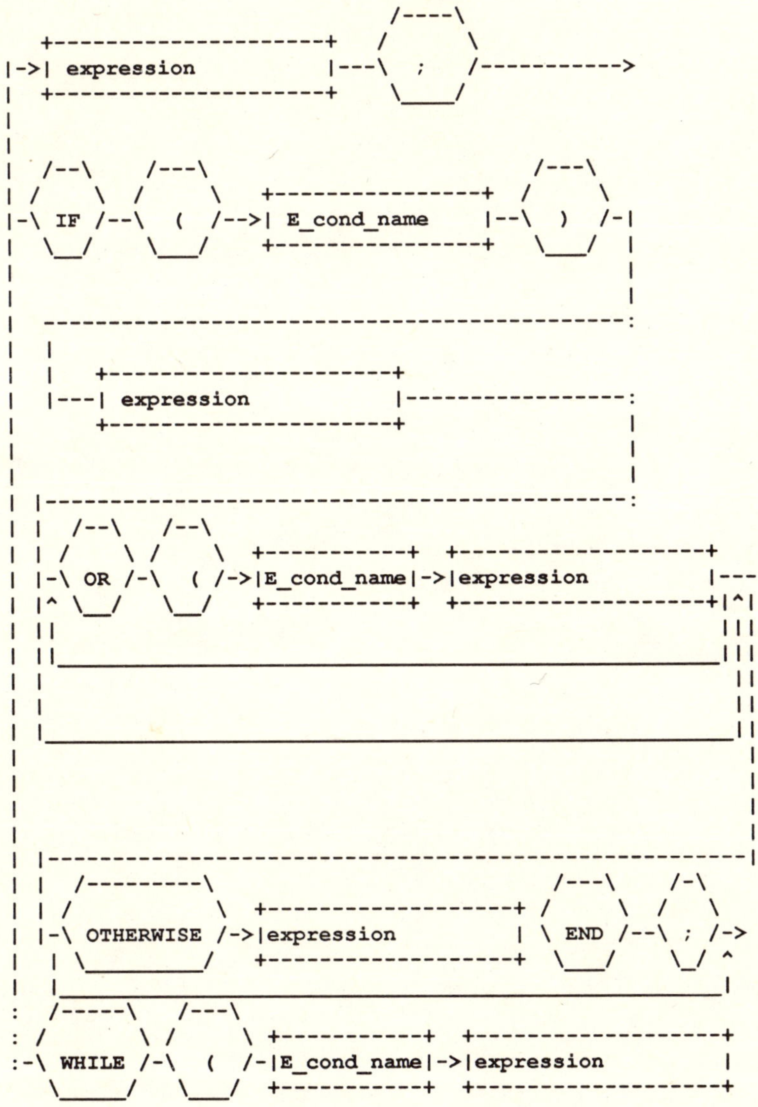

76 ID

```
   +--------+
----| LETTER |----->
  ^ +--------+  |
  |____________|
```

Chapter 6

Estimation of Failure Correlation in Diverse Software Systems with Dependent Components

Francesca Saglietti

6.1 Introduction

The intention of this chapter is to investigate on the inaccuracy resulting from fault-tolerance estimations, which are based on the assumption of failure independence among diverse versions.

An upper bound of the consequences of this error on the final result may permit to draw conservative conclusions on system reliability.

This error bound clearly depends upon the correlation among the failure probabilities of the single programs. In case that a sufficient number of failure observations is available, the underlying correlation factor is estimated by statistical inference; otherwise, we propose a static comparison of diverse programs to obtain a measure of structural dissimilarity, which can be regarded as related to the expected common failure behaviour of diverse components.

6.2 Evaluation of the Inaccuracy Resulting from the Independence Assumption

In the following let S_1 and S_2 denote two software programs developed on the basis of the same specification and executing simultaneously.

An arbitrary failure can then be interpreted as being caused by one of three independent sources, according to the three possibilities of the failure being only in the first version, only in the second one, or in both of them.

We assume the three independent random time-variables representing these processes to be exponentially distributed with rates λ_1, λ_2 and λ_{12} respectively.

This means that the random variables

U_1 representing the time to the next failure occurring only in S_1,

U_2 representing the time to the next failure occurring only in S_2

U_{12} representing the time to the next failure of both S_1 and S_2

have the following probabilities of surviving time x:

$$P\{U_1 > x\} = \exp(-\lambda_1 x)$$

$$P\{U_2 > x\} = \exp(-\lambda_2 x)$$

$$P\{U_{12} > x\} = \exp(-\lambda_{12} x)$$

Thus the random life lengths

$$T_1 = \min(U_1, U_{12}) \text{ of } S_1$$

and

$$T_2 = \min(U_2, U_{12}) \text{ of } S_2$$

are exponentially distributed with rates $\lambda_1 + \lambda_{12}$ and $\lambda_2 + \lambda_{12}$ respectively:

$$R_1(x) := P\{T_1 > x\} = \exp(-(\lambda_1 + \lambda_{12})x)$$

$$R_2(x) := P\{T_2 > x\} = \exp(-(\lambda_2 + \lambda_{12})x)$$

whereas their joint distribution is bivariate exponential:

$$R_j(x,y) := P\{T_1 > x, T_2 > y\} = \exp(-(\lambda_1 x + \lambda_2 y + \lambda_{12}\max(x,y)))$$

The main goal of diversity is to increase the reliability of the system by continuously comparing the results of both parallel versions and by requiring immediate external intervention as soon as they disagree. Therefore, as long as at least one of both components is performing correctly, no erroneous output will be passed to the following segments.

Under these assumptions the reliability of the 1-out-of-2 configuration is thus given by the function R(x):

$$
\begin{aligned}
R(x) &= 1 - P\{T_1 \leq x, T_2 \leq x\} = \\
&= P\{T_1 \leq x, T_2 > x\} + P\{T_1 > x, T_2 \leq x\} + P\{T_1 > x, T_2 > x\} = \\
&= (1 - \exp(-\lambda_1 x))\exp(-(\lambda_2 + \lambda_{12})x) + \\
&\quad + \exp(-(\lambda_1 + \lambda_{12})x)(1 - \exp(-\lambda_2 x)) + \\
&\quad + \exp(-(\lambda_1 + \lambda_2 + \lambda_{12})x) = \\
&= \exp(-(\lambda_1 + \lambda_{12})x) + \exp(-(\lambda_2 + \lambda_{12})x) - \exp(-(\lambda_1 + \lambda_2 + \lambda_{12})x)
\end{aligned}
$$

This expression shows that the only knowledge of the single failure rates $\lambda_1 + \lambda_{12}$ and $\lambda_2 + \lambda_{12}$ does not yet suffice to estimate the system reliability R(x) without knowing the common failure rate λ_{12}. The estimation of this value may lead to difficulties, e.g. when no failure observations are available or the number of common failure observations is too small to permit to apply the classical reliability models to estimate λ_{12}, as for ultrahigh reliable software.

If failure independence could be assumed, one could easily express the joint distribution of the life lengths as the product of the single exponential distributions, merely needing an evaluation of the single failure rates of both programs.

But as in general the independence assumption does not hold, such a simplified calculation would generally render an optimistic value for the common failure probability.

Nonetheless, this estimation, together with its maximal discrepancy from the true value, represents a first step towards the goal of estimating the reliability of a diverse system.

For this reason we consider the maximum discrepancy given in [MAR67]:

$$\max \{R_j(x,y) - R_1(x) \cdot R_2(y)\} = \{\rho^\rho/(1+\rho)^{(1+\rho)}\}^{1/\rho} =: \varepsilon(\rho)$$

as a function of the correlation ρ (proof in appendix a):

$$\rho := \lambda_{12}/(\lambda_1+\lambda_2+\lambda_{12}).$$

With the following equation, which is fulfilled for any bivariate distributed pair (T_1,T_2) (see appendix b):

$$P\{T_1 > x, T_2 > y\} - P\{T_1 > x\} \cdot P\{T_2 > y\} =$$

$$= P\{T_1 \leq x, T_2 \leq y\} - P\{T_1 \leq x\} \cdot P\{T_2 \leq y\},$$

and with the error bound $\varepsilon(\rho)$, we obtain upper and lower bounds for the system reliability (proof in appendix c):

$$R_1(x) + R_2(x) - R_1(x) \cdot R_2(x) - \varepsilon(\rho) \leq R(x) \leq R_1(x) + R_2(x) - R_1(x) \cdot R_2(x)$$

This formula gives a band in which the reliability function R(x) must be situated, as shown in the following figure 6.1.

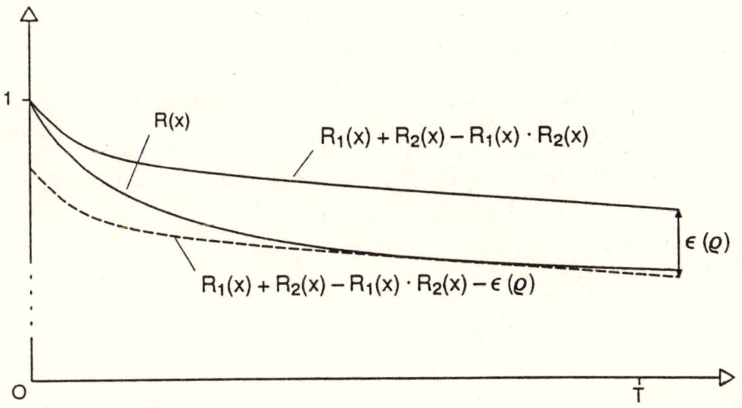

Fig. 6.1.   Band of reliability function

If a minimum reliability requirement R during mission time T has been evaluated by considering the admissible risk:

$$R(T) \geq R,$$

with the help of estimations for the single reliabilities $R_1(x)$ and $R_2(x)$ of S_1 and S_2 as well as for the error bound $\varepsilon(\rho)$ we can thus verify this requirement if the following inequality is fulfilled:

$$R_1(T) + R_2(T) - R_1(T) \cdot R_2(T) - \varepsilon(\rho) \geq R.$$

Conversely, given only an estimate of $\varepsilon(\rho)$, the last inequality determines how long to test the single versions before having achieved the reliability requirement desired.

In order to apply these considerations, we have to evaluate the maximal error $\varepsilon(\rho)$ done by following the independence assumption.

In particular, we may note that the function $\varepsilon(\rho)$ is strictly monotonically increasing with ρ (proof in appendix d), so the error is bounded by:

$$\varepsilon(\rho) < \varepsilon(1) = 1/4 \quad \forall \rho \in]0,1[$$

Thus the special case where the error assumes this maximum value occurs under the condition:

$$\rho=1, \text{ or equivalently } \lambda_1+\lambda_2=0$$

This is fulfilled in the degenerate case of developing two almost identical versions, which fail on exactly the same inputs.

In the general case, accounting for experimental data and theoretical considerations (see chapter 3), we expect λ_{12} to be lower than $\lambda_1+\lambda_2$:

$$\lambda_{12} < \lambda_1+\lambda_2, \text{ implying } \rho<1,$$

so that the discrepancy $\varepsilon(\rho)$ to be considered can be expected to be reasonably small.

In order to quantify the error bound, the correlation ρ will be estimated in the following sections.

6.3   The Case of Available Failure Observations

In the case of failure occurrence, the correlation coefficient ρ can be estimated during a testing phase without corrections. Herein we follow the notation and the considerations suggested in [ARN68]. Given the bivariate distributed random vector $T = (T_1,T_2)$ we consider the random variable Y defined by:

$$Y := \begin{cases} 1 & \text{if } T_1=T_2 \\ 0 & \text{if } T_1 \neq T_2 \end{cases}$$

Clearly:

$$P\{Y=1\} = E(Y) = \lambda_{12}/(\lambda_1+\lambda_2+\lambda_{12}) = \rho,$$

so that Y is binomially distributed with parameters $(1,\rho)$. Thus the obvious procedure for estimating ρ consists of using N observations of T to obtain a consistent estimate of ρ given by:

$$\hat{\rho} = \sum_{j=1}^{n} Y_j /N,$$

where $Y_1,...,Y_N$ represent the N observations of Y based on the sample of size N.

Since $N \cdot \hat{\rho}$ has a binomial distribution with parameters N and ρ, expected value and variance of the estimate of ρ are simply given by:

$$E(\hat{\rho}) = \rho,$$

$$\mathrm{Var}(\hat{\rho}) = \rho(1-\rho)/N$$

and the efficiency of the estimation procedure proposed is given by an improvement of Tchebychev's inequality due to Bernstein [REN62]:

$$P\{|\hat{\rho}-\rho|\geq\varepsilon\} \leq 2 \cdot \exp\left[-\frac{N \cdot \varepsilon^2}{2\rho(1-\rho)(1+\varepsilon/2\rho(1-\rho))^2}\right]$$

At the end of the testing phase, the errors causing the failures observed are corrected.

Each time an error is removed, the rates λ_{12} and $\lambda_1+\lambda_2+\lambda_{12}$ may decrease, so that nothing can be stated with certainty about their quotient. If we, however, assume equal contributions of the errors detected to the total failure rate we can define:

$$\lambda_{12new} = \lambda_{12}-c$$

$$\lambda_{1new}+\lambda_{2new} = \lambda_1+\lambda_2-c'$$

where c and c' are constants with $c/c'=\lambda_{12}/(\lambda_1+\lambda_2)$, λ_{12new} represents the new common failure rate after the correction phase and $\lambda_{1new}+\lambda_{2new}$ represents the new single failure rate after the correction phase.

Now we can easily calculate the new correlation coefficient

$$\rho_{new} = \text{new common failure rate / new failure rate}$$

after the correction at the end of the testing phase obtaining (proof in appendix e):

$$\rho_{new} = \lambda_{12new}/(\lambda_{1new}+\lambda_{2new}+\lambda_{12new}) = \lambda_{12}/(\lambda_1+\lambda_2+\lambda_{12}) = \rho$$

Therefore, under the assumptions above, the parameter ρ can be expected to remain constant after the whole debugging phase, so justifying its estimation with the help of the suggested method.

6.4   The Case of No Available Failure Observations

In case of ultrahigh reliability requirements, the test usually consists of verifying correct performance for a given duration and thus no failure occurs during this validation phase.

In this case, we propose a method of estimating an upper bound for ρ based on the comparison of both flow graphs.

In the following the software versions S_1 and S_2 are assumed to be programs with flow graphs G_1 and G_2 respectively, where each of them is a directed graph with two distinguished vertices representing the begin and the end of the program. To every input x correspond unique complete paths $P_1(x)$ and $P_2(x)$ in the flow graphs G_1 and G_2.

Thus we can define for each input x two complexity measures $Z(P_i(x))$, $i \in \{1,2\}$, where the complexity of a path is defined as the number of possible decisions (or predicates) along this path; these are mostly responsible for design errors (s. [HEN81]).

In the following we shall assume:

1. The probability of a failure of S_i executing the input x is proportional to the complexity of the corresponding path $P_i(x)$. The proportionality constant C represents a quality factor which is first assumed to be equal in both cases. This reflects the fact that complex paths are more failure-prone.

2. If x is handled incorrectly by S_i and $Z(P_i(x)) \leq Z(P_j(x))$, then x is also handled incorrectly by S_j.

Fortunately this statement is not true in general; nonetheless, representing the worst case, it may be considered as a conservative way to look at common failure behaviour.

Let $Z(P_i(x)) \leq Z(P_j(x))$. Assumption 2 implies:

x is incorrectly handled by S_i $\Rightarrow$ x is incorrectly handled by S_j

For a fixed input x this yields with assumption 1:

P{x causes common failure} = $C \cdot \min (Z(P_1(x)), Z(P_2(x)))$ =: $\alpha(x)$

P{x causes failure} = $C \cdot \max (Z(P_1(x)), Z(P_2(x)))$ =: $\beta(x)$

Thus we can interpret

$$\rho(x) := \alpha(x)/\beta(x),$$

as a conservative value for our degree of belief that x causes a common failure, given that x leads to a failure.

ρ can then be bounded by the expected value of $\rho(x)$, where x is a random variable occurring at a random time given by the demand profile p:

$$\rho \leq E[\rho(x)] = \sum_x \rho(x) \cdot p(x) =: ub(\rho).$$

Of course, due to the conservative second assumption and to the mere static program analysis, the value obtained for the correlation ρ can only be expected to give a rough upper bound. In case of ultrahigh requirements, however, where no failures are observed, it could reveal as useful to bound the expected dependence.

The technique described reflects the fact that dissimilar diverse programs tend to be less failure-dependent than similar ones, especially with regard to design faults.

As considered by Eckhardt and Lee in their model [ECK85], inputs which are particularly difficult to be treated correctly will probably cause common errors. If the software products are structurally very dissimilar, these errors will be likely to have different consequences affecting different input subsets. In this case they are more probable to cause first single failures than common ones or to result in different wrong outputs; anyway, they can then be detected by means of a back-to-back test.

Beside this essential motivation, the considerations suggested present also some further advantages:

a) The number of branches in the flow graph of a program is essentially represented by Mc Cabe's metric, which was experimentally found to be correlated with the number of errors as well as with the time required to locate and correct the bugs (s. [HEN81] and [CUR79]). These experimental results can be considered as a valid support for our first assumption.

Nonetheless, in principle the approach suggested does not depend on the choice of a specific metric; it can be easily applied to any other path complexity measure, which in future may prove to be more efficient than the mentioned one.

b) Moreover, the method proposed could be generalized to model different programmers' capabilities, estimating the quotient of their failure probabilities. In this case the first assumption would be formulated with two different proportionality constants, the quotient of which had to be estimated considering e.g. the different staffs' skill.

c) An important advantage of this approach is the applicability of a back-to-back test to estimate the common failure rate λ_{12}.

In fact, comparing the results and verifying their agreement for a given test duration, one can apply the statistical theory of confidence intervals, as suggested in chapter 3, obtaining an upper bound $ub(\lambda_1+\lambda_2)$ for the rate $\lambda_1+\lambda_2$ at some confidence level.

Given an upper bound $ub(\rho)$ for the correlation ρ, we can then bound λ_{12} by:

$$\lambda_{12}/(\lambda_1+\lambda_2+\lambda_{12}) \leq ub(\rho)$$

$$\Rightarrow \lambda_{12} \leq [ub(\rho)/(1-ub(\rho))] \cdot ub(\lambda_1+\lambda_2).$$

d) The considerations mentioned above could be also applied in the opposite sense, i.e. enforcing deterministically dissimilarity instead of expecting it as a result of randomness: depending on the specific reliability requirements and expected development costs, a project manager could estimate a maximal correlation ρ, such that the error bound $\varepsilon(\rho)$ would still be acceptable. He could then organize the diverse programming by determining for each staff a different basic structure to follow, in order to ensure a certain degree of dissimilarity and thus to limit the correlation by ρ.

6.5 Conclusion

This chapter presents an attempt to tackle the problem of estimating failure dependence of diverse software systems. We propose two different evaluation methods, according to the case of past failure observations being available or not. In the former case we suggest a statistical technique and in the latter case a static analysis of the flow graphs.

The considerations concentrate on the case of a two-fold diverse system in order to simplify the calculations, but in principle they can be extended not only to any N-version programming configuration, but also to Recovery Block Systems, thus providing a support in the quantitative assessment of any classical fault-tolerant software architecture.

References

[ARN68] B.C. Arnold: Parameter Estimation for a Multivariate Exponential Distribution. American Statistical Association Journal, September 1968

[CUR79] B. Curtis, S.B. Sheppard, D. Milliman: Third Time Charm: Stronger Prediction of Programmer Performance by Software Complexity Metrics. Proc. 4th Int. Conference on Software Engineering, New York, IEEE 1979

[ECK85] D.E. Eckhardt, L.D. Lee: A Theoretical Basis for the Analysis of Multiversion Software Subject to Coincident Errors. IEEE Transactions on Software Engineering, Vol. SE-11, No. 12, Dec. 1985

[HEN81] S. Henry, D. Kafura, K. Harris: On the Relationships Among Three Software Metrics. Association for Computing Machinery ACM 1981

[KNI86] J.C. Knight, N.G. Leveson: An Experimental Evaluation of the Assumption of Independence in Multiversion Programming. IEEE Trans. on Software Engineering, Vol, SE-12, No. 1, January 1986

[MAR67] A.W. Marshall, I. Olkin: A Multivariate Exponential Distribution. American Statistical Association Journal, March 1967

[REN62] A. Rényi: Wahrscheinlichkeitsrechnung. Berlin: Deutscher Verlag der Wissenschaften 1962

Appendix

a) To determine the greatest discrepancy:

$$\max_{x,y}(R_J(x,y) - R_1(x)\cdot R_2(y)),$$

note that if $x<y$:

$$R_J(x,y) - R_1(x)\cdot R_2(y) = \exp(-(\lambda_1 x + \lambda_2 y + \lambda_{12} y)) -$$
$$\exp(-(\lambda_1 x + \lambda_{12} x + \lambda_2 y + \lambda_{12} y)) =$$
$$\exp(-(\lambda_1 x + (\lambda_2 + \lambda_{12})y)) \cdot (1 - \exp(-\lambda_{12} x))$$

is decreasing in y, so that:

$$R_J(x,y) - R_1(x)\cdot R_2(y) \leq \exp(-(\lambda_1 + \lambda_2 + \lambda_{12}) \cdot \min(x,y)) \cdot$$
$$(1 - \exp(-\lambda_{12} \cdot \min(x,y))) =$$
$$= \exp(-\lambda t)\cdot(1 - \exp(-\lambda_{12} t)),$$

where $\lambda := \lambda_1 + \lambda_2 + \lambda_{12}$, $t := \min(x,y)$.

The maximum of $h(t) := \exp(-\lambda t) \cdot (1 - \exp(-\lambda_{12} t))$

occurs at $t_0 = (1/\lambda_{12})\cdot\ln(1+\lambda_{12}/\lambda) = (1/\lambda_{12})\cdot\ln(1+\rho)$

and is equal to:

$$\max_{x,y}(R_J(x,y) - R_1(x)\cdot R_2(y)) =$$
$$= \exp(-(1/\rho)\cdot\ln(1+\rho))\cdot(1 - \exp(-\ln(1+\rho))) =$$
$$= (1+\rho)^{-(1/\rho)}\cdot (1 - (1+\rho)^{-1}) =$$
$$= \rho / (1+\rho)^{(1+\rho)/\rho} =$$
$$= \{\rho^\rho/(1+\rho)^{(1+\rho)}\}^{(1/\rho)} = \varepsilon(\rho) \qquad \text{q.e.d.}$$

b) I. $\quad P\{T_1 \leq x\}\cdot P\{T_2 \leq y\} = (1 - P\{T_1 > x\})\cdot(1 - P\{T_2 > y\}) =$
$$= 1 - P\{T_1 > x\} - P\{T_2 > y\} + P\{T_1 > x\}\cdot P\{T_2 > y\}$$

II. $\quad P\{T_1 > x, T_2 > y\} = 1 - P\{T_1 \leq x\} - P\{T_2 \leq y\} + P\{T_1 \leq x, T_2 \leq y\}$

Equations I. and II. yield:

$$P\{T_1 > x, T_2 > y\} - P\{T_1 > x\}\cdot P\{T_2 > y\} =$$
$$= 1 - P\{T_1 \leq x\} - P\{T_2 \leq y\} - P\{T_1 \leq x, T_2 \leq y\} - P\{T_1 > x\}\cdot P\{T_2 > y\} =$$
$$= -1 + P\{T_1 > x\} + P\{T_2 > y\} - P\{T_1 > x\}\cdot P\{T_2 > y\} + P\{T_1 \leq x, T_2 \leq y\} =$$
$$= P\{T_1 \leq x, T_2 \leq y\} - P\{T_1 \leq x\}\cdot P\{T_2 \leq y\} \qquad \text{q.e.d.}$$

c) I. $R(x)$ = $1 - P\{T_1 \leq x, T_2 \leq x\}$ =

         = $R_1(x) + R_2(x) - R_j(x,x) \leq$

         $\leq$ $R_1(x) + R_2(x) - R_1(x) \cdot R_2(x)$

   II. $R(x)$ = $R_1(x) + R_2(x) - R_j(x,x) \geq$

         $\geq$ $R_1(x) + R_2(x) - R_1(x) \cdot R_2(x) - \varepsilon(\rho)$

         (with part a)   q.e.d.

d) Let f represent the function given by:

   $f(x)$ $= x \,/\, (1 + x)^{(1 + x)/x}$

   $\Rightarrow$ $f'(x)$ = $\dfrac{(1+x)^{(1+x)/x} \cdot \{1 - (1-(1/x) \cdot \ln(1+x))\}}{\{(1+x)^{(1+x)/x}\}^2}$ > 0 $\forall\, x \in\,]0,1]$

   $\Rightarrow$ $f(x)$ is strictly monotonically increasing for $x \in\,]0,1]$

   $\Rightarrow$ $f(x) \,<\, f(1) \,=\, 1/4$ $\forall\, x \in\,]0,1[$ q.e.d.

e) ρ_{new} = $\lambda_{12new} / (\lambda_{1new} + \lambda_{2new} + \lambda_{12new})$ =

         = $(\lambda_{12} - c)/(\lambda_1 + \lambda_2 + \lambda_{12} - c' - c)$ =

         = $(\lambda_{12} - c)/(\lambda_1 + \lambda_2 + \lambda_{12} - c - c(\lambda_1 + \lambda_2)/\lambda_{12})$ =

         = $\lambda_{12}/(\lambda_1 + \lambda_2 + \lambda_{12}) = \rho$ q. e. d.

Chapter 7

Measurement of Diversity Degree by Quantification of Dissimilarity in the Input Partition

Francesca Saglietti

7.1 Input Partition and Coverage Diversity

Apart from the observable program features mentioned in previous chapters (failure times and structural complexity measures), an additional characteristic, which might be analyzed in order to investigate on the reliability achieved by redundancy, is represented by the difference in the input partition of parallel versions.

With respect to a predefined equivalence relation on the set of flow graph paths resulting in disjoint classes of paths, as suggested in [MÄR77], each program induces a partition of the input set into subsets of inputs, which are "commonly handled" by the program, as their execution will activate paths belonging to the same equivalence class.

Relative to design errors affecting whole input classes, we can then evaluate the efficiency of a redundant system by comparing the input partitions of diverse versions, as sketched in Fig. 7.1.

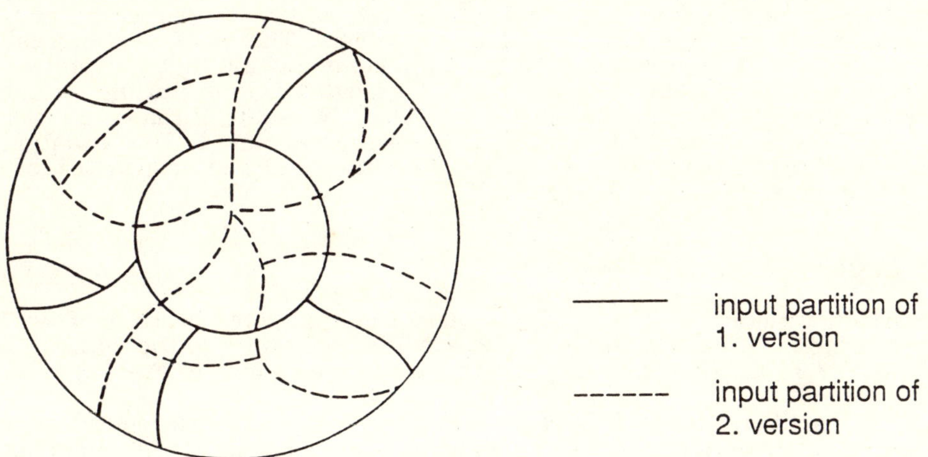

Fig. 7.1.   Input partition of diverse programs

In case of identical input subsets, which may possibly be uniquely determined by a very detailed specification, we have to expect a similar reasoning during the program development and thus a lower error detection capability of the automatic test performed on the alternates by result comparison.

On the other hand, in case of different partitions, a common error affecting the input x situated in the intersection of different input classes might be expected to propagate for each program in another direction, thus increasing the probability of being found by the voter, as shown in Fig. 7.2.

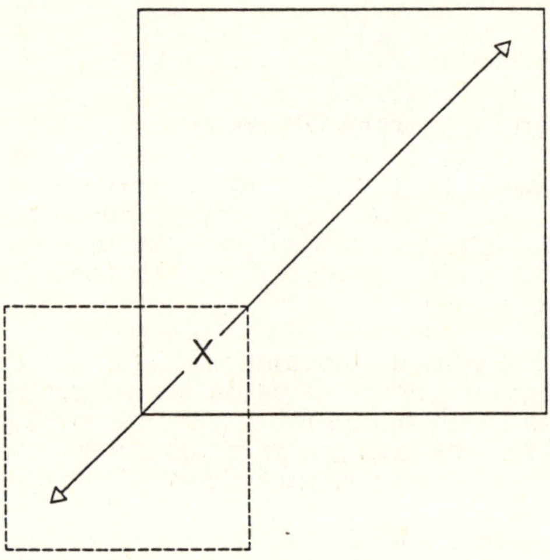

Fig. 7.2.   Different propagation of common error

Although the just defined diversity is a purely structural one, it will in general be very difficult to recognize or even quantify the degree of the partition difference by means of a static analysis. Therefore, we suggest to make use of the dynamic program behaviour to obtain a graphical representation of the diversity achieved. This can be done during a random testing phase executing all alternates with the same inputs and taking gradually into account the path class coverage achieved. The deviation of the resulting coverage curves can then be interpreted as a measure of the partition diversity.

Example:

Fourteen randomly selected inputs yield the complete coverage of two diverse programs, each with eight path classes, according to the figures given in Table 7.1 The corresponding coverage growth is shown in Fig. 7.3.

The partition metric defined as the sum of all absolute deviations can then be easily determined as 1.6, whereas the case with identical partitions is obviously represented by the zero value.

Together with a graphical quantification of the diversity degree, this technique also permits to obtain a proof of correctness with respect to the errors affecting all of a path class.

Of course, all errors of this kind could be easily detected by a conventional testing phase covering each class. For a high number of classes, however, this method could require an unrealistic effort.

Table 7.1. Coverage measures of diverse versions

TEST CASE	COVERAGE 1	COVERAGE 2
1	1\8	1\8
2	2\8	1\8
3	3\8	1\8
4	4\8	2\8
5	5\8	3\8
6	5\8	3\8
7	5\8	4\8
8	5\8	5\8
9	5\8	6\8
10	5\8	6\8
11	6\8	7\8
12	6\8	8\8
13	7\8	8\8
14	8\8	8\8

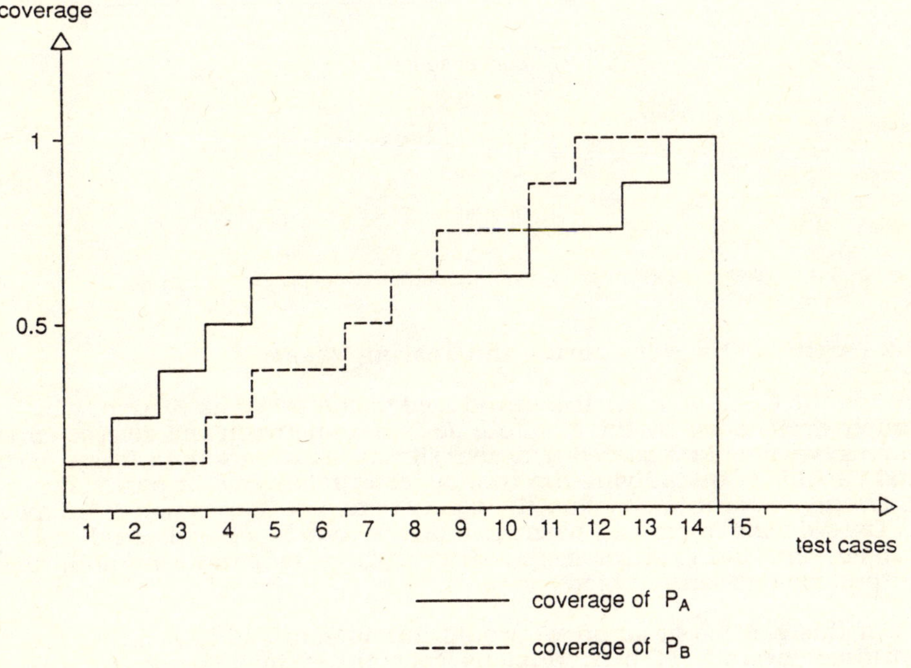

Fig. 7.3.   Coverage growth of diverse versions

In case of substantial partition diversity, on the contrary, the same restricted proof of faultlessness can be carried out at a considerably lower cost according to the following test strategy:

For each input x the coverage growth curves of two diverse versions are compared at x:

a) If there is no change in any of the curves at x, x is ignored.

b) If only one of both curves grows at x, the corresponding path class has already been tested in the other program; thus we only need to verify the result agreement by means of a back-to-back test.

c) If both curves grow, the corresponding path classes have not been tested yet; this will be done by conventionally verifying the correctness of the output to x.

A high partition diversity degree will ensure that step b) is performed more often than step c), thus contributing to a decrease of the testing costs.

Example

The case described in the previous example requires only the systematic verification of four random tests, i.e. half as many as would have been needed by a conventional testing strategy. They yield a complete test covering each path class if they are integrated with some automatic test runs, according to the test sequence sketched in Fig. 7.4.

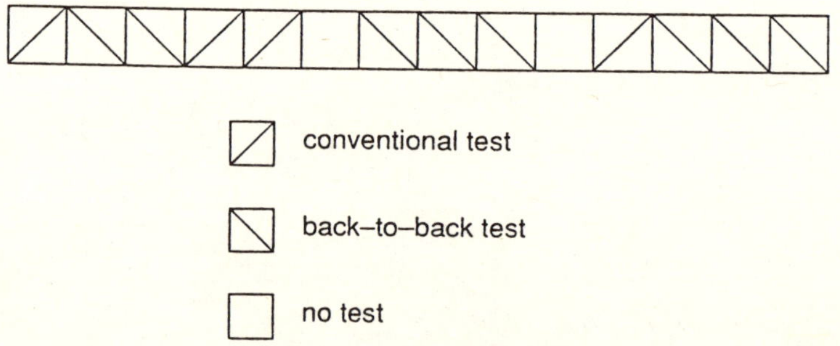

Fig. 7.4.   Test case sequence to achieve complete coverage

7.2 Partition Diversity during the Testing Phase

Beside the elementary metric introduced in the previous section, which was simply determined by the absolute deviations between the diverse coverage curves, we should also define a diversity measure based on input partition and capable of quantifying the confidence in reliability. In particular, in the following we want to consider the case where a single version is intended to be used during operation, whereas a diverse one has only been developed to support the testing phase of the main program by permitting an automatic output comparison.

In this special situation we would like to estimate how much the input partition diversity of both versions contributes to increase our degree of confidence in the correctness of the primary program at the end of a random testing phase.

In order to formalize the following evaluations, we assume the input space I of the program P_A to be partitioned into n disjoint subsets $A_1,....,A_n$, according to Fig. 7.5.

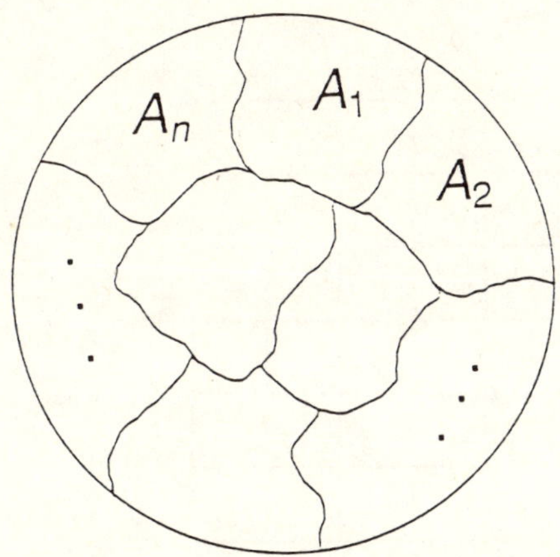

Fig. 7.5.   Input partition of program P_A

As before we will still consider classes as being totally correct or totally incorrect. An error affecting the whole input class A_i will not be detected during a back-to-back test covering each subset in case of an analogous fault in the alternate version P_B. But, in the case of different partitions of P_A and P_B, the agreement of the results on all subset intersections increases the input set concerned by the error. In other words, if A_1 and A_2 are two classes of P_A linked by a class B_1 of P_B, two test runs x,y without disagreement on the subsets $A_1 \cap B_1$ and $A_2 \cap B_1$ will cause the partitions A_1 and A_2 to be both correct or both incorrect, as illustrated in Fig. 7.6.

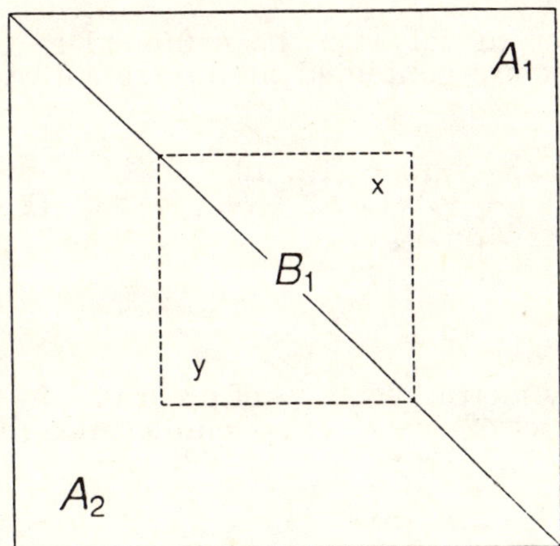

Fig. 7.6.   Back-to-back test runs x and y

   This means that an extensive automatic testing phase without result disagreement between two programs with high partition diversity (as the one shown in Fig. 7.7) forces the undetected class errors to concern a much wider area than programs with identical partition and thus decreases the probability of errors not being detected during conventional testing.

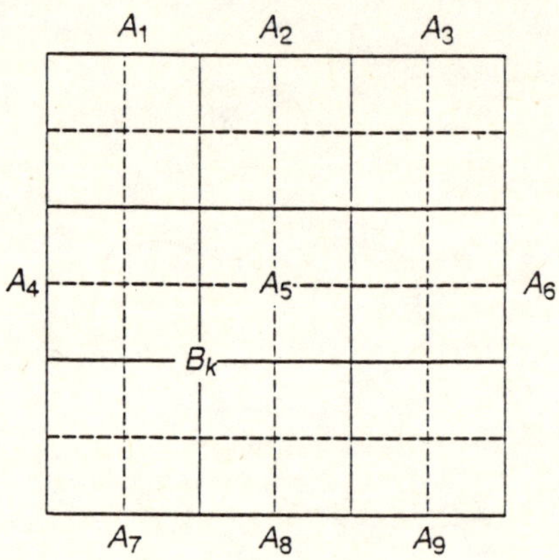

Fig. 7.7.   Example of high partition diversity

   In the example shown in Fig. 7.7 we easily identify the link between two subsets A_i, A_j defined if both of them intersect with the same partition class B_k ($1 \leq i, j, k \leq n$), formally:

$$A_i \sim A_j : \Leftrightarrow \exists k : \quad \begin{array}{l} A_i \cap B_k \neq \varnothing \\ A_j \cap B_k \neq \varnothing \end{array}$$

This is the case e.g. for the pairs (A_1, A_2) and (A_3, A_5):

$$A_1 \sim A_2$$
$$A_3 \sim A_5$$

   The property observed can even be extended to pairs, which are not linked by "~" and yet are contained in the transitive envelope "$\cong$" of this symmetric relation, i.e.:

$$A_i \cong A_j : \quad \Leftrightarrow \exists k_1,...,k_t \in \{1,...,n\}: \\ A_i \sim A_{k_1}, \; A_{k_q} \sim A_{k_{q+1}} \quad \forall q \in \{1,...,t-1\} \\ A_j \sim A_{k_t}$$

Definition

The partition diversity metric $\langle P_A, P_B \rangle$ of programs P_A and P_B is defined as n divided by the number of classes of the equivalence relation "$\cong$".

Examples

a) All the subsets in Fig. 7.7 are connected by the equivalence relation. This means $\langle P_A, P_B \rangle = n$.

b) In case of two programs with identical partitions, i.e. $A_i = B_i \; \forall i \in \{1,...,n\}$, it easily follows $\langle P_A, P_B \rangle = 1$.

In particular, the metric $<P_A, P_B>$ provides an exact measure of the relation between the number of path classes and the number of conventional tests required to be added to an exhaustive back-to-back testing phase to prove the class faultlessness. In fact, as each equivalence class is assumed to be either completely correct or totally affected by some error, the verification of a single test case out of each equivalence class is sufficient to identify which of both cases has occurred. Of course, in addition to these conventional tests, an extensive automatic testing phase, without disagreement, covering each possible subset is necessary in order to justify all the considerations which led us to this final result.

The diversity metric defined can be calculated on the basis of an extensive antecedent random input choice. For each input selected both partition classes A_i, B_j, to which it belongs, are determined and a "1" will be marked at coefficient (i,j) of matrix C. The random selection is concluded when it can be expected that all possible intersections have appeared, i.e. when zero coefficients at position (i,j) are assumed to represent combinations of disjoint A_i and B_j.

At this point the matrix C has to be transformed by line and row permutations into a matrix C' of block-diagonal form, as shown in Fig. 7.8, where r is the maximal number of non-zero blocks and thus n/r represents exactly the diversity metric $<P_A, P_B>$.

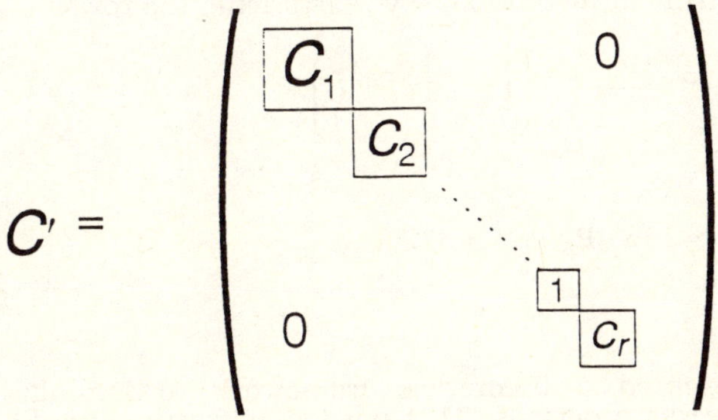

$$
C' = \begin{pmatrix}
\boxed{C_1} & & & & 0 \\
& \boxed{C_2} & & & \\
& & \ddots & & \\
& & & \boxed{1} & \\
0 & & & & \boxed{C_r}
\end{pmatrix}
$$

Fig. 7.8.   Block-diagonal matrix C'

Both extreme cases we considered before in the examples are then just given by the matrix C_1 exclusively consisting of coefficients 1 and by the identity matrix C_I with zero coefficients only outside the main diagonal $\{(i,i) \mid i \geq 1\}$.

A few simple non-trivial examples as the following one easily show that the defined metric can take any rational value between the boundaries 1 and n occurring in the special situations just seen.

Example

Both programs P_A and P_B consist of 2 classes connected as illustrated in Fig.7.9.

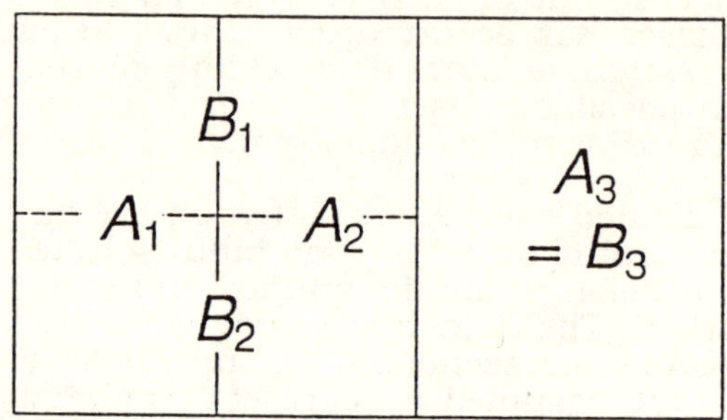

Fig. 7.9.   Example of relation among input partitions

The matrix C may first be obtained during random input selection as

$$C \quad = \quad \begin{pmatrix} 1 & 0 & 1 \\ 1 & 0 & 1 \\ 0 & 1 & 0 \end{pmatrix}$$

and can be easily transformed into C' by rearranging the rows:

$$C' \quad = \quad \begin{pmatrix} 1 & 1 & 0 \\ 1 & 1 & 0 \\ 0 & 0 & 1 \end{pmatrix}$$

This yields:

$$r=2 \Rightarrow <P_A,P_B> = 3/2$$

7.3 Conclusion

This chapter presented a theoretical framework to formalize partition dissimilarity in diverse programs. This particular feature should reflect the diversity degree in the design of alternative versions of redundant software systems.

As common failures primarily occur and remain undetected as a result of similar programming reasoning, the metrics suggested are meant to provide information on the expected failure behaviour of the system and its testability by means of conventional and automatic verification runs.

The major restriction regards the classes of errors considered, which are assumed to affect all of a partition class. Therefore, the relation inducing the underlying input partition should be chosen to be as detailed as to allow a fine subdivision of the input space into sufficiently small subsets.

Both metrics are based on a dynamic software analysis permitting their simple evaluation: the first (and more elementary one) will depend on the input selection process (and may be averaged by replications), whereas the second one is absolutely quantifiable in principle, but may be realistically estimated by analysing a random input sequence.

References

[ECK85] D.E. Eckhardt, L.D. Lee: A Theoretical Basis for the Analysis of Redundant Software Subject to Coincident Errors. NASA Technical Memorandum 86369

[KNI86] J.C. Knight, N.G. Leveson: An Experimental Evaluation of the Assumption of Independence in Multiversion Programming. IEEE Trans. on Software Engineering, Vol. SE-12, No. 1, January 1986

[LIT87] B. Littlewood, D.R. Miller: A Conceptual Model of Multi-Version Software. Digest of 17th Annual Symposium on Fault-Tolerant Computing (FTCS-17), IEEE Computer Society Press 1987

[MÄR77] J. Märtz: Definition von Äquivalenzklassen auf der Pfadmenge eines schleifenlosen Programms zum Zweck der Auswahl von Testpfaden. Internal IRS-Report, 1977

Chapter 8

Comparison of Mnemonics for Software Diversity Assessment

Michael Martin Burke, David Nicholas Wall

This approach to determine the diversity of two pieces of software investigated the possibility of making a comparison of the machine code representations of two versions, via their mnemonics. The approach is based on the observation that the use of optimising compilers may be detrimental to developing diverse versions. That is, efforts to introduce diversity into the development process may be negated when a version is translated into a machine code representation. In other words the crudest but possibly the most effective way of assessing the diversity of two versions may be to compare their machine code representations.

It should be noted here that the use of the expression software diversity in the context of this work is not that normally recognised in software engineering. In usual parlance the term software diversity is used in the context of two pieces of software with identical functionality being free from common mode failures. In this work the term software diversity and its assessment are simply used to indicate differences in the two pieces of software under consideration. The measurement of diversity output from the work reported here would thus be input to a software diversity assessment which considers diverse and common mode failures. It is suggested that this second step could be performed by an approach using a fuzzy logic expert system similar to that also developed during the REQUEST project and described in chapter 9.

8.1 The Initial Prototype Investigation

The original idea of matching mnemonics to assess software diversity involved comparing the hexadecimal machine codes of two versions. However, there was concern about the legality of matching two identical codes, one of which may represent an opcode, the other an operand. This problem was resolved by comparing the instruction mnemonics.

A pattern recognition system written in POP 11, an Artificial Intelligence Language, was developed to perform the task of comparing machine code representations. The system is based on a simple pattern matching algorithm which compares the ordered sequence of mnemonics associated with the listings of the assembly language statements for the two versions to determine the matching frequency at shift i which is defined in the following way:

Let V_1 and V_2 be two versions and let $(M_1,M_2,....,M_r)$ and $(N_1,N_2,....,N_s)$ denote the sets of mnemonics corresponding to the assembly listings of V_1

and V_2 respectively. For convenience we shall assume r=s. Then we define the matching frequency at shift i to be the number of corresponding matches when comparing $(M_1, M_2, ..., M_r)$ and $(N_1, N_2, ..., N_s)$ when the sequence $N_1, N_2, ..., N_s$ has been shifted i places. More precisely we define:

- matching frequency at shift 0 to be the number of times $M_j = N_j$ for $1 \leq j \leq r$

- for $1 \leq i \leq r-1$: matching frequency at shift i to be the number of times $M_j = N_k$ for $1 \leq j \leq r$ where k=j+i for j+i$\leq$r and k=j+i-r for r<j+i

- for $-(r-1) \leq i \leq -1$: matching frequency at shift i to be the number of times $M_j = N_k$ for $1 \leq j \leq r$ where k=j+i+r for j+i$\leq$0 and k=j+i for j+i>0.

Using this data a histogram $H(V_1, V_2)$ can be constructed whose x-axis represents the mnemonic shift and the y-axis the mnemonic match frequency. The resulting histogram from matching two identical patterns (ie H(V,V) and referred to as a self-matching histogram) is a symmetrical histogram around a central peak at shift zero. Fig 8.1 provides an example to illustrate these definitions, showing how the mnemonics are shifted past one another and how the results are presented.

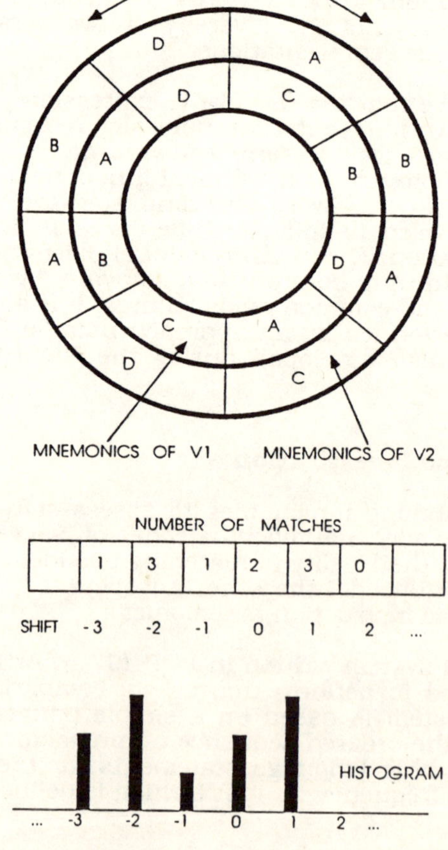

Fig. 8.1. Example of the pattern matching technique

Since this was a preliminary investigation into the feasibility of this approach it was not considered necessary to develop a mnemonic pattern recognition system that performs an exhaustive correlation of all mnemonic patterns of all lengths.

For this technique to be relevant to diversity it must be able to be applied to programs implemented in a wide variety of assembly languages. To achieve this the two sets of mnemonics to be compared are first rigourously translated into equivalent sets composed of mnemonics from a universal set of mnemonics.

8.1.1 Initial Tests and Results

An initial test of the technique was based on solutions to the ARCSINE problem. This was a small experiment in which staff from both CAP Scientific and UKAEA produced 10 independently developed programs to meet the following common requirement:

- determine the arcsine of a real number between -1 and +1.

Three of the solutions denoted V_1, V_2 and V_3, were selected to test the pattern matching technique. V_1 and V_2 were selected because they seemed intuitively similar. V_3 was selected because it seemed intuitively diverse to both V_1 and V_2. A fourth program developed for an entirely different requirement specification, and denoted V_4, was also obtained and was used as a bogus solution. All four versions were coded in Pascal and compiled on the same machine.

From the assembler language listings produced by the compiler, four ordered sets of mnemonics MV_1, MV_2, MV_3 and MV_4 were constructed corresponding to the versions V_1, V_2, V_3 and V_4 respectively. These mnemonic lists were then compared using the pattern matching algorithm in the following ways:

- MV_1 with itself
- MV_1 with MV_2
- MV_2 with itself
- MV_1 with MV_3
- MV_3 with itself
- MV_1 with MV_4

The resulting 6 histograms are depicted in figures 8.2 through 8.7 (pattern shift on the X-axis versus match frequency on the Y-axis).

It can be seen from examination of the histograms, that the outcome of matching two identical patterns is a symmetrical histogram around a central peak. The 'side bands' indicate a lower degree of matching when the patterns are shifted relative to each other. The general shape of a self-match is a characteristic of the pattern. Of particular note is the resemblance in shape of the self-matchings of MV_1 and MV_2 (which were judged as being intuitively 'similar' versions before the tests). The self-matching of MV_3 (where V_3 was subjectively judged to be diverse with respect to V_1 and V_2) has far less in common with either of the former plots. When MV_1 and MV_2 are cross-matched, the result is a histogram which has both a high degree of symmetry and maintains the same basic shape. A cross-match of MV_1 with MV_3 gives a result with a lesser degree of symmetry and with lower peaks. Finally a cross-matching between MV_1 and the bogus solution MV_4 gives a very low indication of similarity.

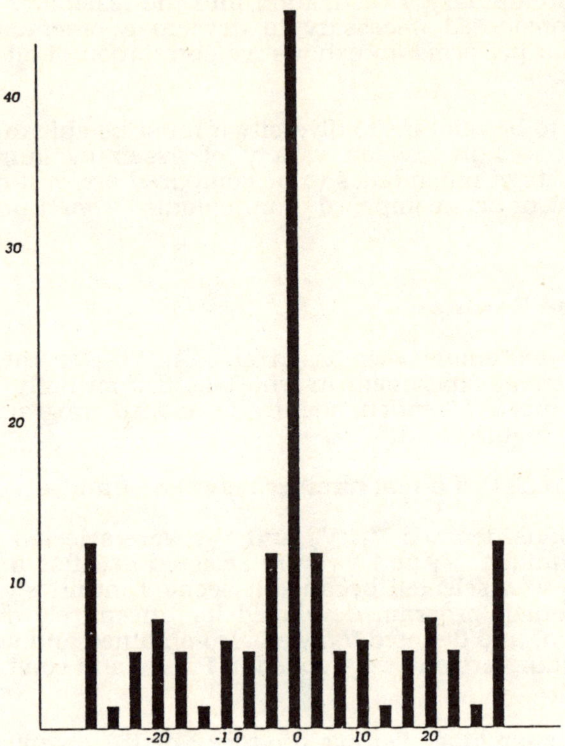

Fig. 8.2. Histogram H(V1,V1)

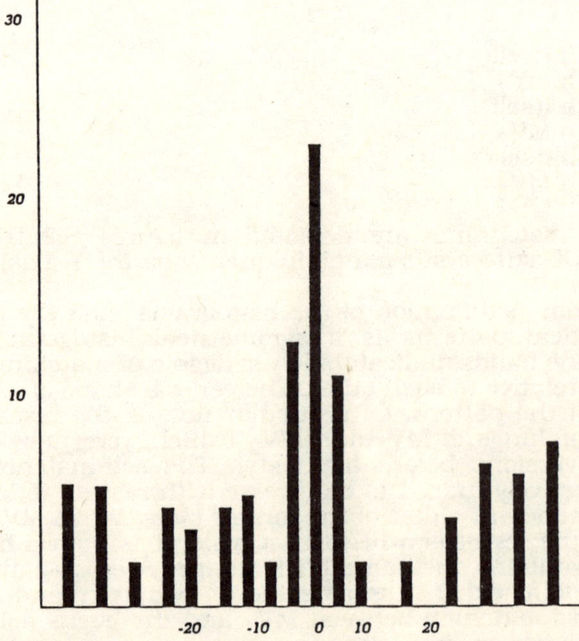

Fig. 8.3. Histogram H(V1,V2)

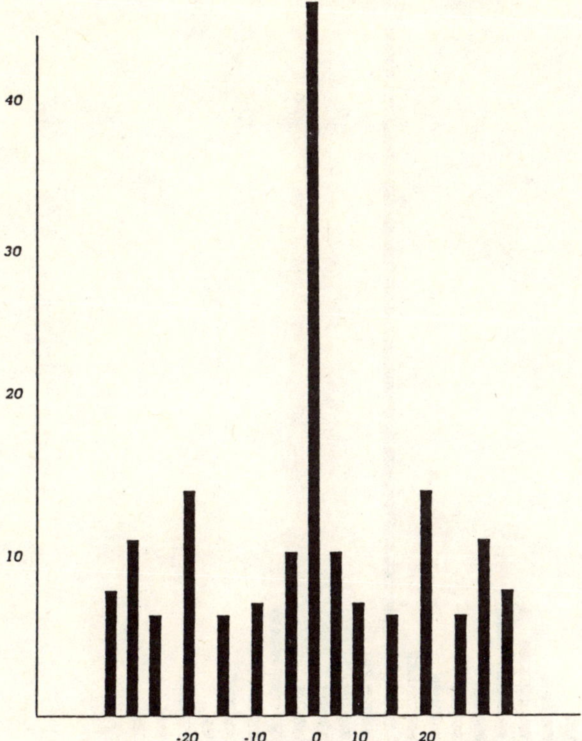

Fig. 8.4. Histogram H(V2,V2)

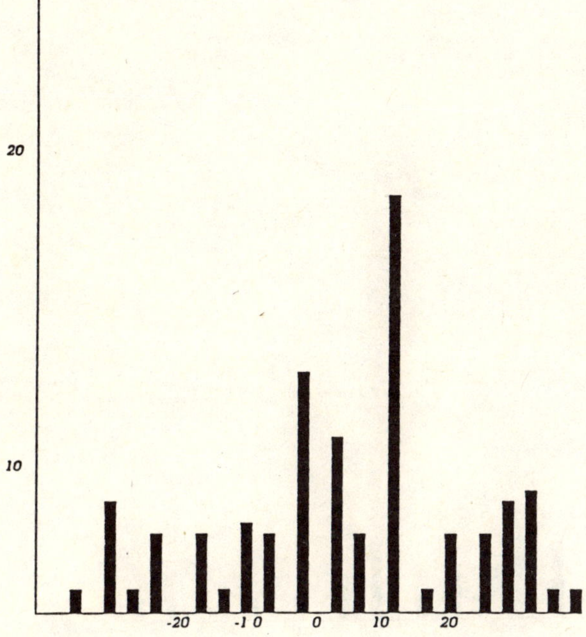

Fig. 8.5. Histogram H(V1,V3)

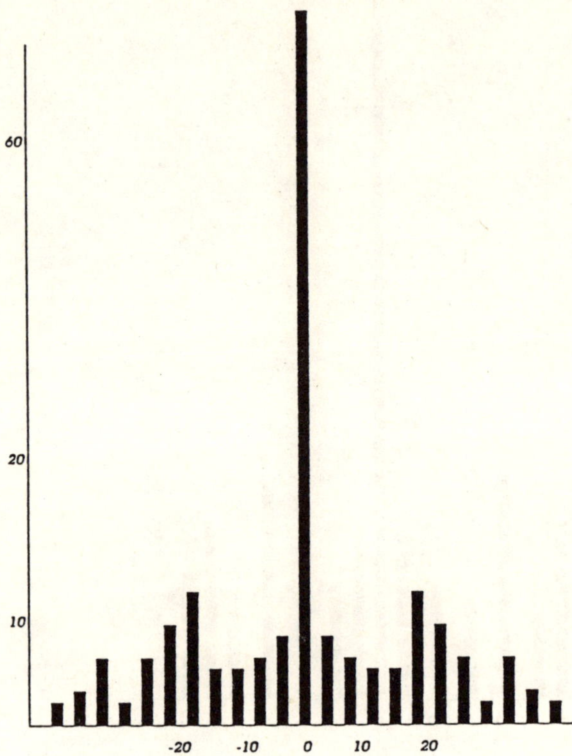

Fig. 8.6.Histogram H(V3,V3)

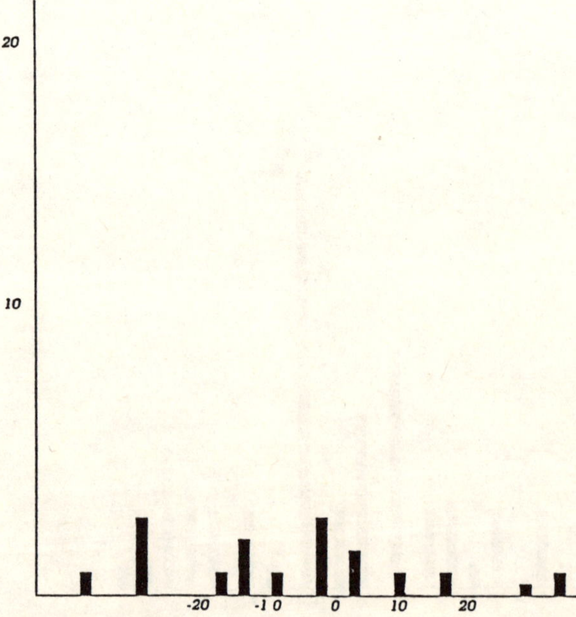

Fig. 8.7. Histogram H(V1,V4)

From analysing the resulting 4 histograms, the following conjectures were proposed:

- 'similar' versions have similar self-matching histograms

- if V_1 and V_2 are 'similar' then $H(V_1,V_2)$ has a high degree of symmetry about the y-axis

- a necessary condition for V_1 and V_2 to be similar (ie not diverse) is that the histograms $H(V_1,V_1)$, $H(V_2,V_2)$ and $H(V_1,V_2)$ are similar.

- if V1 and V2 are 'diverse' then H(V1,V2) has a low degree of symmetry about the y-axis and low match frequency with respect to each shift.

8.1.2 Shortcomings of the Prototype Technique

While the prototype technique appeared to work very well, critical examination and discussion of the results led to the identification of a number of potential problems and shortcomings of the technique. These shortcomings are discussed below.

8.1.2.1 Length of Programs

The programs chosen were all very short and only contained a few lines of source code. When the assembly level code for these programs was analysed by hand it was found that programs written in PASCAL all contained a large area of common code. This common code set up and accessed the Input/Output functions of the computer and was automatically inserted by the compiler. It was not related to the diversity of the algorithms within the programs. When the common code was removed there were too few remaining mnemonics for the matching program to produce any meaningful results.

8.1.2.2 Suitability of Trial Data

The programs chosen were produced by giving a simple specification to ten programmers who worked independently. The eleventh program was of similar length but for a completely different specification. This meant that there was no control over the diversity of the programs and no expected results to compare the actual results with.

8.1.2.3 Matching Algorithm

The matching program counted the number of mnemonics which were in the same positions at each step of the rotation of the buffers. All assembly languages contain a limited number of mnemonics and a single source code instruction may require several mnemonics to be implemented. The same mnemonics can be used in various combinations to implement different source code instructions. This means that a number of mnemonic matches may be found even in source codes which are very dissimilar. These spurious matches can be regarded as noise. This noise results in a distorted measure of diversity.

8.1.2.4 Programming Style

This method did not consider the effects of changing the order of statements within a program or of adding one or two extra statements to a program. This would make a dramatic difference to the results as blocks of mnemonics would match in different places.

8.1.2.5 Lack of Automation

The file containing only the mnemonic codes was been produced by hand-editing the listing file generated by the microvax compiler. This would not be an acceptable method to use with larger programs. The histograms were also produced by manipulating the result files manually. An automated process would be much better.

8.1.2.6 Assessment of Results

For these tests, the diversity was judged by plotting the results and making subjective estimates as to how symmetrical the resulting graph was. This was not a very accurate guide of diversity. What was required was a numerical method of determining the symmetry of the results.

8.2 Enhancement of the Prototype

In order to fully evaluate the idea of mnemonic pattern matching it was chosen to address the shortcomings that had been identified. The work was undertaken in two steps. First the measures taken to overcome the shortcomings are identified and then the results of the repeated exercise are described.

8.2.1 Improvements to Overcome Identified Shortcomings

Three principle measures were taken to overcome the shortcomings that were identified in 8.1.2. These measures are described below.

8.2.1.1 Automation of Mnemonic Code File Generation

It was clear that in order to test and develop this method of measuring diversity, much larger programs would have to be used. This would make it impractical to produce this file by hand-editing as was previously done. A PASCAL program was therefore written to automatically create the mnemonic code file from the compiler listing file. This program was selective as to which mnemonics were actually used. Mnemonics which were added by the compiler but were not actually related to the algorithm were discarded. Typical of these mnemonics were no-operation commands inserted to put page boundaries at the correct addresses and standard sequences used at the beginning and end of every procedure.

8.2.1.2 Selection of Trial Data

For the next series of tests, three procedures which each contained about 70 source code instructions were chosen. These procedures were all written in PASCAL to perform the same function, calibrating input signals in a reactor trip program, but each used a different method. As the procedures had been written for a real-time application they did not contain the common Input/Output area instructions which were inserted into the first set of test programs.

8.2.1.3 Reducing the Effect of Noise

The noise caused by random matches can be reduced by matching sequences of more than one mnemonic - if two sequences of five mnemonics match, then it is quite likely that their respective lines of source code are functionally identical.

The matching program was modified to enable any size of block to be specified for the matching. Changes were also made so that the size of the circular buffers was determined by the number of instructions in the mnemonic code files (they previously had a fixed length).

8.2.2 Tests with Improved Technique

Each procedure was matched with itself and the other two using block sizes of one to five. A block size of three gave the best results - filtering out random matches (noise) whilst preserving the locations of the peaks. None of the histograms produced showed any sign of symmetry, the indication of areas of common code. This was surprising as there were significant areas of the source codes which were similar.

8.3 Further Improvements to Technique

Despite the setback that the results of Section 8.2.2 represented it was considered that there was still scope for improvement particularly in the mechanics of the analysis of the results.

8.3.1 Selection of a Better Set of Test Data

It was decided to analyse larger programs with known diversity in order to get more conclusive results. Nine PASCAL programs, each containing between 100 and 500 instructions were chosen.

The details of the programs are given below:

A,B,C.   Three reactor protection system programs created as part of an exercise in serial diversity. These involve reading input values, calculating results using "look-up" tables and generating a safe or trip flag. They were designed to be diverse by use of different algebra for their calculations, different control structures and by doing operations in a different order wherever possible.

D.   Program A compiled with a different option (NO OPTIMIZE).

E.   Program A with its internal procedures declared in a different order and with the order of a few trivial instructions altered.

F.   A reactor trip module from a program written for a different project to A, B and C.

G.   Program F compiled with a different option (NO OPTIMIZE).

H. Program F with three functionally neutral (WRITELN) statements added in different locations.

I. Program F with five functionally neutral (WRITELN) statements added in different locations.

8.3.2 Mathematical Comparison of Results and Presentation

A mathematical method was chosen to analyse the symmetry of the results. If the results are treated as a numerical series, the symmetry can be measured by finding the correlation between values on either side of the peak value. The peak value may not be the middle value due to data skew. To overcome this the results need to be placed in a circular buffer and the correlation calculated for every point. The maximum value of the correlation and the corresponding point can then be recorded.

The correlation function used is the standard correlation function used to compare discrete time series.

$$\frac{\sum_{n}(u_n-\bar{u})(v_n-\bar{v})}{\sqrt{\sum_{n}(u_n-\bar{u})^2\sum_{n}(v_n-\bar{v})^2}}$$

where

u = matches with positive shifts

v = matches with negative shifts

$\bar{u}$ = mean of u

$\bar{v}$ = mean of v

The correlation will be

1.0 for symmetrical results (ie identical codes)

0.0 for results with no symmetry (ie completely dissimilar codes)

Finally the graphics program on the microVAX computer used was adapted to automatically produce scaled bar graphs from the results when requested.

8.3.3 Testing of Further Improvements

The codes were matched against themselves and each other using block sizes of one to five. To do this, the codes were put into circular buffers and the number of matches between two buffers recorded at each step (shift) as the buffers were rotated relative to each other through 360 degrees. The matching and cross-correlation of all nine codes was done using a single batch file to automate the process.

8.3.4 Results

The results of the cross-correlation for block sizes of one to five are given in [REQ89], and are summarised briefly here.

The cross-correlation between the similar programs F, G, H and I, identical programs except for use of different optimisation and introduction of functionally neutral "writeln" statements, appears to be promising. It takes values greater than 0.5 for a block size of one and tends to stay about the same value as the block size is increased.

The cross-correlation between the similar programs A, D and E appears to be no better than between the "diverse" programs A, B and C for a block size of one. The graphs for matching A and A, A and D, and A and E with a block size of one showed very few similarities. However, the correlation between A and D was seen to improve as the block size is increased and the noise becomes less.

A quite dissimilar result was obtained for the correlation between programs A and B as the block size is changed. The correlation drops as the block size is increased from one to two to three, and the noise becomes less. This is the expected result as programs A and B are designed to be diverse. As the block size is further increased, the correlation starts to rise. This is because there are less data points to consider.

It was generally observed that comparing larger sized blocks can initially give a more accurate correlation but will ultimately give a completely false result. The histograms for matching program A against program H, two programs written for different projects with very different structures had only 2 matches for a block size of five and this resulted in a correlation of 1.0 implying identical codes.

8.4 Conclusions

A process to automatically compare the diversity of programs using the mnemonics from their assembly language code listings has been developed. The process was limited to PASCAL programs in order to give a more controlled test environment. The process calculates the correlation between the codes by matching groups of mnemonics and looking for symmetry. Unfortunately this method of measuring the diversity doesn't give very reliable results. If too small a size of block is used, then the results are masked by noise due to random matches. If the block size is too large, then not enough matches are found for the mathematical method used to be accurate.

The method did not take account of the number of consecutive mnemonics which matched. It was found that this could cause the measured "diversity" between programs differing in only a single line to be as good as between very dissimilar programs.

The attempts at analysis of the results assume that similar programs whose mnemonic sequences are matched will produce a histogram which is symmetrical about a single point whilst dissimilar programs will produce asymmetrical histograms. This assumption has been shown to be invalid. Consequently, if the approach is to be further developed, a more rigorous method of analysis is required.

A better way of measuring the diversity between two program codes would be to compare the size and distribution of identical blocks of mnemonics: a higher proportion of the mnemonics for similar programs will be contained in large identical blocks.

It is hoped to develop a more reliable method of measuring the diversity of computer programs from this process based on the size and distribution of identical blocks of mnemonics in the codes.

References

[HIL88] I. W. Hill: Assembler Code Level Pattern Matching as a Diversity Metric. Safety and Engineering Science Division,UKAEA Winfrith, February 1988

[REQ89] D. N. Wall: Software Diversity - Its Role and Measurement. Phase 2 REQUEST Report R 2.3.6, August 1989

Chapter 9

The FRIL Model Approach for Software Diversity Assessment

Michael Martin Burke, David Nicholas Wall

The approach consisted of developing a conceptual model and subsequently implementing it as a prototype knowledge based system to assess both the similarity and dissimilarity of two software systems developed from the same requirement. In essence the model tries to determine the diversity of two programs by comparing whatever evidence is available regarding those attributes that have the potential of influencing diversity. Some of the information upon which such an assessment is made will be of variable quality and in some cases information will be completely lacking. In order to enable all of this information to be represented in a consistent way the model was implemented in FRIL (Fuzzy Relational Inference Language) as FRIL is capable of representing knowledge bases containing uncertainties of a probabilistic, fuzzy and evidential nature.

It should be noted here that the use of the expression software diversity in the context of this work is not that normally recognised in software engineering. In usual parlance the term software diversity is used in the context of two pieces of software with identical functionality having common mode failures. In this work the term software diversity and its assessment are simply used to indicate differences in the two pieces of software under consideration. The measurement of diversity difference output from the work reported here would thus be input to a software diversity assessment which considers diverse and common mode failures. It is suggested that this second step could be performed by an approach using a fuzzy logic expert system similar to that developed here. This second step is not considered here.

The description of the work given here outlines the principles of the approach and the attributes of the software as considered in the model. The internal structure of the model and the rules used by the inference engine at the heart of the model are not discussed as space does not permit their inclusion and explanation.

9.1 Software Attributes Affecting Diversity

With the advent of sophisticated software development tools such as high level languages, programs are no longer thought of as a collection of machine executable instructions. Instead they are viewed as a collection of objects, such as the code and supporting documentation, together with an associated set of attributes which characterise both the processes used in the development of the software and the properties of the software. One of the first aspects of the study was concerned with defining a set of attributes which can influence and characterise software diversity in terms of the processes associated with developing the software, referred to as process attributes, and the properties of the software itself, referred to as product attributes. These attributes include not only those that have the potential for enhancing diversity but also those that have the potential for inhibiting diversity. For example, the use of a design methodology which dictates the use of a particular implementation language, is considered as inhibiting diversity. It should be noted that certain attributes may only be applicable to specific applications. For example, at present the use of formal methods is only practiced for small systems, less than 2000 lines of code, or critical parts of a large system.

The fundamental reason for using diversity in multi version software systems is to reduce the likelihood of common-mode failures. Therefore it seems reasonable to assume that in order to assist in determining a set of attributes that characterise diversity, an understanding of the type, frequency and distribution of errors that can occur, is required. This in turn requires an understanding of the activities involved in software development. The software engineering industry has proposed a variety of life-cycle models for representing the activities involved in developing a software product. The process of software development can be viewed in an abstract sense as an iterative translation process, translating an initial concept of what is thought is required into a sequence of representations (intermediate states) and culminating in a computer-based implementation, see fig. 9.1.

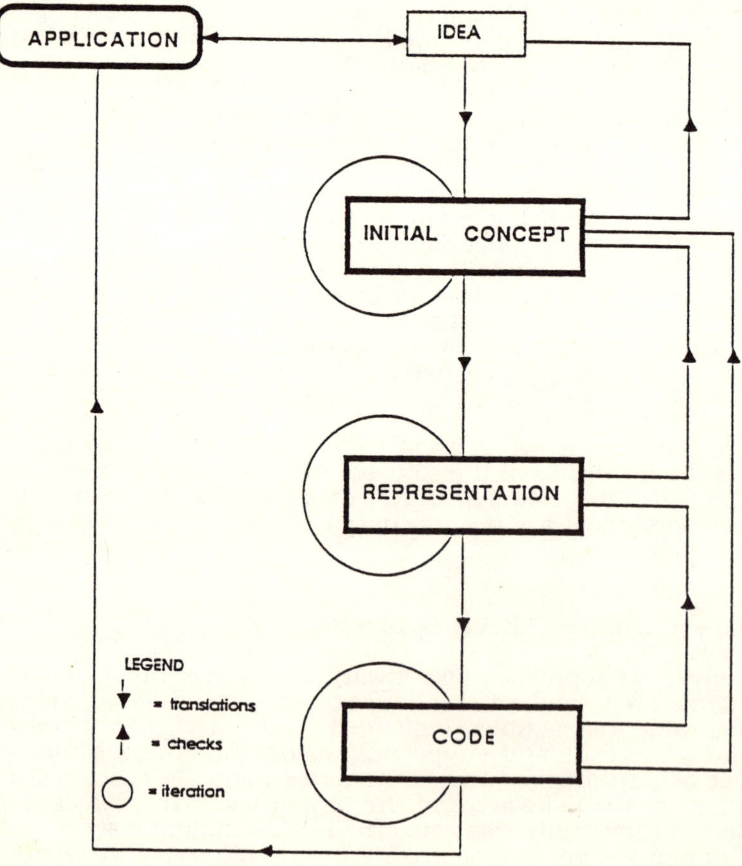

Fig. 9.1. Process of software development

The activities associated with developing software can:

- introduce uncertainties into the intermediate states due to a variety of reasons such as errors resulting from non rigorous translations;

- raise the level of assurance that errors are not present by the use of various techniques such as verification and validation.

Throughout the process of software development, software errors can be introduced for a variety of reasons, such as misinterpretation of what is to be translated. As errors can occur throughout the development process and diversity can be influenced at all stages of the development process, the strategy adopted to ascertain a set of attributes focused on the following activities, which in general, are common to any software development:

- defining initial concept/application
- requirements analysis
- choosing a development methodology
- modelling
- specification
- design
- implementation
- verification, validation and testing
- maintenance
- tool support
- personnel

Based on these activities two distinct lists of attributes were produced, namely:

- those attributes which characterise the process of developing the software and referred to as process attributes;

- those attributes which characterise the properties of the software itself and referred to as product attributes.

We now list these attributes in two groups, for the process and then for the product.

9.1.1 Process Attributes

This section describes the attributes associated with the process of transforming a set of requirements into an implementation that can be executed on a computer. Fig. 9.2 depicts the hierarchical structure of the process attributes.

9.1.1.1 Process Character

The following attributes will be used to characterise a high level impression of the process used to develop the software:

Type of Methodology

- formal
- rigorous
- systematic
- prototyped

- ad hoc
- consistent (ability of different teams to use method in a consistent manner)

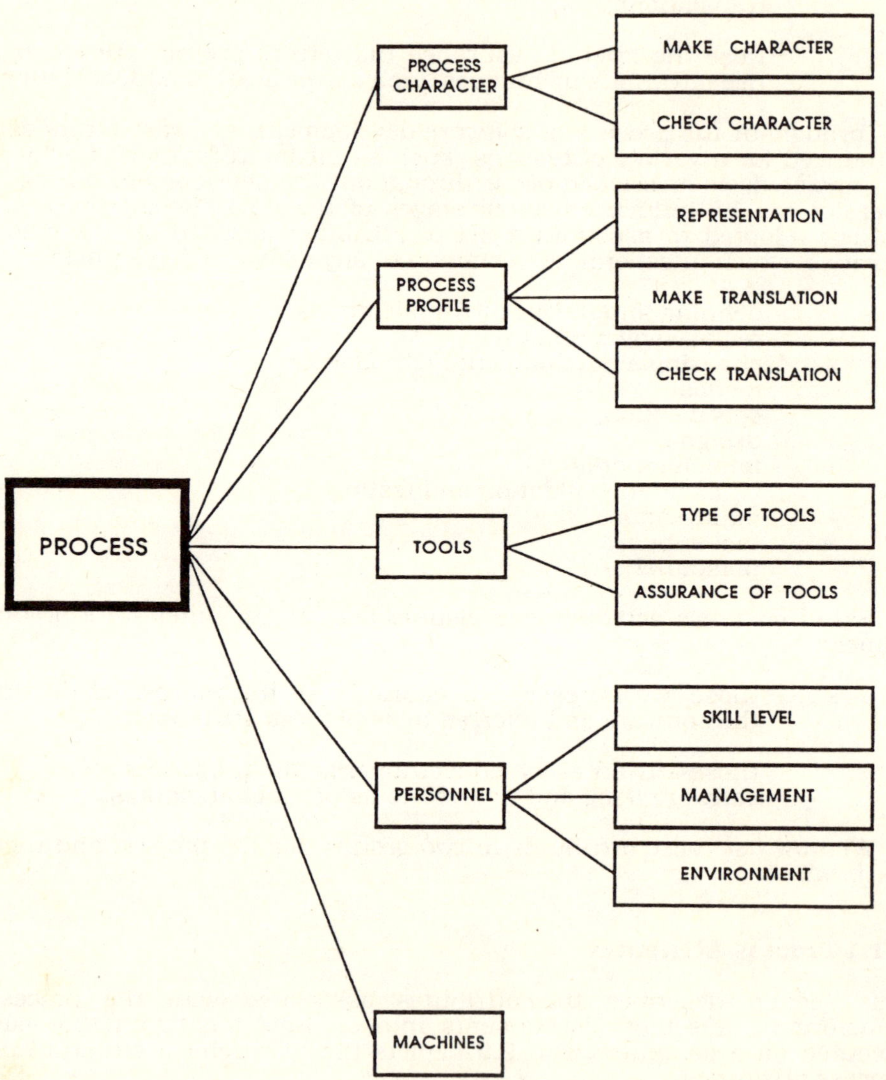

Fig. 9.2. Hierarchical structure of process attributes

9.1.1.2 Process Profile

The following attributes will be used to characterise the strategy used to transform the requirements into an implementation. The approach used is based on the abstract process of development depicted in fig. 9.1. The characterisation is complementary to that of 'Process Character'. However, it is a much more detailed breakdown than that used in 'Process Character' which uses vague but easily acquired evidence.

Representation

The following attributes will be used to categorize a representation:

- type of representation
- decomposition
- specification
- design
- implementation etc
- level and preciseness of detail
- level of abstraction
- device dependence
- language dependence
- specialist resources

Make Translation

The following attributes will be used to categorize how a representation is translated into a more detailed representation:

- automatic
- manual
- level of formality

Check Translation

The following attributes will be used to categorize how checks are performed to determine the accuracy and validity of a translation of a representation into a more detailed representation:

- simulation
- prototyping
- modelling
- level of formality
- type of analysis (symbolic, static, dynamic etc)
- audits
- certification
- dependability
- level and type of verification
- level and type of validation
- level and type of testing
- unit, module, integration, system
- acceptance tests
- path coverage

9.1.1.3 Tools

The following attributes will be used to categorize the tools used in development:

Type of Tools Used

- static analysers
- dynamic analysers
- debugging environments (test harnesses etc)
- library files
- expert systems to aid design, debugging etc
- IPSEs (integrated project support environments)
- compiler

- operating system
- project management system

Assurance of Tools

- maturity of tools
- certification

9.1.1.4 Personnel

The following attributes will be used to categorize the development team and their working environment:

Skill Level

- experience of personnel
- skill level of analysts, designers, programmers and testers
- specialist personnel
- training

Management

- management style
- team structure
- resource utilisation (for example use of separate test teams)
- communications

Environment

- working environment

9.1.1.5 Machines

The following attributes will be used to categorize the machines used in the development process:

Type of Machines

- PCs
- host machines
- target machines
- word processors

9.1.2 Product Attributes

This section describes the attributes associated with the properties of the product itself. Some of these attributes may relate to attributes that can only be measured at run time (i.e. certain performance characteristics). Fig. 9.3 depicts the hierarchical structure of the product attributes.

9.1.2.1 Product Character

The following attributes will be used to characterise a high level impression of the software:

Type of Product

-	formal
-	rigorous
-	systematic
-	prototyped
-	ad hoc

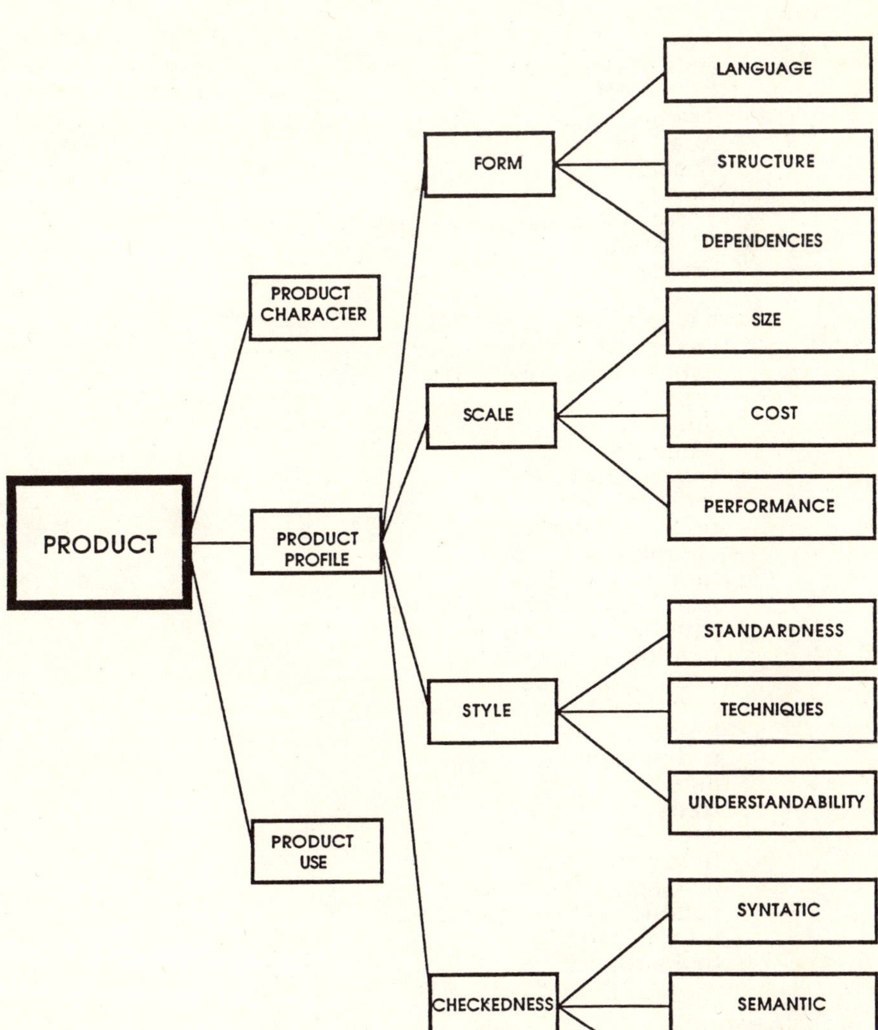

Fig. 9.3. Hierarchical structure of product attributes

9.1.2.2 Product Profile

The following attributes will be used to characterise the properties of the
software in a more detailed way than 'Product Character'. The two
characterisations are complementary, enabling vague easily assessed
evidence to be used, as well as more precise, and in general, more difficult
to acquire evidence in the same model.

Form

- type of language
- high level
- Traditional
- Ada
- Pascal
- Coral
- Fortran etc
- AI based
- Prolog
- Lisp
- low level
- structure
- control structure
- type
- dijkstra
- while do
- repeat until
- reducible
- non reducible
- complexity
- module coupling
- number of decision points
- number of jumps
- nesting of procedures
- nesting of loops
- data structure
- types
- n-dimensional arrays
- lists
- trees etc
- dependencies
- hardware
- disc space required
- volatile memory requirement
- interfaces
- tool support

Scale

- size
- number of executable statements
- number of global variables
- amount of redundancy
- use of recursion
- cost
- amount of effort
- breakdown of effort into phases of development
- performance
- execution time

- precision and accuracy of calculations
- storage requirements

Style

- standardness
- generality
- off the shelf
- bespoke
- manufacturer
- maturity of product
- available in public domain
- common code usage
- reusability of modules
- use of library files
- standards compliance
- conformance to standards '
- configuration management (version control etc)
- programming
- documentation
- serviceability
- use of specialist tools
- use of specialist engineers
- cost of service contract
- techniques
- algorithms
- integrity
- defensive programming
- understandability
- use of structured code
- legibility
- self descriptiveness
- consistency
- comments embedded in the code
- error messages
- documentation
- self documentation
- use of diagrams (flow charts)
- how well documentation covers features of software

Checkedness

These attributes concern evidence about how well the software has been checked throughout the development process.

- documentation
- documentation of test cases
- number of write statements in the code
- syntactic
- semantic
- theorem checking
- threat analysis
- algebraic description (SPADE)
- coverage
- number of lines used by test harness
- number of paths executed in testing and trials

9.2   Measuring Diversity

The diversity of software versions developed to meet the same requirement cannot be determined solely by simply combining counting functions associated with the product attributes, for example the number of executable statements. Measurement of diversity is far more complex and requires sophisticated techniques to be employed.

9.2.1 Measurement of Attributes

The following points should be considered when trying to measure attributes that have a potential for affecting diversity, namely:

- Highly accurate measurements do not necessarily have a significant influence on assessing diversity. For example, many of the attributes associated with implementation are easily measurable to a high degree of accuracy, but do not necessarily have a very significant effect on diversity.

- Not all attributes will be measurable in full.

- Not all attributes will be relevant to the goal of using diversity to minimise common mode failure in a multi- version software system.

- Only subjective measurements may be possible on some attributes.

- Where possible, information that is available should be used to measure diversity taking into account its importance and relevance relative to other information.

- Diversity attributes can be structured into a hierarchical frame work which categorizes attributes at a number of levels. For example,

- High level attributes, that is those attributes that can be measured before compilation of source code

- Medium level attributes, that is those attributes that can be measured during compilation of source code

- Low level attributes, that is those attributes that can be measured after compilation of source code.

In general, measurement of low level attributes will infer something about high level attributes and visa versa. Furthermore attributes at the lowest level can, in general, be measured to a high degree of accuracy, hence part of the reason for their identification.

- Only those attributes which are 'compiler-insensitive', produced as a result of compilation or measurable after compilation will be significant in the context of diversity.

9.2.2 Tools to Aid in Measuring Attributes

There are a number of tools that can aid in the process of measuring software attributes. We consider the following tools:

9.2.2.1 Compilers

In general, compilers produce useful information for measuring certain software attributes. For example, the following data is usually produced at the compilation stage:

- frequency of use of variables
- statements per module/procedure
- total number of executable statements.

9.2.2.2 Static Analysers

Static analysers can provide a variety of information concerning the structure and semantics of a program including the following information:

Structure

- all starts and ends
- type of control structure (Dijkstra structured etc)
- location of loops with their entry and exit points
- nesting of loops
- executable paths
- superfluous statements

Semantics

- conditions for execution of each path

- extraction of a partial program composed of those statements which may affect the value of the variable at a point in the code

- assisting in establishing how the value of a variable is obtained at some point within the program

- identification of all the possible ways in which the value of a variable at a particular point within the program, may affect subsequent program execution

- for each variable, a dependency list of variables which can contribute to its value.

9.2.3 Measuring Process Attributes

This aspect of the study consists of our initial ideas on techniques that could be used to quantify process attributes. This part of the study was only an initial investigation and requires further work. The following techniques could be used to measure the main groups of process attributes identified in 9.1.1.

9.2.3.1 Process Character

The following techniques could be used to obtain a coarse impression of the process used to develop the software:

- inspection of deliverable documents (code etc)

9.2.3.2 Process Profile

The following techniques could be used to quantify a software development methodology:

- make a list of representations used in the development
- make a list of translations used in the development
- make a list of checks used in the development
- measure time spent on each phase of development
- assess level of specialist knowledge required to apply methodology
- estimate productivity achieved
- assess level of annotation in the form of pre and post conditions
- assess level of abstraction.

9.2.3.3 Tools

Assessment of the tools used in software development could be made in terms of:

- the quality of support offered by available toolsets
- level of validation of compiler
- ease of use

9.2.3.4 Personnel

The following techniques could be used to make an assessment of the suitability of personnel and their effective deployment:

- assess resource utilisation

- count number of years of experience of analysts, designers and programmers

- measure time taken to learn how to operate system

9.2.3.5 Machines

Assessment of the machines used in software development could be made in terms of:

- performance
- memory
- support facilities
- ease of use

9.2.4 Measuring Product Attributes

The exercise of establishing how product attributes can be measured can follow on from that for the process attributes described in section 9.2.3. The attributes and the resultant measurements would appear to be better defined and amenable to simple measuring (counting) techniques. The following techniques could be used to measure the main groups of product attributes identified in 9.1.2.

9.2.4.1 Product Character

The following techniques could be used to obtain a coarse impression of the character of a software product:

- inspection of code
- inspection of supporting documentation

9.2.4.2 Product Profile

The following assessments and counts could be used to quantify the product profile of a software system:

Form

- structure
- control structure
- assess call structure
- assess modularity of structure
- count number of loops
- count nesting of loops
- assess type of data structures
- count average number of statements that affect the value of a variable at any point in the program
- count number of basic control structures (while do, if then else, etc)
- count frequency of use of basic control structures
- count number of branch points
- count number of jumps
- complexity
- count number of superfluous statement
- count number of distinct operator
- count number of occurrences of each operator
- count number of global variables
- count number of executable statements
- count number of executable paths
- count average length of paths
- count average number of statements per module/procedure
- count average number of statements that affect the value of a variable at any point in the program
- count depth of nesting of procedures
- count depth of nesting of loops
- data structures
- count number of different data structures
- dependencies
- count number of interfaces

Scale

- performance
- measure execution time
- measure time each module takes to run
- estimate efficiency

Style

- standards compliance
- assess conformance to standards
- assess conformance to specification
- techniques
- assess maturity of algorithms
- assess precision of calculations
- understandability
- count number of comments
- assess sophistication of error messages

Checkedness

- measure time spent on testing
- estimate reliability
- count the number and type of errors that occurred during development
- measure time taken to correct errors
- count proportion of errors detected during distinct phases of development
- estimate reliability of individual subsystems.

9.2.4.3 Product Use

The intended application of the product is determined by assessment of its ability to satisfactorily perform a number of acceptance tests.

9.3   The FRIL Model for Software Diversity Assessment

The FRIL model approach for software diversity assessment consisted of developing a conceptual model, which was subsequently implemented as a prototype system, to assess both the similarity and dissimilarity of two software systems developed from the same requirement. Fundamental to this approach was the use of a set of attributes based on those defined in section 9.1, which characterise a software system both in terms of the processes associated with its development and the properties of the software itself.

The aim of the work at this point was to establish the viability of the approach consequently the primary objectives of developing the prototype system to measure the diversity of two versions were:

- to provide a broad coverage of our high level ideas

- to incorporate the most important features

- to enable the prototype to be easily extended to incorporate additional features

- to be able to model any software development that can be represented by the abstract software development process depicted in fig. 9.1.

- to allow the prototype to be compared with other models.

In essence the model tries to determine the diversity of two versions by comparing whatever evidence is available regarding the attributes identified as influencing software diversity.

The input to the model consists of evidence about each version's attributes which can come from a variety of sources such as:

Attribute	*Source of Evidence*
Development methodology	Documentation
Personnel	Documentation, interviews
Control structure	Static analysis
Operational behaviour	Trials

The quality of the input information will be variable and in some cases information will be completely lacking. Consequently representing all of this information in a consistent way requires a sophisticated and subtle mechanism which can handle both quantitative and qualitative evidence about the attributes. The output from the model is a measure of the support given to the belief that the two versions under examination are diverse.

9.3.1 Description of Model

The five essential features of the model are now described:

Representation

The model represents software in terms of a set of both process and product attributes together with the subtle and often complex relationships between these attributes. The model uses a collection of rules in the form of logical statements which define the sophisticated relationships which must, in general, hold between the various attributes of two versions for there to be support to the conclusion that they are diverse. For example:

- the relative importance of each attribute in terms of their ability to either contribute to enhancing diversity or conversely contribute to inhibiting diversity

- the relationships between attributes, such as:

- how the choice of a particular development methodology affects the choice of an implementation language

- how the maintainability of a system will affect its reliability.

Certain information concerning the nature of attributes and their inter-dependencies will be imprecise and involve uncertainties. For example, the relationship between the skill level of a development team and the use of development tools. To cope with such situations the model can represent information of a probabilistic, fuzzy and evidential nature.

Evidence

The model provides a means of handling both quantitative and qualitative evidence about the attributes of software products, both by direct observation and by indirect inference from the processes used in their development. Provision of this evidence and information for certain attributes of a particular version may require the expert, subjective knowledge of experienced software engineers. Other information such as that associated with testing, verification and validation can be treated in a more objective manner.

Comparison

The model compares two software versions in terms of evidence about their software attributes. Given evidence, either of a quantitative or qualitative nature, about any or all of the attributes of two particular versions, the model provides the means for inferring the extent to which the versions are diverse.

For example, if the only information available is that one version is implemented in Ada and the other version implemented in Pascal, then the support that the versions are diverse would be lower than if they were implemented in Prolog and Fortran.

If evidence about the processes used to develop the versions is available then the model will determine the degree to which this affects their diversity. For example how the use of independent development teams using diverse development methodologies affects diversity.

Diversity Metric

The model produces a single metric for the diversity of two versions in the form of a measure which quantifies the support given to the belief that the versions under consideration are diverse.

Implementation

The model is implemented as a knowledge based system in FRIL (Fuzzy Relational Inference Language [BAL86]), a powerful computer language for Artificial Intelligence applications. FRIL can handle knowledge bases containing uncertainties of a probabilistic, fuzzy and evidential nature through its facilities such as support logic programming ([BAL87]), and so is well suited to model the diversity of software.

9.3.2 Design of The FRIL Program

This section briefly describes the design of the FRIL program to assess the diversity of two software versions. As no standard FRIL design method existed, a novel design technique was used to develop the FRIL program. It is hoped that this design technique is sufficiently flexible to be used for any FRIL design.

The data structures used in the model, organize the attributes identified in section 9.1, into structures which emphasise their meaning. In conjunction with these data structures there is an associated set of rules that represent the logical relationships between the elements of the data structures. Furthermore there is also a set of rules that allow comparisons of two data structures associated with two versions to be made.

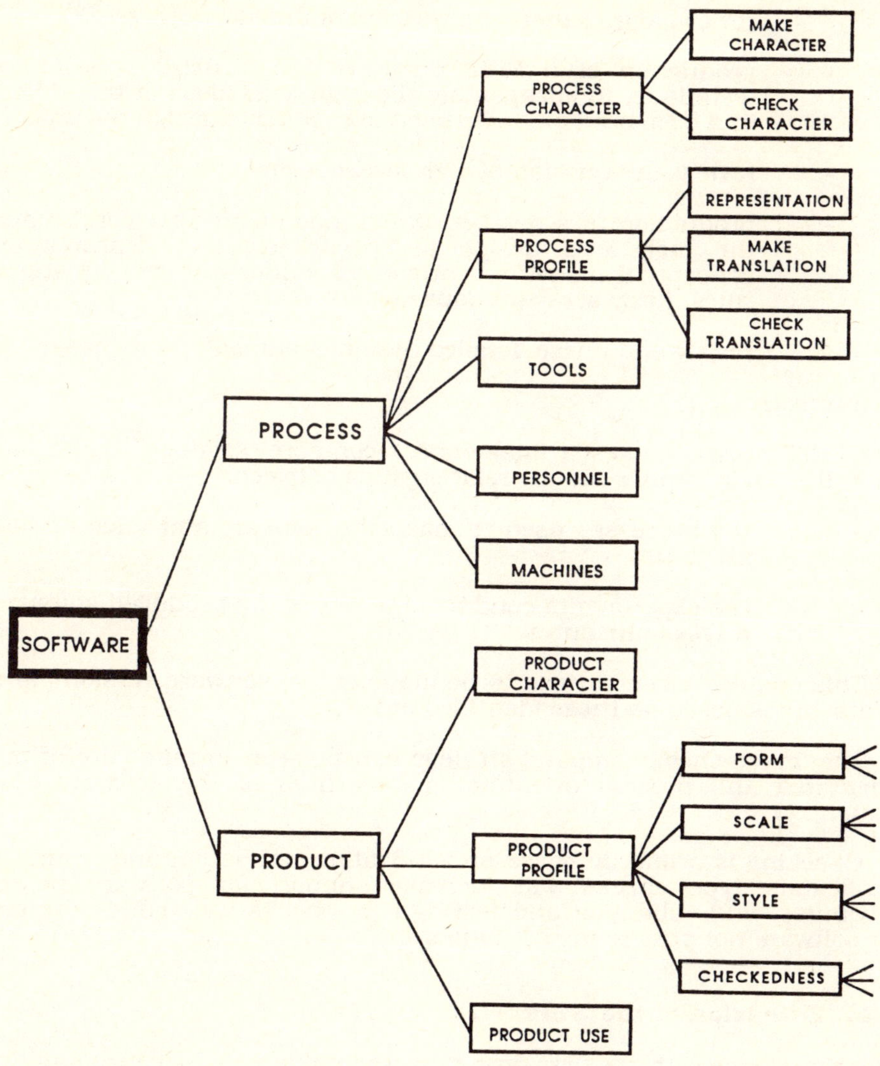

Fig. 9.4. Hierarchical structure of high level attributes

The data structures have been designed to reflect the hierarchical nature of the attributes and to enable the model to represent any software development that can be described by the abstract software development process depicted in fig. 9.1. Fig. 9.4 depicts the hierarchical structure of the high level attributes. The rules take into account how the comparison of a low level attribute contributes to the comparison of other, high level attributes.

The model design activities consisted of the following steps:

    production of a natural language document by the members of the study describing their perception of the appropriate software attributes

-    review, aggregation and revision of this document

-    production of a FRIL program design using a semi formal technique, to encapsulate the high level ideas of this document in a form suitable to be used to produce a design document

-    review and revision of high level design

-    production of a detailed design document as a continuation of the high level design to specify low level features of the conceptual model and numerical values on partially supported rules, fuzzy set definitions etc.

-    review and revise detailed design document.

Strategy

The FRIL program uses a 'make-check-compare' strategy. Using support logic, the model represents the relationships between:

-    the processes used to make the software and a set of software attributes

-    the experiments conducted to check the produced software and a set of attributes.

This enables a comparison to be made of two software versions in terms of attributes based on those identified in 9.1.

The 'make-check-compare' strategy can be seen to take care of product orientated and process orientated perspectives of the software diversity issue.

Checking is primarily based on verification, validation and testing where verification type checks will increase support for software possessing attributes, and validation and testing type checks will reduce the support for software not possessing attributes.

9.4   Extension of the Work

The experience with the first prototype was sufficiently encouraging that the work was extended by improving the model and its internal structure and providing it with a menu driven user interface. The latter is considered important as it allows experts to make use of the model and investigate its properties. The feedback available from such exercises allows the model structure and the relationship of the attributes to be further developed to capture such expert knowledge and opinion.

9.4.1 Prototype Development

The results of the experiment conducted on the prototype system showed that there were two areas where significant improvement would be possible. The first was the structure and importance attributed to the different attributes, the second was the definitions of the attributes. In addition it was recognised that the human interface with the model was in significant need of improvement to allow experts not familiar with the FRIL programming language to use the model.

9.4.1.1 The Attributes

During the experimentation with and subsequent review of the prototype model it was found that the definitions of the attributes for which information was to be provided were not sufficiently tightly drawn. Consequently it was necessary for the developers to provide advice and information to the experimenters so prejudicing their independence. The information gained by the developers during this phase of the development provided much needed and very valuable input to the development of the conceptual model to be represented by the FRIL expert system. It also lead to a considerable improvement in the definition of the attributes and their relation in the hierarchical structure, the foundation and essential elements of the model. The definitions of the attributes used to construct the conceptual model are given below. The references numbers uniquely define each attribute the daughter taking the reference number of the parent as the base for its reference number as can be seen by reference to fig. 9.5. Those attributes marked 'leaf' are at ends of the structure and are those and only those attributes for which information is provided.

Software(0) is all programs, procedures, rules, and possibly associated documentation and data pertaining to the operation of a programmable system. Software is defined in terms of the sub- attributes process and product.

Process (0.1) is an attribute which describes the processes used in the development of software. It is defined in terms of the sub- attributes process profile, tools, personnel and machines.

Product(0.2) is an attribute which describes software when regarded as an artefact or commodity. It is defined in terms of the sub-attributes product profile and use.

Process profile (0.1.1) is an attribute which describes the nature of the processes used in the development of the software. The attribute product profile is defined in terms of sub-attributes representations, make-translations and check-translations.

Tools(0.1.2) is a process attribute which describes the software engineering tools used in developing the software. Tools is defined in terms of sub-attributes software tools and hardware tools.

Personnel(0.1.3) is a process attribute which describes the people involved in the development of the software. It is defined in terms of sub-attributes skills, management and environment.

Machines (0.1.4) is a process attribute. It is a list of the various machines used in the development of software.

Representations (0.1.1.1) is a process attribute. It is a list of the various descriptions of the software produced during development. Typical examples of elements of representation lists are requirements specifications, functional specifications, design, object code, machine code, etc.

Make-translations (0.1.1.2) is a process attribute. It is a list of the processes by which the various representations of the software are transformed into another more detailed representations. Typical examples of elements of make-translations lists are systems analysis, designing, coding etc.

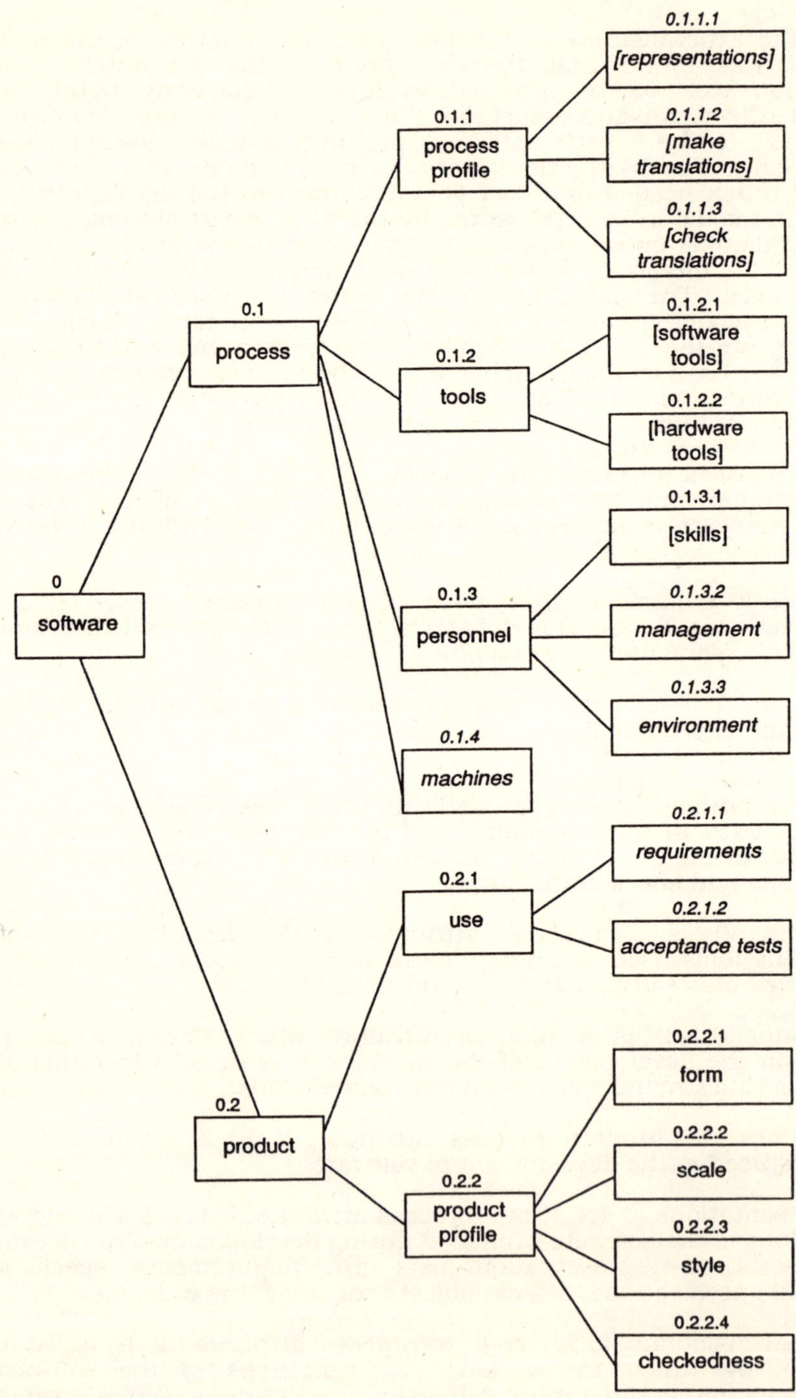

Fig. 9.5. Attributes used to construct the conceptual model

Check-translations (0.1.1.3) is a process attribute. It is a list of the processes by which checks are made that the various representations of the software have been faithfully transformed into other more detailed representations. Typical examples of elements of check-translations lists are design reviews, walkthroughs, unit tests, integration tests, sneak analysis, etc.

Software tools (0.1.2.1) is a process attribute which describes the computer programs used to help implement, test, analyse or maintain software. It is a list whose elements are defined in terms of the sub-attributes software tool name and assurance of software tool.

Hardware tools (0.1.2.2) is a process attribute which describes the hardware devices used to help implement, test, analyse or maintain software. It is a list whose elements are defined in terms of the sub-attributes hardware tool name and assurance of hardware tool.

Software tool name (0.1.2.1.1, leaf) is a process attribute which identifies a software tool used in the development of software.

Assurance of software tool (0.1.2.1.2, leaf) is a process attribute which describes the level of maturity of a software tool used in the development of the software.

Hardware tool name (0.1.2.2.1, leaf) is a process attribute which identifies a hardware tool used in the development of software.

Assurance of hardware tool (0.1.2.2.2, leaf) is a process attribute which describes the level of maturity of a hardware tool used in the development of the software.

Skills (0.1.3.1) is a process attribute which describes the abilities of the personnel involved in the development of software.

Person name (0.1.3.1.1, leaf) is a process attribute which identifies a person involved in the development of software.

Skill name (0.1.3.1.2, leaf) is a process attribute which identifies the skill of a person involved in the development of software.

Skill level (0.1.3.1.3, leaf) is a process attribute which describes the level of expertise of the personnel involved in the development of the software.

Management(0.1.3.2) is a process attribute which describes the approach to managerial control used in the development of the software.

Environment (0.1.3.3) is a process attribute which describes the culture in which the software was developed.

Use (0.2.1) is a product attribute which describes the set of functions that the software is intended to perform. Use is defined in terms of sub-attributes requirements and acceptance tests.

Product profile (0.2.2) is an attribute which describes the nature of software. The attribute product profile is defined in terms of sub-attributes form, style, scale and checkedness.

Requirements (0.2.1.1) is a product attribute which describes the set of requirements or the requirement specification that the software has been developed to satisfy.

Acceptance tests (0.2.1.2) is a product attribute which describes the set of acceptance tests that the software has been developed to satisfy.

Form (0.2.2.1) is a product attribute which describes the configuration of software. The attribute form is defined in terms of sub-attributes, languages, structure and dependencies.

Scale (0.2.2.2) is a product attribute which describes the magnitude of the software. The attribute scale is defined in terms of sub-attributes, size, costs and performance.

Style (0.2.2.3) is a product attribute. The attribute style is defined in terms of sub-attributes, standardness, techniques and understandability.

Checkedness (0.2.2.4) is a product attribute which describes the apparent extent and thoroughness of checking that the software has undergone. The attribute checkedness is defined in terms of sub- attributes testedness and proveness.

Languages (0.2.2.1.1) is a product attribute which describes the implementation language used to generate or express the software. The attribute language is defined in terms of the sub-attributes high-level languages and low-level languages.

Structure (0.2.2.1.2) is a product attribute which describes how the software are internally organised. It describes the inter- relationships of the software's component parts. The attribute structure is defined in terms of sub-attributes control structure and data structures.

Dependencies (0.2.2.1.3) is a product attribute which describes how software relies on or is inter-related to other entities. The attribute dependencies is defined in terms of sub-attributes, hardware dependencies and interface types.

Size (0.2.2.2.1) is a product attribute which describes the dimensions of the software. The attribute size is defined in terms of sub-attributes number of executable statements, number of global variables, level of use of recursion and storage requirements.

Costs (0.2.2.2.2) is a product attribute which describes the levels of expenditure for the software. The attribute costs is defined in terms of sub-attributes time and money.

Performance (0.2.2.2.3) is a product attribute which describes the execution behaviour of the software. The attribute performance is defined in terms of sub-attributes execution time, precision, accuracy and throughput.

Standardness (0.2.2.3.1) is a product attribute which describes the orthodoxy of the software. The attribute standardness is defined in terms of sub-attributes common practice usage, common code usage and standards compliance.

Techniques (0.2.2.3.2) is a product attribute which describes the nature of the approaches and methods used in the development of the software. The attribute techniques is defined in terms of sub- attributes algorithms and integrity.

Understandability (0.2.2.3.3) is a product attribute which describes how easily software can be understood with respect to its requirements by personnel other than those involved in its development. The attribute understandability is defined in terms of sub-attributes consistency, self-descriptiveness and legibility.

Testedness (0.2.2.4.1) is a product attribute which describes the apparent extent and thoroughness of testing that software has undergone. Testedness is defined in terms of sub-attributes planned test coverage and actual test coverage.

Proveness (0.2.2.4.2) is a product attribute which describes the apparent extent and thoroughness of verification proof that the software has undergone. Proveness is defined in terms of sub- attributes planned proof coverage and actual proof coverage.

Control structure (0.2.2.1.1.3) is a product attribute which describes the pattern of flow of control in the software. The attribute control structure is defined in terms of sub-attributes, control structure type, module coupling type and complexity.

Data structures (0.2.2.2.1.1.4, leaf) is a product attribute. It is a list of the representations used in the software for the ordering and accessibility relationships between data items. Typical examples of elements of data structure lists are lists, trees, tables, strings, arrays, etc.

Hardware dependencies (0.2.2.1.1.5, leaf) is a product attribute. It is a list of the inter-relationships of the software with physical equipment.

Interface types (0.2.2.1.1.6, leaf) is a product attribute. It is a list of the shared boundaries by which software communicates with other system components.

Control structure type (0.2.2.1.1.3.1, leaf) is a product attribute which categorizes the control structures of the software into one of the following three types, well-formed, reducible and irreducible.

Module coupling type (0.2.2.1.1.3.2, leaf) is a product attribute which categorizes the control structures between modules within the software into one of the following three types, well-formed, reducible and irreducible.

Complexity (0.2.2.1.1.3.3) is a product attribute which describes the intricacy of the software control structures. It is defined in terms of sub-attributes, number of decision points and number of loops.

Number of decision points (0.2.2.1.1.3.3.1, leaf) is a product attribute which accounts for the number of decision points in software. A decision point is a program statement which tests for some condition or set of conditions and dependent upon the result of the test affects the subsequent execution of the program.

Number of loops (0.2.2.1.1.3.3.2, leaf) is a product attribute which accounts for the number of loops in software. A loop is a set of instructions that may be executed repeatedly while a certain condition prevails.

Common practice usage (0.2.2.3.1, leaf) is a product attribute which describes the extent to which software makes use of popular or commonly accepted methods or 'tricks of the trade'.

Common code usage (0.2.2.3.1.2, leaf) is a product attribute which describes the degree to which software makes use of identical pieces of code.

Standards compliance (0.2.2.3.1.3, leaf) is a product attribute. It is a list of the software engineering standards which the software adheres to.

Number of executable statements (0.2.2.2.1.1, leaf) is a product attribute which accounts for the number of instructions which may be executed by the software.

Number of global variables (0.2.2.2.1.2, leaf) is a product attribute which accounts for the number of variables in the software which are available to the whole of that program.

Use of recursion (0.2.2.2.1.3, leaf) is a product attribute which describes the degree to which the software uses recursion.

Storage requirements (0.2.2.2.1.4, leaf) is the product attribute which describes the memory needs of the software.

Time (0.2.2.2.2.1) is a product attribute which describes the elapsed time and effort involved in the development of the software. It is defined in terms of sub-attributes duration and person months.

Money (0.2.2.2.2.2, leaf) is a product attribute which describes the financial cost of developing the software.

Duration (0.2.2.2.2.1.1, leaf) is a product attribute which describes the actual time elapsed in developing software.

Person days (0.2.2.2.2.1.2, leaf) is a product attribute which describes the number of days effort spent by the development team on the software.

Execution time (0.2.2.2.3.1) is a product attribute which accounts for the amount of time used in executing the software. It is defined in terms of sub-attributes actual time and CPU time.

Precision(0.2.2.2.1.2, leaf) is a product attribute which measures the abilities of the software to distinguish between nearly equal values. The metric of precision is the number of digits used to represent the fraction of a floating-point number.

Accuracy (0.2.2.2.3.3, leaf) is a product attribute which describes the abilities of software to avoid the introduction of systematic errors. A number is accurate in n digits if there are n significant digits. A digit (leading zeros neglected) is significant, if the error is smaller than half the unit of its position. An error is a discrepancy between a computed, observed, or measured value or condition and the true, specified, or theoretically correct value or condition.

Throughput (0.2.2.2.3.4, leaf) is a product attribute which describes the amount of work performed by software over a period of time

Algorithms (0.2.2.3.2.1, leaf) is the product attribute which describes the sets of rules or sequence of operation used by the software in performing their required functions.

Integrity (0.2.2.3.2.2) is the product attribute which describes the degree to which software deploys special techniques to avoid or tolerate errors. The attribute integrity is defined in terms of sub-attributes defensive programming and hazards containment.

Consistency (0.2.2.3.3.1, leaf) is a product attribute which describes the degree to which software is coherent and avoids internal conflict or self-contradiction.

Self-descriptiveness (0.2.2.3.3.2, leaf) is a product attribute which describes the degree to which software is self-explanatory and can be understood without reference to additional or supplementary material.

Legibility (0.2.2.3.3.3, leaf) is a product attribute which describes the ease with which software can be read.

Planned test coverage (0.2.2.4.1.1, leaf) is a product attribute which describes the extent and stringency of the planned testing to be performed on the software.

Actual test coverage (0.2.2.4.1.2, leaf) is a product attribute which describes the extent to which the planned tests have been carried out on the software.

Planned proof coverage (0.2.2.4.2.1, leaf) is a product attribute which describes the extent and stringency of the planned proof activities to be performed on the software.

Actual proof coverage (0.2.2.4.2.2, leaf) is a product attribute which describes the extent to which the planned proof activities have been carried out on the software.

High-level languages (0.2.2.1.1.1, leaf) is a product attribute. It is a list of the high-level languages used to write the software. A high-level language is a problem-orientated programming language in which each instruction may be equivalent to several machine-code instructions.

Low-level languages (0.2.2.1.1.2, leaf) is a product attribute. It is a list of the low-level languages used to write the software. A low-level language is a machine-orientated language in which each program instruction corresponds to a single machine-code instruction.

Actual time (0.2.2.2.3.1.1, leaf) is a product attribute which describes the duration of the execution of software.

CPU time (0.2.2.2.3.1.2, leaf) is a product attribute which describes the amount of central processor time used in executing a program.

Defensive programming (0.2.2.3.2.2.1, leaf) is a product attribute which describes the extent to which the software has been written to detect and tolerate erroneous input and output values and erroneous control flow.

Hazards containment (0.2.2.3.2.2.2, leaf) is a product attribute which describes the extent to which the software has been written to eliminate, or reduce the risk from hazards. A hazard is a condition that can lead to an accident.

9.4.1.2 Model Development

The changes and improvements in attribute definitions that resulted from the experiments conducted by the developers and others coupled with the recognition that additional attributes of relevance could be identified and defined lead to the need to review the model and its structure. it was recognised that a new improved model could be defined that better captured and expressed the features of interest. Despite the quite major changes the bulk of the model is similar to that of the prototype it has however an increased level of development of the lower levels of the hierarchy. This is particularly significant as this is where the evidence on which the assessment is based is provided and results in an increase in the amount of evidence that can be used to make the assessment. The new hierarchical structure of the model is presented in part in figures 9.5, 9.6 and 9.7. These figures show the higher levels to be identical to those of the first prototype, however the lower levels are significantly expanded in detail. The numbering scheme adopted for the attributes and included in the figures not only uniquely identifies the attribute but also defines its position in the hierarchy.

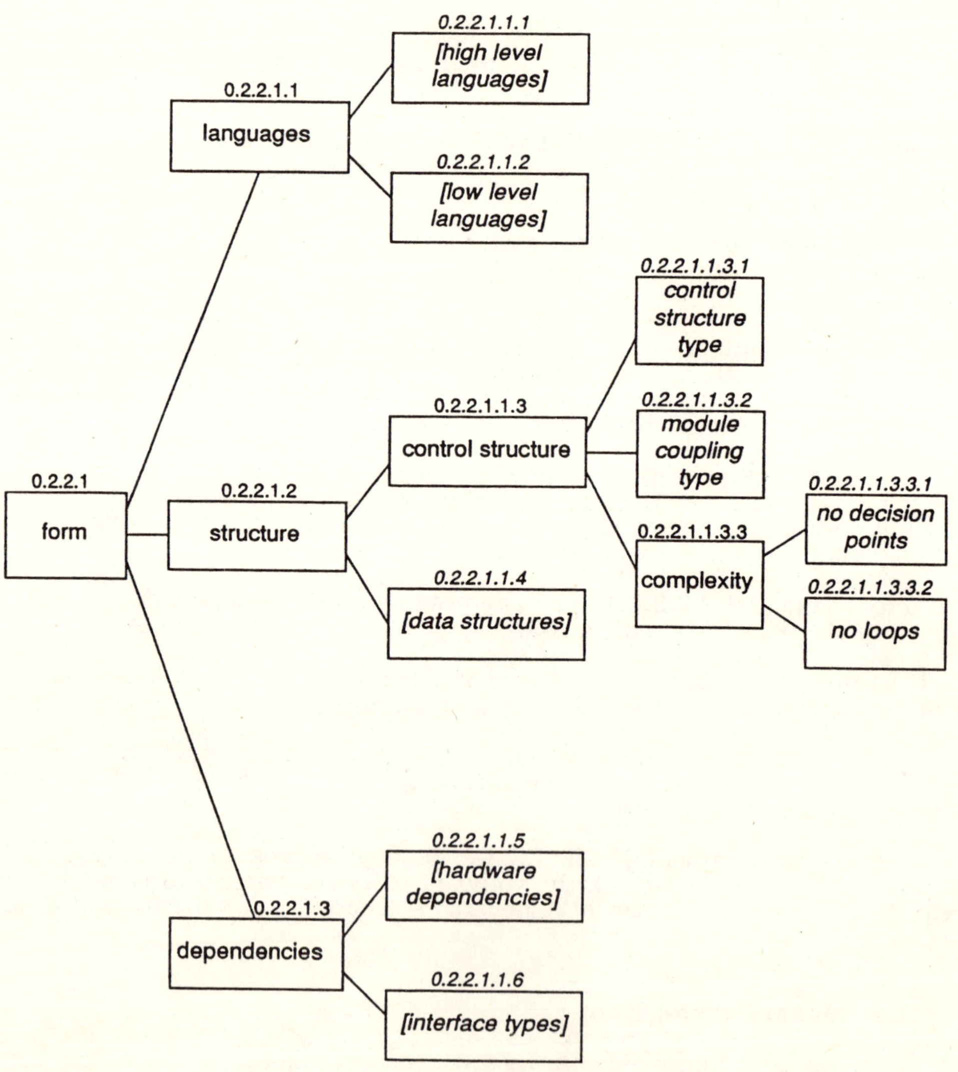

Fig. 9.6. Hierarchical structure of the model (part 1)

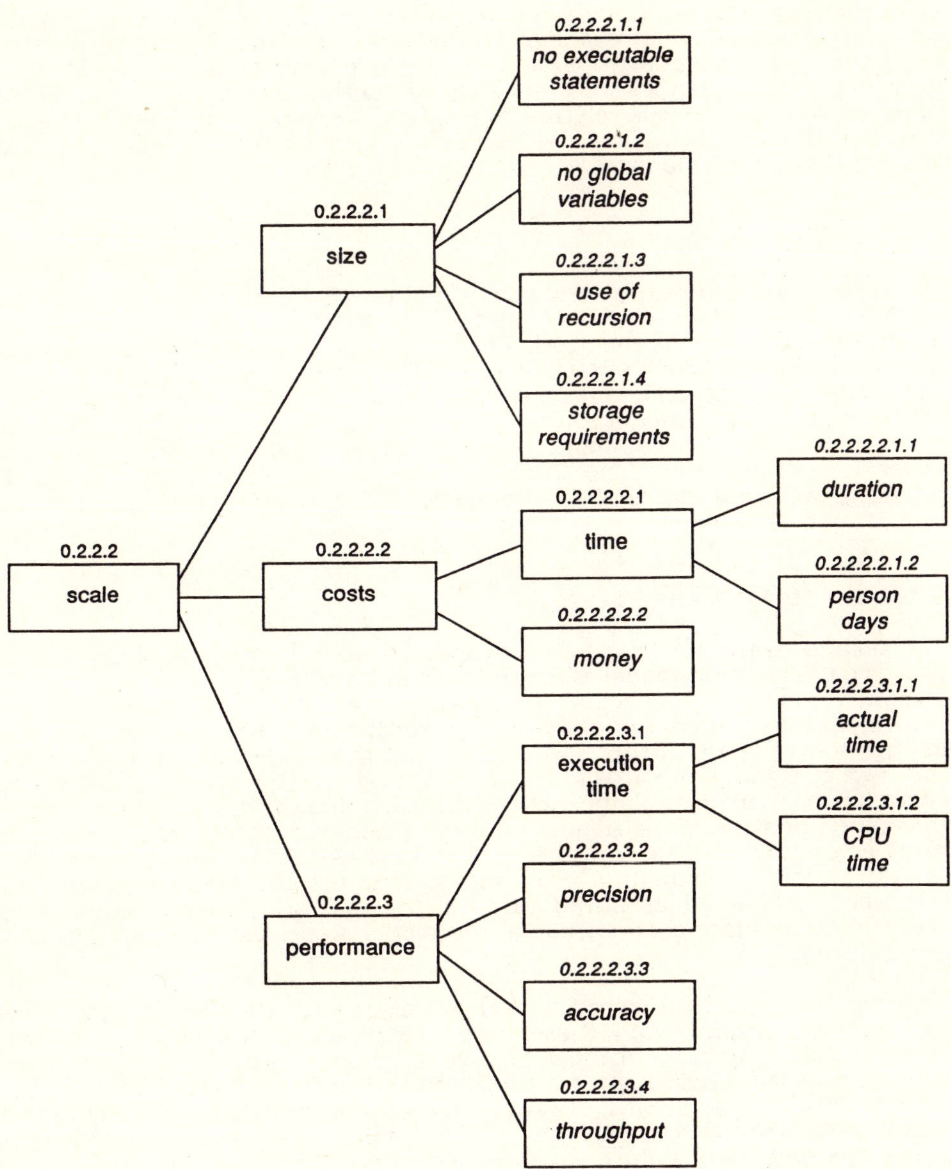

Fig. 9.7. Hierarchical structure of the model (part 2)

9.4.1.3   The Rules and Inference

The experimental exercises conducted by both developers and independent experts showed that the rules and reasoning contained in the prototype were adequate but could be improved. However it was also recognised that there was scope for improvement in the way the attribute information was combined and in the way different attributes interacted and modified the outcome. These schemes were modified along the lines of the opinion of the developers. The reader is referred to [WAL89] for details of the rules used in this model and [BAL86] and [BAL87] for further information of a more general nature on this topic.

9.4.1.4   The Interface

The data input and output and the execution of the prototype was in terms of FRIL shell and language commands. This was found unsatisfactory in the experimental phase of the work as it was not possible to use the model without being able to program in FRIL. This prevented independent use of the model by independent experts whose opinions must be gathered and encapsulated in the model if it were to be of value. The model was therefore provided with a simple menu driven/highlight bar interface to facilitate wider use of the tool. The interface was also provided with simple file handling and editing facilities to ease and further speed the use and execution of the model.

9.4.2 The Results and Future

The results of the new model were broadly similar to those of the original prototype. The new model was however subject to an extensive range of sensitivity and other checks. The overall conclusion was the results were consistent and understandable. There were however a number of anomalies in the view of some of those who examined the model. For example one of the most significant attributes was found to be the leaf standards compliance. While compliance with a common standard would in the view of the experimenters work against diversity some expected attributes such number of lines of code, number of loops and similar mechanistic features to figure more prominently. This and similar results were not unexpected but were considered as stimulating as through such discussion and the widespread (ie more experts) use of the model so professional opinion could be captured.

It was seen that the experimental exercises with the revised model were far more successful than those with the prototype as more cases were examined by a greater number of experts primarily because of the better definition of the attributes and the improved menu driven interface of the model. This change greatly improved the ease of capture of expert opinion and it is the captive and expression of the opinion of the experts that is the key to the success or failure of expert system models of this type.

The success of the work indicates this type of approach could be adopted to make the step from the expression of diversity considered here to making an assessment of common mode failure. Clearly in such a scheme the model described above would only be one part of the input perhaps becoming one attribute of the model. A second attribute, at which data could be input, might be the output from a mnemonic pattern matching exercise of the type described in chapter 8.

References

[BAL86] J.F. Baldwin: Support Logic Programming. In: Fuzzy Sets Theory and Applications, A. Jones et al. (eds.), pp 133-170, D. Reidel Pub. Co. NATO ASI Series, Series C: Mathematical and Physical Sciences Vol. 177, 1986

[BAL87] J.F. Baldwin: Evidential Support Logic Programming. Fuzzy Sets and Systems 24, pp 1-26, Elsevier Science Publishers, North-Holland, 1987

[WAL89] D.N. Wall: Software Diversity - Its Role and Measurement. Phase 2, REQUEST report R2.3.6, 1989

Chapter 10

Reliability Evaluation

Maria Teresa Mainini

10.1 Introduction

This chapter describes an approach to fault tolerant software architecture modelling. The defined model allows to evaluate the probability of an erroneous behaviour of a fault tolerant architecture, on the basis of the intrinsic reliabilities of the system components and of the conditional failure probabilities of the versions.

The main model innovative feature is its ability to take into account the correlation among errors in different versions. The modelling approach is general enough to be applied to a generic architecture, meaning that it can deal with every N version programming and recovery block architecture, independently from the number of versions composing the system and from the number of versions required to achieve the majority. In order to automatically generate the formulae related to a specific architecture, a computerized algorithm has been implemented, which allows to instantiate the general approach for the specific case under consideration.

In the next sections, to indicate the fault tolerant typical architectures, the following abbreviations will be used:

NVP: N version programming; RB: Recovery block programming.

Furthermore, N will conventionally indicate the number of versions composing an architecture and M will indicate the number of versions required to agree in order to achieve a majority in an NVP architecture.

10.2 State of the Art of Reliability Models for Fault Tolerant Software

The traditional fault tolerant architecture models, having been designed for hardware components, are not portable to software, due to the different nature of errors: in fact, they must not handle random errors due to breakage or aging of components, but design errors.

On the other hand, many computer scientists have dealt with software reliability modelling on the basis of two different approaches: a topological one, aiming to predict reliability considering the program architecture, or a black-box one considering a program as a source of errors having a certain rate that can be calculated as a function of the observed error distribution. Anyway, none of these models takes into account redundancy and its implications on system reliability. Scott's model (see [SCO84] and [SCO84a]) is the only one meeting these requirements. The approach explained in the following section is inspired by it. The main differences consist in the formalism used and in the capability of dealing with common error probabilities.

10.3 System States of Fault Tolerant Architectures

From the point of view of its external behaviour, a system implemented by means of a fault tolerant architecture can be in one of the following states:

- the correct one, meaning that the system is able to deliver a correct output. In the case of a NVP architecture, this state corresponds to the fact that at least M versions deliver a correct output. In the case of a RB architecture, it corresponds to the fact that at least one version delivers a correct output and the acceptance test accepts it.

- the incorrect but safe one, meaning that the system decides that the outputs of the versions are incorrect and then it is not able to deliver any output. In the case of a NVP architecture, this state corresponds to the fact that there are not M versions delivering the same output. In the case of a RB architecture, it corresponds to the fact that the acceptance test does not accept the output of any version.

- the incorrect and unsafe one, meaning that the system delivers an incorrect output, not perceiving that it is incorrect. In the case of a NVP architecture, this state corresponds to the fact that M versions deliver the same incorrect output. In the case of a RB architecture, it corresponds to the fact that the acceptance test accepts the incorrect output of a version.

These three system states are determined by the behaviours of the versions and, in the case of a RB architecture, of the acceptance test. Each possible combination of versions and acceptance test behaviours implies a certain system state. These combinations will be called system sub-states.

In particular it is possible to identify:

- Sc: the set of the possible system sub-states implying a correct system state

- Ss: the set of the possible system sub-states implying an incorrect but safe system state

- Su: the set of the possible system sub-states implying an incorrect unsafe system state

Starting from an initial system state So, each combination belonging to Sc changes the system state to correct, whilst each combination belonging to Ss changes the system state to incorrect but safe, etc.

10.4 Analysis of System Sub-States

An important consideration concerns the identification of all the possible system sub-states of a fault tolerant system.

A version, considered as an independent entity, can be either correct or incorrect. It is possible to assume that the correct output is unique, whilst the incorrect one can be equal to the one of another version or may be different.

It is important to consider separately the two situations of: two versions producing equal incorrect outputs and of two versions producing two different incorrect outputs, because the fault tolerant architectures may present a different behaviour in the two cases.

In the case of N versions programming, if the majority of versions produces the same incorrect output, this will be accepted, leading to an incorrect unsafe system state, whilst, if they produce different incorrect outputs, they are detected but not masked, leading to an incorrect but safe system state.

In the case of recovery block, the implications mainly concern the probability of failure detection. If two versions produce the same incorrect output, the probability that the acceptance test can detect the error is lower than in the case of two different outputs, in fact, if an error has not been detected in a version, there is no chance that it is detected in the other one, which has delivered the same output. On the contrary, if the two outputs are different, the probabilities of detecting the two errors may be assumed to be independent and then the probability that the second one is detected is not correlated to the probability that the first one has been detected.

Each incorrect system state may be achieved in multiple ways, corresponding to different system sub-states leading to the corresponding system state. For example, in the simple case of a NVP where N=3 and M=2, Su, set of the system sub-states implying an incorrect unsafe system state, contains the following elements:

System Sub-State 1:
versions 1 and 2 deliver the same incorrect output and version 3 is correct.

System Sub-State 2:
versions 1 and 2 deliver the same incorrect output and version 3 delivers a different incorrect output.

System Sub-State 3:
versions 1 and 3 deliver the same incorrect output and version 2 is correct.

System Sub-State 4:
versions 1 and 3 deliver the same incorrect output and version 2 delivers a different incorrect output.

System Sub-State 5:
versions 2 and 3 deliver the same incorrect output and version 1 is correct.

System Sub-State 6:
versions 2 and 3 deliver the same incorrect output and version 1 delivers a different incorrect output.

System Sub-State 7:
the three versions deliver all the same incorrect output.

In the case of a RB architecture, where N=3, Su contains the following elements:

System Sub-State 1:
version 1 delivers an incorrect output that is accepted.

System Sub-State 2:
version 1 delivers a correct output that is not accepted, whilst version 2 delivers an incorrect output that is accepted.

System Sub-State 3:
version 1 delivers an incorrect output that is not accepted, whilst version 2 delivers a different incorrect output that is accepted.

System Sub-State 4:
version 1 and 2 deliver a correct output that is not accepted, whilst version 3 delivers an incorrect output that is accepted.

System Sub-State 5:
versions 1 and 2 deliver the same incorrect output that is not accepted, whilst version 3 delivers a different incorrect output that is accepted.

System Sub-State 6:
versions 1 and 2 deliver two different incorrect outputs that are not accepted, whilst version 3 delivers a further different incorrect output that is accepted.

System Sub-State 7:
version 1 delivers an incorrect output that is not accepted, version 2 delivers a correct output that is not accepted, whilst version 3 delivers a different incorrect output that is accepted.

System Sub-State 8:
version 1 delivers a correct output that is not accepted, version 2 delivers an incorrect output that is not accepted, whilst version 3 delivers a different incorrect output that is accepted.

10.5 Modelling Approach

The objective of the model is to evaluate the probability that the system is in one of the two incorrect states. This probability is represented by a sum whose terms are the separate and independent probabilities of the system sub-states belonging to Ss or to Su.

The probabilities of the sub-states are expressed by means of the probabilities of the corresponding behaviours of the versions and of the acceptance test (only for the RB architecture).

For the considerations already presented in the previous chapters, the assumption of independence in failure behaviour of the versions is not realistic, so it is necessary to take into account common error probabilities.

The common error probabilities are treated using the conditional probability formalism consisting in expressing the probability of two correlated events A and B as the event A probability multiplied by the probability that the event B happens, assuming that the event A has happened, i.e.:

$$P(A,B) = P(A)*P(B/A)$$

Following this approach, the system sub-states probabilities may be expressed as a product of: probability of a given behaviour of a version assumed as the primary one, conditional probabilities of a given behaviour of the other versions and, in the case of RB, probability of a given behaviour of the acceptance test.

The limitations of the model are mainly two:

- the assumption that the voter and the recovery procedure are error free,
- the assumption that the acceptance test is independent from the versions.

These restrictions are not completely realistic, but can be accepted in the major part of the cases.

10.6 Modelling Methods

Two separate reliability models have been defined: one for N version programming architectures and another one for recovery block architectures, but the methods followed to implement them are very similar. Two different methods have been pursued to define these models. The first one was developed to apply the approach in the simple cases of architectures composed by three versions. It was easy to be used, especially in the case of few versions, but it was difficult to be generalized in case of many versions. For this reason, it will be identified as "special purpose method".

Then a second method was followed, aiming to extend the previous one to include all the architectures independently from the number of versions composing them. This method will be identified as "general purpose method".

10.6.1 The Special Purpose Method

This method is based on the representation of the models through markovian diagrams and equations aiming to evaluate the failure probability of the above mentioned architectures.

The followed approach consists in representing a number of chains of logical transitions from the initial state, in which the behaviours of the versions are unknown, to the final system sub-states belonging to Su or Ss, in which the informations about the version behaviours permit to assess that the system is failing.

Each chain starts from the unique initial state and ends with its own final system sub-state; between the initial and the final state in the chain, there is a certain number of intermediate states; the kth state of the chain represents the current behaviour of the first k versions. Each transition from a state to the following one in the markovian chain represents the achievement of an information about the behaviour of a version. In the case of the RB architecture, the last transition represents the achievement of information about the acceptance test behaviour.

The probability of transition from the kth state of the chain to the (k+1)st one is the probability that, given that the previous k versions of the chain had a certain behaviour, the (k+1)st version has the behaviour corresponding to the achievement of the (k+1)st state conditioned by the fact that the previous k versions had the behaviours corresponding to the kth state.

In figures 10.1 and 10.2, two examples of markovian diagrams respectively for a 2 out of 3 N version programming architecture and for a 3 versions recovery block architecture are presented.

The system failure probability is then evaluated as the sum of the probabilities that the system sub-states belonging to Su or to Ss are reached.

Each term of the sum, corresponding to a chain, is represented as a product of the incorrectness (or correctness) probability of the first version (conventionally version 1) multiplied by the conditional probabilities that the remaining transitions belonging to the chain happen.

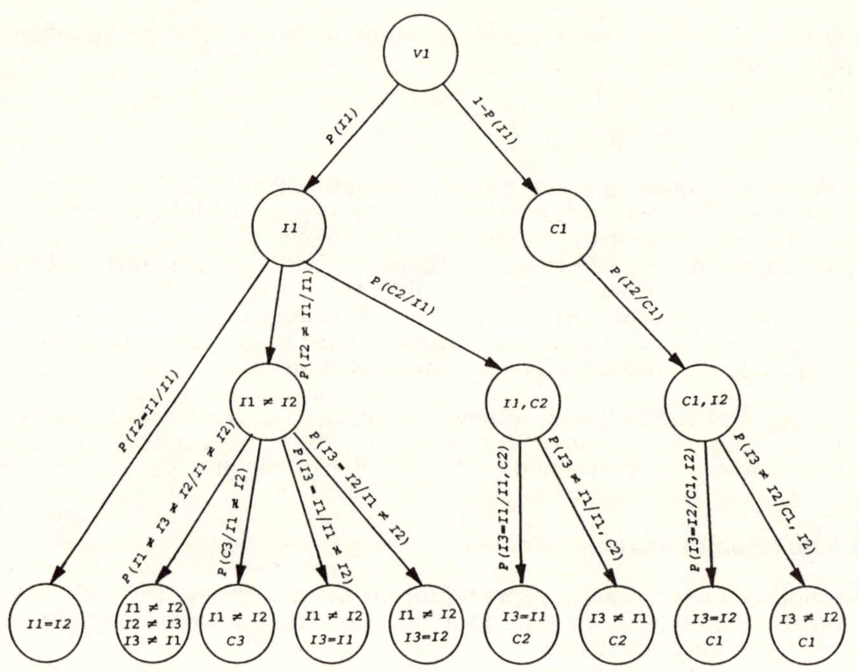

Fig. 10.1. Markovian diagram of a 2-out-of-3 versions NVP architecture

For instance, the probability of achieving the incorrect unsafe state of a NVP architecture where N=3 and M=2 by means of the chain: version 1 and 2 incorrect in the same way and version 3 correct (system sub-state 1), is expressed as:

$$P=P(I1)*P(I2=I1/I1)*P(C3/I2=I1)$$

where:

P(I1) = probability that version 1 is incorrect,

P(I2=I1/I1) = probability that version 2 delivers the same incorrect output of version 1, given that version 1 is incorrect,

P(C3/I2=I1) = probability that version 3 is correct, given that version 1 and 2 deliver the same incorrect output.

While the probability of achieving the incorrect unsafe state of a RB architecture where N=3 by means of the chain: version 1 incorrect rejected, version 2 correct rejected and version 3 incorrect accepted (system sub-state 7) is expressed as:

$$P=P(I1)*P(C2/I1)*P(I3{\neq}I1/I1,C2)*P(Ri)*P(Rc)*R(Ai)$$

where:

P(I1) =   probability that version 1 is incorrect,

P(C2/I1) =   probability that version 2 is correct, given that version 1
                         is incorrect,

P(Ri) =   probability that the acceptance test rejects an incorrect
                         output,

P(Rc) =   probability that the acceptance test rejects a correct
                         output,

P(Ai) =   probability that the acceptance test accepts an incorrect
                         output.

$P(I3 \neq I1/I1,C2)$ represents the probability that version 3 delivers an incorrect output different from the one delivered by version 1, given that version 1 is incorrect and version 2 is correct.

This approach is very useful for a manual study, because it permits the user to take into consideration only the possible behaviours of one version at each step. In the case of a small number of versions, the problem can be easily managed manually, but, in the case of a greater number of versions, it can become untreatable without the support of a formula implementable by a computer program.

Then a first attempt was done to formalize the approach through general formulae applicable in the case of a generic number of versions. Anyway, due to the number of intermediate states to be considered, the approach appeared difficult to be followed.

For instance, to give an order of magnitude of the problem, in the case of a 3 out of 5 NVP architecture, the number of final states is higher than 80 and the total number of states is higher than 200.

10.6.2 The General Purpose Method

In order to overcome the limitations of the special purpose method, it was decided to modify the initial approach, in order to make it more manageable in the general case and easily representable through a formula. The new method was based on the approach of generating all the possible system sub-states and then selecting among them the ones that could lead to an incorrect system state, i.e. the ones belonging to Su or to Ss.

The problem of generating all the possible system sub-states is not trivial. In fact, as a maximum, given N versions, they can deliver N different erroneous outputs. But, considering the behaviour of the previous k versions, the number of possible incorrect outputs of the (k+1)st to be considered may be different from case to case.

For instance, if N=5 and if versions 1, 2, 3 and 4 have been all correct, version 5 can only be correct or incorrect; on the contrary, if versions 1, 2 and 3 were correct and 4 was incorrect, version 5 has 3 possibilities that must be distinguished: correct, incorrect in the same way as the previous four versions or incorrect in a different way. In the case where the first four versions were all incorrect in a different way, the fifth version has six possibilities: correct, incorrect in four different ways equal to one of the first four versions, incorrect in a way different from the other ones.

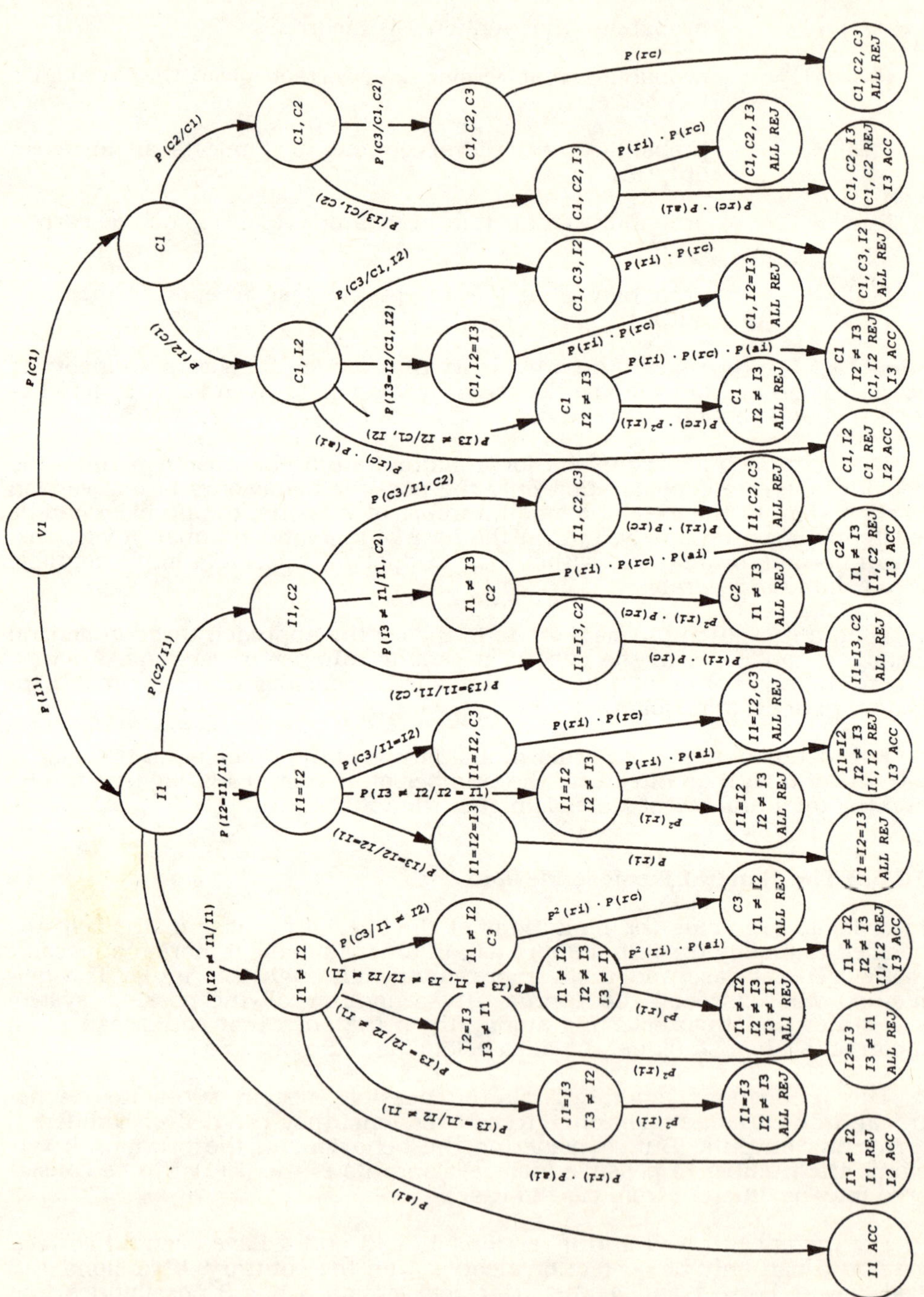

Fig. 10.2. Markovian diagram of a 3 versions RB architecture

This implies that the system sub-states generation requires a particular care in selecting the range of possible behaviour of a certain version because the range is not fixed, but may change in accordance with the behaviour of the previous versions. The selection of system sub-states in order to identify those belonging to Su or to Ss is done in a different way, depending on the architecture type.

NVP Architecture

In the case of this architecture, to assess that a combination of version behaviours leads to an incorrect and unsafe state, it is necessary to check if at least M versions deliver the same incorrect output. On the contrary, to assess that a combination of version behaviour leads to an incorrect but safe state, it is necessary to check if the maximum number of equal outputs delivered by the versions is less than M.

RB Architecture

In the case of a RB architecture, it is also necessary to consider partial combinations, including only a subset of versions, because, as their execution is sequential and conditioned by the result of the acceptance test, many times, in the case of an incorrect unsafe system state, not all of the N versions are activated.

In the case of an incorrect unsafe system state, firstly it is necessary to check if the combination does not end with a version delivering a correct output, secondly it is necessary to reduce the combinations ending with more than one version delivering the same incorrect output; the reduction is made cancelling the ending versions delivering the same incorrect output except the last one.

For instance, a combination where the first version is correct and the others are incorrect in the same way is reduced to a combination of version 1 correct and version 2 incorrect. Thirdly, among the remaining combinations, a further purge must be done to cancel the combinations including more versions delivering the same incorrect output of the last one. For instance, the case where version 1 and 3 deliver the same incorrect output and version 2 is incorrect in a different way will be cancelled.

The first operation is necessary because, if the last version delivers a correct output, there are two possibilities: either the correct output is accepted or it is rejected; in both cases an incorrect output is not issued.

The second operation is necessary to exclude combinations where more versions deliver the same incorrect output; in fact, either this output is accepted the first time it is delivered, or it is rejected every time.

The third operation has the same meaning with the difference that in the previous case a subset of combinations may exist, whilst the second case is impossible because if an incorrect output is accepted the following versions will never be activated.

In the case of an incorrect but safe system state, no version is cancelled, because whichever combination may lead to an incorrect safe state, the acceptance test rejects both the correct and incorrect outputs.

After having considered the behaviour of the versions it is necessary to consider the acceptance test's one. The longest chain leading to the incorrect unsafe state occurs when the acceptance test rejects (incorrect or correct) outputs of all but the last version and subsequently accepts the incorrect output of the last version. In the case of the incorrect safe state the acceptance test rejects all the outputs.

In considering the probabilities of rejection and acceptance, it is necessary to count the number of times a specific version behaviour happens; if two or more versions deliver the same incorrect output the probability of this event must be counted only once. For instance, if versions 1 and 2 deliver the same incorrect output and version 3 delivers an incorrect but different one, from the point of view of the acceptance test, the probability of an incorrect unsafe state is the probability of rejecting one incorrect output multiplied by the probability of accepting an incorrect one, whilst the probability of an incorrect safe state is the square of the probability of rejecting an incorrect output.

10.6.3 Implementation Choice

The special purpose method was applied to the simple cases of a NVP architecture based on a 2 out of 3 majority voting and to a RB architecture composed by 3 versions. The implementation consists in the markovian diagrams of figures 10.1 and 10.2 with the related equations for reliability evaluation.

The general purpose method was implemented by means of a computerized program allowing to generate the equations for reliability evaluation in an automatic way for whichever NVP and RB architecture. In the case of NVP architectures, the program is based on two main algorithms: one generating all the possible system sub-states and one checking each of them to control if it can lead to an incorrect system state. In the case of RB architectures, two further algorithms must be introduced to reduce the combinations and to evaluate the probabilities of behaviour of the acceptance test.

For both the architectures, finally, an algorithm has been introduced to express the system sub-states probabilities in a conditional format. All the probabilities, except the one of correctness of all the versions, have been represented as probability of the system sub-state conditioned by the fact that the first incorrect version of the sub-state is incorrect multiplied by the absolute probability that such a version is incorrect. The output of the program is stored in an ASCII file. In the Appendix the outputs generated in the case of an NVP architecture based on a 3 out of 5 majority voting and in the case of a RB architecture composed by 5 versions are included.

10.7 Evaluation of the Equations

Having defined the model equations, it is now necessary to fix a methodology for the evaluation of their terms. Before presenting the expressions of the probabilistic terms, it is anyway necessary to introduce the framework and the assumptions made constituting the basis of the evaluation.

It is assumed that a fault tolerant system is tested in two different steps: test of the single versions and test of the integrated fault tolerant system. In both cases, the concept of testing session, intended as launch of a sequence of test cases, is not taken into account in order to treat the problem in a more general way, i.e. not taking into consideration the testing strategy adopted. In fact, while the first activities of the testing phase are typically based on testing sessions, the last ones use strategies like alfa test, beta test, simulation of the operational environment etc. that can be considered as part of the operational phase, from the point of view of the system solicitation type.

10.7.1 Single Component Test

In the first step, all the versions and the acceptance test are tested separately and their failure behaviour is traced and modelled using a single component reliability model (e.g. Musa-Okumoto or Littlewood model).

From the evaluated error rate, the probability that a version fails is computed as:

$$P(I_i) = q_i * t_i$$

where

q_i = failure rate of component i
t_i = duration of each execution of component i

In the case of versions, the only information needed is $P(I_i)$, absolute failure probability of version i. In the case of the acceptance test, three separate informations are required:

$P(R_c)$ = probability that the acceptance test rejects a correct output,

$P(A_i)$ = probability that the acceptance test accepts an incorrect output,

$P(R_i)$ = probability that the acceptance test rejects an incorrect output.

The first two terms correspond to an erroneous behaviour, whilst the third one corresponds to a correct performance. Then two separate test sessions will be needed. During the first session the acceptance test is solicited only with correct version outputs and the failure rate evaluated allows to determine the value of $P(R_c)$. During the second session the acceptance test is solicited only with incorrect version outputs and the failure rate evaluated allows to determine the value of $P(A_i)$. Then $P(R_i)$ is evaluated as:

$$P(R_i) = 1 - P(A_i)$$

It is assumed that the mean time to fail $(1/q_i)$ is higher than the execution duration; this hypothesis is reasonable considering the nature of fault tolerant systems requiring a high reliability of all the components. The concept of execution must be better clarified to avoid misunderstandings. In the case of off-line programs (e.g. a compiler or a pure computational program) the concept of execution is clear, because typically the program is activated by an user request, the program performs its computations and then stops; the execution duration can be different depending from the input type (e.g. the length and complexity of the code to be compiled in the case of a compiler), but anyway the starting and ending points are clearly identified.

In the case of real time systems, that is the typical kind of systems where fault tolerant features are required, the starting and ending points and then the execution duration are more difficult to be identified because the characteristic of these systems is to provide a continuous service and the high number of different processes involved and of random events to be treated (interrupts, asynchronous user requests, etc.) generally do not permit to identify typical process cycles. Anyway, in the case of fault tolerant systems, the situation is slightly different. The presence of adjudication mechanisms (voters or acceptance tests) requires periodic synchronizations among the different versions in order to permit them to operate on coherent data.

This fact implies that also the software must be organized in such a way to identify some basic "meeting" points where the versions are "lined up" in their computations. For this reason and for simplicity sake, that historically constitutes a basic requirement for ultra reliable systems, the usage of asynchronous events is carefully avoided. Then a sort of cyclic behaviour can be usually identified in the structure of fault tolerant software. Probably it will be possible to identify many internal cycles due to the necessity of voting outputs that must be delivered with different frequency; in fact, usually some outputs will be delivered at a high rate (e.g. every 100 msec), others will be delivered at a medium rate (e.g. every 500 msec or 1 sec, etc) and others at a low rate (e.g. every minute).

In this context, the execution duration is intended as "the duration of the maximum internal cycle of the software" or "the time period elapsing between two ensuing synchronizations related to the voting of the outputs that are less frequently voted".

10.7.2 Fault Tolerant System Integration Test

In the second step, the various versions are set up to build the chosen fault tolerant architecture and the complete system is tested. The failures occurred can be classified on the basis of the versions involved as: failures due to only one version, failures due to two versions incorrect in the same way, failures due to two versions incorrect in different ways, etc.

The conditional probabilities may be simply evaluated as ratios of numbers of failure events of the related types; this approach has the advantage of being based on a well defined number and type of events.

From the point of view of the equations terms evaluation, it is necessary to take into consideration the system sub-states belonging to Ss or to Su and to try to express their probabilities in a conditional form. The most suitable conditioning is the one with respect to an incorrect version.

For example, the probability that versions 2, 3 and 4 have the same incorrect behaviour and version 1 is correct can be expressed as the probability that version 2 is incorrect multiplied by the probability that versions 3 and 4 have the same incorrect behaviour as version 2, and that version 1 is correct, given that version 2 is incorrect, i.e.:

$$P(I2=I3=I4,C1) = P(I2=I3=I4,C1/I2)*P(I2)=$$

$$\frac{N(I2=I3=I4,C1)}{N(I2)}$$

where:

$N(I2=I3=I4,C1) =$ number of times this system sub-state occurred during the test,

$N(I2) =$ number of times version 2 was incorrect.

As all the final states imply that at least one version is incorrect, whichever is the number of versions, this method is always applicable and offers all the advantages already explained.

References

[AND84] T. Anderson: Can Design Faults be tolerated? Univ. of Newcastle upon Tyne, Technical Report, 1984

[AVI84] A. Avizienis, J. Kelly: Fault-tolerance by Design Diversity: Concepts and Experiments. IEEE COMPUTER, August 1984

[AVI85] A. Avizienis: The N-Version Approach to Fault Tolerant Software. IEEE Transactions on Software Engineering, Dec. 1985

[BIS85] P. Bishop, D. Esp, M. Barnes, et al.: Project on Diverse Software; An Experiment in Software Reliability. Proc. of Safecomp '85, 1985, Pergamon Press

[ECK85] D.E. Eckhardt, L. D. Lee: A Theoretical Basis for the Analysis of Multiversion Software Subject to Coincident Errors. IEEE Transactions on Software Engineering, Dec. 1985

[KEL86] J. Kelly, A. Avizienis, et al.: Multi-Version Software development. Proc. of Safecomp '86, 1986, Pergamon Press

[KNI86] J. Knight, N. Leveson: An Experimental Evaluation of the Assumption of Independence in Multiversion Programming. IEEE Trans. on Software Engineering, Vol SE-12, No. 1, 1986

[RAN75] B. Randell: System Structure for Software Fault Tolerance. Proc. of the International Conference on Reliable Software, 1975

[SCO84] R. K. Scott, J. W Gault, D. F. McAllister, J. Wiggs: Experimental Validation of Six Fault Tolerant Software Reliability Models. IEEE 1984

[SCO84a] R. K. Scott, J. W Gault, D. F. McAllister, J. Wiggs: Investigating Version Dependence in Fault Tolerant Software. IEEE 1984

[SHO83] M. L. Shooman: Software Engineering. McGraw Hill, 1983

Appendix

Notation:

Ck: Version k delivers a correct output
Ik=X, Y,...: Version k deliver an incorrect output (X, Y,...)

(3 out of 5) - NVP Architecture

Probability of an incorrect unsafe system state =

```
P(C1,C2,I3=X,I4=X,I5=X/I3)*P(I3)  +
P(C1,I2=X,C3,I4=X,I5=X/I2)*P(I2)  +
P(C1,I2=X,I3=X,C4,I5=X/I2)*P(I2)  +
P(C1,I2=X,I3=X,I4=X,C5/I2)*P(I2)  +
P(C1,I2=X,I3=X,I4=X,I5=X/I2)*P(I2)  +
P(C1,I2=X,I3=X,I4=X,I5=Y/I2)*P(I2)  +
P(C1,I2=X,I3=X,I4=Y,I5=X/I2)*P(I2)  +
P(C1,I2=X,I3=Y,I4=X,I5=X/I2)*P(I2)  +
P(C1,I2=X,I3=Y,I4=Y,I5=Y/I2)*P(I2)  +
P(I1=X,C2,C3,I4=X,I5=X/I1)*P(I1)  +
P(I1=X,C2,I3=X,C4,I5=X/I1)*P(I1)  +
P(I1=X,C2,I3=X,I4=X,C5/I1)*P(I1)  +
P(I1=X,C2,I3=X,I4=X,I5=X/I1)*P(I1)  +
P(I1=X,C2,I3=X,I4=X,I5=Y/I1)*P(I1)  +
P(I1=X,C2,I3=X,I4=Y,I5=X/I1)*P(I1)  +
P(I1=X,C2,I3=Y,I4=X,I5=X/I1)*P(I1)  +
P(I1=X,C2,I3=Y,I4=Y,I5=Y/I1)*P(I1)  +
P(I1=X,I2=X,C3,C4,I5=X/I1)*P(I1)  +
P(I1=X,I2=X,C3,I4=X,C5/I1)*P(I1)  +
P(I1=X,I2=X,C3,I4=X,I5=X/I1)*P(I1)  +
P(I1=X,I2=X,C3,I4=X,I5=Y/I1)*P(I1)  +
P(I1=X,I2=X,C3,I4=Y,I5=X/I1)*P(I1)  +
P(I1=X,I2=X,I3=X,C4,C5/I1)*P(I1)  +
P(I1=X,I2=X,I3=X,C4,I5=X/I1)*P(I1)  +
P(I1=X,I2=X,I3=X,C4,I5=Y/I1)*P(I1)  +
P(I1=X,I2=X,I3=X,I4=X,C5/I1)*P(I1)  +
P(I1=X,I2=X,I3=X,I4=X,I5=X/I1)*P(I1)  +
P(I1=X,I2=X,I3=X,I4=X,I5=Y/I1)*P(I1)  +
P(I1=X,I2=X,I3=X,I4=Y,C5/I1)*P(I1)  +
P(I1=X,I2=X,I3=X,I4=Y,I5=X/I1)*P(I1)  +
P(I1=X,I2=X,I3=X,I4=Y,I5=Y/I1)*P(I1)  +
P(I1=X,I2=X,I3=X,I4=Y,I5=Z/I1)*P(I1)  +
P(I1=X,I2=X,I3=Y,C4,I5=X/I1)*P(I1)  +
P(I1=X,I2=X,I3=Y,I4=X,C5/I1)*P(I1)  +
P(I1=X,I2=X,I3=Y,I4=X,I5=X/I1)*P(I1)  +
P(I1=X,I2=X,I3=Y,I4=X,I5=Y/I1)*P(I1)  +
P(I1=X,I2=X,I3=Y,I4=X,I5=Z/I1)*P(I1)  +
P(I1=X,I2=X,I3=Y,I4=Y,I5=X/I1)*P(I1)  +
P(I1=X,I2=X,I3=Y,I4=Y,I5=Y/I1)*P(I1)  +
P(I1=X,I2=X,I3=Y,I4=Z,I5=X/I1)*P(I1)  +
P(I1=X,I2=Y,C3,I4=X,I5=X/I1)*P(I1)  +
P(I1=X,I2=Y,C3,I4=Y,I5=Y/I1)*P(I1)  +
P(I1=X,I2=Y,I3=X,C4,I5=X/I1)*P(I1)  +
P(I1=X,I2=Y,I3=X,I4=X,C5/I1)*P(I1)  +
P(I1=X,I2=Y,I3=X,I4=X,I5=X/I1)*P(I1)  +
P(I1=X,I2=Y,I3=X,I4=X,I5=Y/I1)*P(I1)  +
P(I1=X,I2=Y,I3=X,I4=X,I5=Z/I1)*P(I1)  +
P(I1=X,I2=Y,I3=X,I4=Y,I5=X/I1)*P(I1)  +
```

```
P(I1=X,I2=Y,I3=X,I4=Y,I5=Y/I1)*P(I1)  +
P(I1=X,I2=Y,I3=X,I4=Z,I5=X/I1)*P(I1)  +
P(I1=X,I2=Y,I3=Y,C4,I5=Y/I1)*P(I1)  +
P(I1=X,I2=Y,I3=Y,I4=X,I5=X/I1)*P(I1)  +
P(I1=X,I2=Y,I3=Y,I4=X,I5=Y/I1)*P(I1)  +
P(I1=X,I2=Y,I3=Y,I4=Y,C5/I1)*P(I1)  +
P(I1=X,I2=Y,I3=Y,I4=Y,I5=X/I1)*P(I1)  +
P(I1=X,I2=Y,I3=Y,I4=Y,I5=Y/I1)*P(I1)  +
P(I1=X,I2=Y,I3=Y,I4=Y,I5=Z/I1)*P(I1)  +
P(I1=X,I2=Y,I3=Y,I4=Z,I5=Y/I1)*P(I1)  +
P(I1=X,I2=Y,I3=Z,I4=X,I5=X/I1)*P(I1)  +
P(I1=X,I2=Y,I3=Z,I4=Y,I5=Y/I1)*P(I1)  +
P(I1=X,I2=Y,I3=Z,I4=Z,I5=Z/I1)*P(I1)  .
```

Probability of an incorrect safe system state =

```
P(C1,C2,I3=X,I4=X,I5=Y/I3)*P(I3)  +
P(C1,C2,I3=X,I4=Y,I5=X/I3)*P(I3)  +
P(C1,C2,I3=X,I4=Y,I5=Y/I3)*P(I3)  +
P(C1,C2,I3=X,I4=Y,I5=Z/I3)*P(I3)  +
P(C1,I2=X,C3,I4=X,I5=Y/I2)*P(I2)  +
P(C1,I2=X,C3,I4=Y,I5=X/I2)*P(I2)  +
P(C1,I2=X,C3,I4=Y,I5=Y/I2)*P(I2)  +
P(C1,I2=X,C3,I4=Y,I5=Z/I2)*P(I2)  +
P(C1,I2=X,I3=X,C4,I5=Y/I2)*P(I2)  +
P(C1,I2=X,I3=X,I4=Y,C5/I2)*P(I2)  +
P(C1,I2=X,I3=X,I4=Y,I5=Y/I2)*P(I2)  +
P(C1,I2=X,I3=X,I4=Y,I5=Z/I2)*P(I2)  +
P(C1,I2=X,I3=Y,C4,I5=X/I2)*P(I2)  +
P(C1,I2=X,I3=Y,C4,I5=Y/I2)*P(I2)  +
P(C1,I2=X,I3=Y,C4,I5=Z/I2)*P(I2)  +
P(C1,I2=X,I3=Y,I4=X,C5/I2)*P(I2)  +
P(C1,I2=X,I3=Y,I4=X,I5=Y/I2)*P(I2)  +
P(C1,I2=X,I3=Y,I4=X,I5=Z/I2)*P(I2)  +
P(C1,I2=X,I3=Y,I4=Y,C5/I2)*P(I2)  +
P(C1,I2=X,I3=Y,I4=Y,I5=X/I2)*P(I2)  +
P(C1,I2=X,I3=Y,I4=Y,I5=Z/I2)*P(I2)  +
P(C1,I2=X,I3=Y,I4=Z,C5/I2)*P(I2)  +
P(C1,I2=X,I3=Y,I4=Z,I5=X/I2)*P(I2)  +
P(C1,I2=X,I3=Y,I4=Z,I5=Y/I2)*P(I2)  +
P(C1,I2=X,I3=Y,I4=Z,I5=Z/I2)*P(I2)  +
P(C1,I2=X,I3=Y,I4=Z,I5=W/I2)*P(I2)  +
P(I1=X,C2,C3,I4=X,I5=Y/I1)*P(I1)  +
P(I1=X,C2,C3,I4=Y,I5=X/I1)*P(I1)  +
P(I1=X,C2,C3,I4=Y,I5=Y/I1)*P(I1)  +
P(I1=X,C2,C3,I4=Y,I5=Z/I1)*P(I1)  +
P(I1=X,C2,I3=X,C4,I5=Y/I1)*P(I1)  +
P(I1=X,C2,I3=X,I4=Y,C5/I1)*P(I1)  +
P(I1=X,C2,I3=X,I4=Y,I5=Y/I1)*P(I1)  +
P(I1=X,C2,I3=X,I4=Y,I5=Z/I1)*P(I1)  +
P(I1=X,C2,I3=Y,C4,I5=X/I1)*P(I1)  +
P(I1=X,C2,I3=Y,C4,I5=Y/I1)*P(I1)  +
P(I1=X,C2,I3=Y,C4,I5=Z/I1)*P(I1)  +
P(I1=X,C2,I3=Y,I4=X,C5/I1)*P(I1)  +
P(I1=X,C2,I3=Y,I4=X,I5=Y/I1)*P(I1)  +
P(I1=X,C2,I3=Y,I4=X,I5=Z/I1)*P(I1)  +
P(I1=X,C2,I3=Y,I4=Y,C5/I1)*P(I1)  +
P(I1=X,C2,I3=Y,I4=Y,I5=X/I1)*P(I1)  +
P(I1=X,C2,I3=Y,I4=Y,I5=Z/I1)*P(I1)  +
P(I1=X,C2,I3=Y,I4=Z,C5/I1)*P(I1)  +
```

```
P(I1=X,C2,I3=Y,I4=Z,I5=X/I1)*P(I1)  +
P(I1=X,C2,I3=Y,I4=Z,I5=Y/I1)*P(I1)  +
P(I1=X,C2,I3=Y,I4=Z,I5=Z/I1)*P(I1)  +
P(I1=X,C2,I3=Y,I4=Z,I5=W/I1)*P(I1)  +
P(I1=X,I2=X,C3,C4,I5=Y/I1)*P(I1)  +
P(I1=X,I2=X,C3,I4=Y,C5/I1)*P(I1)  +
P(I1=X,I2=X,C3,I4=Y,I5=Y/I1)*P(I1)  +
P(I1=X,I2=X,C3,I4=Y,I5=Z/I1)*P(I1)  +
P(I1=X,I2=X,I3=Y,C4,C5/I1)*P(I1)  +
P(I1=X,I2=X,I3=Y,C4,I5=Y/I1)*P(I1)  +
P(I1=X,I2=X,I3=Y,C4,I5=Z/I1)*P(I1)  +
P(I1=X,I2=X,I3=Y,I4=Y,C5/I1)*P(I1)  +
P(I1=X,I2=X,I3=Y,I4=Y,I5=Z/I1)*P(I1)  +
P(I1=X,I2=X,I3=Y,I4=Z,C5/I1)*P(I1)  +
P(I1=X,I2=X,I3=Y,I4=Z,I5=Y/I1)*P(I1)  +
P(I1=X,I2=X,I3=Y,I4=Z,I5=Z/I1)*P(I1)  +
P(I1=X,I2=X,I3=Y,I4=Z,I5=W/I1)*P(I1)  +
P(I1=X,I2=Y,C3,C4,I5=X/I1)*P(I1)  +
P(I1=X,I2=Y,C3,C4,I5=Y/I1)*P(I1)  +
P(I1=X,I2=Y,C3,C4,I5=Z/I1)*P(I1)  +
P(I1=X,I2=Y,C3,I4=X,C5/I1)*P(I1)  +
P(I1=X,I2=Y,C3,I4=X,I5=Y/I1)*P(I1)  +
P(I1=X,I2=Y,C3,I4=X,I5=Z/I1)*P(I1)  +
P(I1=X,I2=Y,C3,I4=Y,C5/I1)*P(I1)  +
P(I1=X,I2=Y,C3,I4=Y,I5=X/I1)*P(I1)  +
P(I1=X,I2=Y,C3,I4=Y,I5=Z/I1)*P(I1)  +
P(I1=X,I2=Y,C3,I4=Z,C5/I1)*P(I1)  +
P(I1=X,I2=Y,C3,I4=Z,I5=X/I1)*P(I1)  +
P(I1=X,I2=Y,C3,I4=Z,I5=Y/I1)*P(I1)  +
P(I1=X,I2=Y,C3,I4=Z,I5=Z/I1)*P(I1)  +
P(I1=X,I2=Y,C3,I4=Z,I5=W/I1)*P(I1)  +
P(I1=X,I2=Y,I3=X,C4,C5/I1)*P(I1)  +
P(I1=X,I2=Y,I3=X,C4,I5=Y/I1)*P(I1)  +
P(I1=X,I2=Y,I3=X,C4,I5=Z/I1)*P(I1)  +
P(I1=X,I2=Y,I3=X,I4=Y,C5/I1)*P(I1)  +
P(I1=X,I2=Y,I3=X,I4=Y,I5=Z/I1)*P(I1)  +
P(I1=X,I2=Y,I3=X,I4=Z,C5/I1)*P(I1)  +
P(I1=X,I2=Y,I3=X,I4=Z,I5=Y/I1)*P(I1)  +
P(I1=X,I2=Y,I3=X,I4=Z,I5=Z/I1)*P(I1)  +
P(I1=X,I2=Y,I3=X,I4=Z,I5=W/I1)*P(I1)  +
P(I1=X,I2=Y,I3=Y,C4,C5/I1)*P(I1)  +
P(I1=X,I2=Y,I3=Y,C4,I5=X/I1)*P(I1)  +
P(I1=X,I2=Y,I3=Y,C4,I5=Z/I1)*P(I1)  +
P(I1=X,I2=Y,I3=Y,I4=X,C5/I1)*P(I1)  +
P(I1=X,I2=Y,I3=Y,I4=X,I5=Z/I1)*P(I1)  +
P(I1=X,I2=Y,I3=Y,I4=Z,C5/I1)*P(I1)  +
P(I1=X,I2=Y,I3=Y,I4=Z,I5=X/I1)*P(I1)  +
P(I1=X,I2=Y,I3=Y,I4=Z,I5=Z/I1)*P(I1)  +
P(I1=X,I2=Y,I3=Y,I4=Z,I5=W/I1)*P(I1)  +
P(I1=X,I2=Y,I3=Z,C4,C5/I1)*P(I1)  +
P(I1=X,I2=Y,I3=Z,C4,I5=X/I1)*P(I1)  +
P(I1=X,I2=Y,I3=Z,C4,I5=Y/I1)*P(I1)  +
P(I1=X,I2=Y,I3=Z,C4,I5=Z/I1)*P(I1)  +
P(I1=X,I2=Y,I3=Z,C4,I5=W/I1)*P(I1)  +
P(I1=X,I2=Y,I3=Z,I4=X,C5/I1)*P(I1)  +
P(I1=X,I2=Y,I3=Z,I4=X,I5=Y/I1)*P(I1)  +
P(I1=X,I2=Y,I3=Z,I4=X,I5=Z/I1)*P(I1)  +
P(I1=X,I2=Y,I3=Z,I4=X,I5=W/I1)*P(I1)  +
P(I1=X,I2=Y,I3=Z,I4=Y,C5/I1)*P(I1)  +
P(I1=X,I2=Y,I3=Z,I4=Y,I5=X/I1)*P(I1)  +
```

```
P(I1=X,I2=Y,I3=Z,I4=Y,I5=Z/I1)*P(I1)  +
P(I1=X,I2=Y,I3=Z,I4=Y,I5=W/I1)*P(I1)  +
P(I1=X,I2=Y,I3=Z,I4=Z,C5/I1)*P(I1)  +
P(I1=X,I2=Y,I3=Z,I4=Z,I5=X/I1)*P(I1)  +
P(I1=X,I2=Y,I3=Z,I4=Z,I5=Y/I1)*P(I1)  +
P(I1=X,I2=Y,I3=Z,I4=Z,I5=W/I1)*P(I1)  +
P(I1=X,I2=Y,I3=Z,I4=W,C5/I1)*P(I1)  +
P(I1=X,I2=Y,I3=Z,I4=W,I5=X/I1)*P(I1)  +
P(I1=X,I2=Y,I3=Z,I4=W,I5=Y/I1)*P(I1)  +
P(I1=X,I2=Y,I3=Z,I4=W,I5=Z/I1)*P(I1)  +
P(I1=X,I2=Y,I3=Z,I4=W,I5=W/I1)*P(I1)  +
P(I1=X,I2=Y,I3=Z,I4=W,I5=H/I1)*P(I1) .
```

RB Architecture with 5 Versions

Probability of an incorrect unsafe system state =

```
P(C1,C2,C3,C4,I5=X/I5)*P(I5)*P(Rc)*P(Ai)  +
P(C1,C2,C3,I4=X/I4)*P(I4)*P(Rc)*P(Ai)  +
P(C1,C2,C3,I4=X,I5=Y/I4)*P(I4)*P(Rc)*P(Ri)*P(Ai)  +
P(C1,C2,I3=X,C4,I5=Y/I3)*P(I3)*P(Rc)*P(Ri)*P(Ai)  +
P(C1,C2,I3=X/I3)*P(I3)*P(Rc)*P(Ai)  +
P(C1,C2,I3=X,I4=X,I5=Y/I3)*P(I3)*P(Rc)*P(Ri)*P(Ai)  +
P(C1,C2,I3=X,I4=Y/I3)*P(I3)*P(Rc)*P(Ri)*P(Ai)  +
P(C1,C2,I3=X,I4=Y,I5=Z/I3)*P(I3)*P(Rc)*P(Ri)**2*P(Ai)  +
P(C1,I2=X,C3,C4,I5=Y/I2)*P(I2)*P(Rc)*P(Ri)*P(Ai)  +
P(C1,I2=X,C3,I4=X,I5=Y/I2)*P(I2)*P(Rc)*P(Ri)*P(Ai)  +
P(C1,I2=X,C3,I4=Y/I2)*P(I2)*P(Rc)*P(Ri)*P(Ai)  +
P(C1,I2=X,C3,I4=Y,I5=Z/I2)*P(I2)*P(Rc)*P(Ri)**2*P(Ai)  +
P(C1,I2=X,I3=X,C4,I5=Y/I2)*P(I2)*P(Rc)*P(Ri)*P(Ai)  +
P(C1,I2=X/I2)*P(I2)*P(Rc)*P(Ai)  +
P(C1,I2=X,I3=X,I4=X,I5=Y/I2)*P(I2)*P(Rc)*P(Ri)*P(Ai)  +
P(C1,I2=X,I3=X,I4=Y/I2)*P(I2)*P(Rc)*P(Ri)*P(Ai)  +
P(C1,I2=X,I3=X,I4=Y,I5=Z/I2)*P(I2)*P(Rc)*P(Ri)**2*P(Ai)  +
P(C1,I2=X,I3=Y,C4,I5=Z/I2)*P(I2)*P(Rc)*P(Ri)**2*P(Ai)  +
P(C1,I2=X,I3=Y,I4=X,I5=Z/I2)*P(I2)*P(Rc)*P(Ri)**2*P(Ai)  +
P(C1,I2=X,I3=Y/I2)*P(I2)*P(Rc)*P(Ri)*P(Ai)  +
P(C1,I2=X,I3=Y,I4=Y,I5=Z/I2)*P(I2)*P(Rc)*P(Ri)**2*P(Ai)  +
P(C1,I2=X,I3=Y,I4=Z/I2)*P(I2)*P(Rc)*P(Ri)**2*P(Ai)  +
P(C1,I2=X,I3=Y,I4=Z,I5=W/I2)*P(I2)*P(Rc)*P(Ri)**3*P(Ai)  +
P(I1=X,C2,C3,C4,I5=Y/I1)*P(I1)*P(Rc)*P(Ri)*P(Ai)  +
P(I1=X,C2,C3,I4=X,I5=Y/I1)*P(I1)*P(Rc)*P(Ri)*P(Ai)  +
P(I1=X,C2,C3,I4=Y/I1)*P(I1)*P(Rc)*P(Ri)*P(Ai)  +
P(I1=X,C2,C3,I4=Y,I5=Z/I1)*P(I1)*P(Rc)*P(Ri)**2*P(Ai)  +
P(I1=X,C2,I3=X,C4,I5=Y/I1)*P(I1)*P(Rc)*P(Ri)*P(Ai)  +
P(I1=X,C2,I3=X,I4=X,I5=Y/I1)*P(I1)*P(Rc)*P(Ri)*P(Ai)  +
P(I1=X,C2,I3=X,I4=Y/I1)*P(I1)*P(Rc)*P(Ri)*P(Ai)  +
P(I1=X,C2,I3=X,I4=Y,I5=Z/I1)*P(I1)*P(Rc)*P(Ri)**2*P(Ai)  +
P(I1=X,C2,I3=Y,C4,I5=Z/I1)*P(I1)*P(Rc)*P(Ri)**2*P(Ai)  +
P(I1=X,C2,I3=Y,I4=X,I5=Z/I1)*P(I1)*P(Rc)*P(Ri)**2*P(Ai)  +
P(I1=X,C2,I3=Y/I1)*P(I1)*P(Rc)*P(Ri)*P(Ai)  +
P(I1=X,C2,I3=Y,I4=Y,I5=Z/I1)*P(I1)*P(Rc)*P(Ri)**2*P(Ai)  +
P(I1=X,C2,I3=Y,I4=Z/I1)*P(I1)*P(Rc)*P(Ri)**2*P(Ai)  +
P(I1=X,C2,I3=Y,I4=Z,I5=W/I1)*P(I1)*P(Rc)*P(Ri)**3*P(Ai)  +
P(I1=X,I2=X,C3,C4,I5=Y/I1)*P(I1)*P(Rc)*P(Ri)*P(Ai)  +
P(I1=X,I2=X,C3,I4=X,I5=Y/I1)*P(I1)*P(Rc)*P(Ri)*P(Ai)  +
P(I1=X,I2=X,C3,I4=Y/I1)*P(I1)*P(Rc)*P(Ri)*P(Ai)  +
P(I1=X,I2=X,C3,I4=Y,I5=Z/I1)*P(I1)*P(Rc)*P(Ri)**2*P(Ai)  +
```

```
P(I1=X,I2=X,I3=X,C4,I5=Y/I1)*P(I1)*P(Rc)*P(Ri)*P(Ai) +
P(I1=X/I1)*P(I1)*P(Ai) +
P(I1=X,I2=X,I3=X,I4=X,I5=Y/I1)*P(I1)*P(Ri)*P(Ai) +
P(I1=X,I2=X,I3=X,I4=Y/I1)*P(I1)*P(Ri)*P(Ai) +
P(I1=X,I2=X,I3=X,I4=Y,I5=Z/I1)*P(I1)*P(Ri)**2*P(Ai) +
P(I1=X,I2=X,I3=Y,C4,I5=Z/I1)*P(I1)*P(Rc)*P(Ri)**2*P(Ai) +
P(I1=X,I2=X,I3=Y,I4=X,I5=Z/I1)*P(I1)*P(Ri)**2*P(Ai) +
P(I1=X,I2=X,I3=Y/I1)*P(I1)*P(Ri)*P(Ai) +
P(I1=X,I2=X,I3=Y,I4=Y,I5=Z/I1)*P(I1)*P(Ri)**2*P(Ai) +
P(I1=X,I2=X,I3=Y,I4=Z/I1)*P(I1)*P(Ri)**2*P(Ai) +
P(I1=X,I2=X,I3=Y,I4=Z,I5=W/I1)*P(I1)*P(Ri)**3*P(Ai) +
P(I1=X,I2=Y,C3,C4,I5=Z/I1)*P(I1)*P(Rc)*P(Ri)**2*P(Ai) +
P(I1=X,I2=Y,C3,I4=X,I5=Z/I1)*P(I1)*P(Rc)*P(Ri)**2*P(Ai) +
P(I1=X,I2=Y,C3,I4=Y,I5=Z/I1)*P(I1)*P(Rc)*P(Ri)**2*P(Ai) +
P(I1=X,I2=Y,C3,I4=Z/I1)*P(I1)*P(Rc)*P(Ri)**2*P(Ai) +
P(I1=X,I2=Y,C3,I4=Z,I5=W/I1)*P(I1)*P(Rc)*P(Ri)**3*P(Ai) +
P(I1=X,I2=Y,I3=X,C4,I5=Z/I1)*P(I1)*P(Rc)*P(Ri)**2*P(Ai) +
P(I1=X,I2=Y,I3=X,I4=X,I5=Z/I1)*P(I1)*P(Ri)**2*P(Ai) +
P(I1=X,I2=Y,I3=X,I4=Y,I5=Z/I1)*P(I1)*P(Ri)**2*P(Ai) +
P(I1=X,I2=Y,I3=X,I4=Z/I1)*P(I1)*P(Ri)**2*P(Ai) +
P(I1=X,I2=Y,I3=X,I4=Z,I5=W/I1)*P(I1)*P(Ri)**3*P(Ai) +
P(I1=X,I2=Y,I3=Y,C4,I5=Z/I1)*P(I1)*P(Rc)*P(Ri)**2*P(Ai) +
P(I1=X,I2=Y,I3=Y,I4=X,I5=Z/I1)*P(I1)*P(Ri)**2*P(Ai) +
P(I1=X,I2=Y/I1)*P(I1)*P(Ri)*P(Ai) +
P(I1=X,I2=Y,I3=Y,I4=Y,I5=Z/I1)*P(I1)*P(Ri)**2*P(Ai) +
P(I1=X,I2=Y,I3=Y,I4=Z/I1)*P(I1)*P(Ri)**2*P(Ai) +
P(I1=X,I2=Y,I3=Y,I4=Z,I5=W/I1)*P(I1)*P(Ri)**3*P(Ai) +
P(I1=X,I2=Y,I3=Z,C4,I5=W/I1)*P(I1)*P(Rc)*P(Ri)**3*P(Ai) +
P(I1=X,I2=Y,I3=Z,I4=X,I5=W/I1)*P(I1)*P(Ri)**3*P(Ai) +
P(I1=X,I2=Y,I3=Z,I4=Y,I5=W/I1)*P(I1)*P(Ri)**3*P(Ai) +
P(I1=X,I2=Y,I3=Z/I1)*P(I1)*P(Ri)**2*P(Ai) +
P(I1=X,I2=Y,I3=Z,I4=Z,I5=W/I1)*P(I1)*P(Ri)**3*P(Ai) +
P(I1=X,I2=Y,I3=Z,I4=W/I1)*P(I1)*P(Ri)**3*P(Ai) +
P(I1=X,I2=Y,I3=Z,I4=W,I5=H/I1)*P(I1)*P(Ri)**4*P(Ai) .
```

Probability of an incorrect safe system state =

```
P(C1,C2,C3,C4,C5)*P(Rc) +
P(C1,C2,C3,C4,I5=X/I5)*P(I5)*P(Rc)*P(Ri) +
P(C1,C2,C3,I4=X,C5/I4)*P(I4)*P(Rc)*P(Ri) +
P(C1,C2,C3,I4=X,I5=X/I4)*P(I4)*P(Rc)*P(Ri) +
P(C1,C2,C3,I4=X,I5=Y/I4)*P(I4)*P(Rc)*P(Ri)**2 +
P(C1,C2,I3=X,C4,C5/I3)*P(I3)*P(Rc)*P(Ri) +
P(C1,C2,I3=X,C4,I5=X/I3)*P(I3)*P(Rc)*P(Ri) +
P(C1,C2,I3=X,C4,I5=Y/I3)*P(I3)*P(Rc)*P(Ri)**2 +
P(C1,C2,I3=X,I4=X,C5/I3)*P(I3)*P(Rc)*P(Ri) +
P(C1,C2,I3=X,I4=X,I5=X/I3)*P(I3)*P(Rc)*P(Ri) +
P(C1,C2,I3=X,I4=X,I5=Y/I3)*P(I3)*P(Rc)*P(Ri)**2 +
P(C1,C2,I3=X,I4=Y,C5/I3)*P(I3)*P(Rc)*P(Ri)**2 +
P(C1,C2,I3=X,I4=Y,I5=X/I3)*P(I3)*P(Rc)*P(Ri)**2 +
P(C1,C2,I3=X,I4=Y,I5=Y/I3)*P(I3)*P(Rc)*P(Ri)**2 +
P(C1,C2,I3=X,I4=Y,I5=Z/I3)*P(I3)*P(Rc)*P(Ri)**3 +
P(C1,I2=X,C3,C4,C5/I2)*P(I2)*P(Rc)*P(Ri) +
P(C1,I2=X,C3,C4,I5=X/I2)*P(I2)*P(Rc)*P(Ri) +
P(C1,I2=X,C3,C4,I5=Y/I2)*P(I2)*P(Rc)*P(Ri)**2 +
P(C1,I2=X,C3,I4=X,C5/I2)*P(I2)*P(Rc)*P(Ri) +
P(C1,I2=X,C3,I4=X,I5=X/I2)*P(I2)*P(Rc)*P(Ri) +
P(C1,I2=X,C3,I4=X,I5=Y/I2)*P(I2)*P(Rc)*P(Ri)**2 +
P(C1,I2=X,C3,I4=Y,C5/I2)*P(I2)*P(Rc)*P(Ri)**2 +
P(C1,I2=X,C3,I4=Y,I5=X/I2)*P(I2)*P(Rc)*P(Ri)**2 +
```

```
P(C1,I2=X,C3,I4=Y,I5=Y/I2)*P(I2)*P(Rc)*P(Ri)**2 +
P(C1,I2=X,C3,I4=Y,I5=Z/I2)*P(I2)*P(Rc)*P(Ri)**3 +
P(C1,I2=X,I3=X,C4,C5/I2)*P(I2)*P(Rc)*P(Ri) +
P(C1,I2=X,I3=X,C4,I5=X/I2)*P(I2)*P(Rc)*P(Ri) +
P(C1,I2=X,I3=X,C4,I5=Y/I2)*P(I2)*P(Rc)*P(Ri)**2 +
P(C1,I2=X,I3=X,I4=X,C5/I2)*P(I2)*P(Rc)*P(Ri) +
P(C1,I2=X,I3=X,I4=X,I5=X/I2)*P(I2)*P(Rc)*P(Ri) +
P(C1,I2=X,I3=X,I4=X,I5=Y/I2)*P(I2)*P(Rc)*P(Ri)**2 +
P(C1,I2=X,I3=X,I4=Y,C5/I2)*P(I2)*P(Rc)*P(Ri)**2 +
P(C1,I2=X,I3=X,I4=Y,I5=X/I2)*P(I2)*P(Rc)*P(Ri)**2 +
P(C1,I2=X,I3=X,I4=Y,I5=Y/I2)*P(I2)*P(Rc)*P(Ri)**2 +
P(C1,I2=X,I3=X,I4=Y,I5=Z/I2)*P(I2)*P(Rc)*P(Ri)**3 +
P(C1,I2=X,I3=Y,C4,C5/I2)*P(I2)*P(Rc)*P(Ri)**2 +
P(C1,I2=X,I3=Y,C4,I5=X/I2)*P(I2)*P(Rc)*P(Ri)**2 +
P(C1,I2=X,I3=Y,C4,I5=Y/I2)*P(I2)*P(Rc)*P(Ri)**2 +
P(C1,I2=X,I3=Y,C4,I5=Z/I2)*P(I2)*P(Rc)*P(Ri)**3 +
P(C1,I2=X,I3=Y,I4=X,C5/I2)*P(I2)*P(Rc)*P(Ri)**2 +
P(C1,I2=X,I3=Y,I4=X,I5=X/I2)*P(I2)*P(Rc)*P(Ri)**2 +
P(C1,I2=X,I3=Y,I4=X,I5=Y/I2)*P(I2)*P(Rc)*P(Ri)**2 +
P(C1,I2=X,I3=Y,I4=X,I5=Z/I2)*P(I2)*P(Rc)*P(Ri)**3 +
P(C1,I2=X,I3=Y,I4=Y,C5/I2)*P(I2)*P(Rc)*P(Ri)**2 +
P(C1,I2=X,I3=Y,I4=Y,I5=X/I2)*P(I2)*P(Rc)*P(Ri)**2 +
P(C1,I2=X,I3=Y,I4=Y,I5=Y/I2)*P(I2)*P(Rc)*P(Ri)**2 +
P(C1,I2=X,I3=Y,I4=Y,I5=Z/I2)*P(I2)*P(Rc)*P(Ri)**3 +
P(C1,I2=X,I3=Y,I4=Z,C5/I2)*P(I2)*P(Rc)*P(Ri)**3 +
P(C1,I2=X,I3=Y,I4=Z,I5=X/I2)*P(I2)*P(Rc)*P(Ri)**3 +
P(C1,I2=X,I3=Y,I4=Z,I5=Y/I2)*P(I2)*P(Rc)*P(Ri)**3 +
P(C1,I2=X,I3=Y,I4=Z,I5=Z/I2)*P(I2)*P(Rc)*P(Ri)**3 +
P(C1,I2=X,I3=Y,I4=Z,I5=W/I2)*P(I2)*P(Rc)*P(Ri)**4 +
P(I1=X,C2,C3,C4,C5/I1)*P(I1)*P(Rc)*P(Ri) +
P(I1=X,C2,C3,C4,I5=X/I1)*P(I1)*P(Rc)*P(Ri) +
P(I1=X,C2,C3,C4,I5=Y/I1)*P(I1)*P(Rc)*P(Ri)**2 +
P(I1=X,C2,C3,I4=X,C5/I1)*P(I1)*P(Rc)*P(Ri) +
P(I1=X,C2,C3,I4=X,I5=X/I1)*P(I1)*P(Rc)*P(Ri) +
P(I1=X,C2,C3,I4=X,I5=Y/I1)*P(I1)*P(Rc)*P(Ri)**2 +
P(I1=X,C2,C3,I4=Y,C5/I1)*P(I1)*P(Rc)*P(Ri)**2 +
P(I1=X,C2,C3,I4=Y,I5=X/I1)*P(I1)*P(Rc)*P(Ri)**2 +
P(I1=X,C2,C3,I4=Y,I5=Y/I1)*P(I1)*P(Rc)*P(Ri)**2 +
P(I1=X,C2,C3,I4=Y,I5=Z/I1)*P(I1)*P(Rc)*P(Ri)**3 +
P(I1=X,C2,I3=X,C4,C5/I1)*P(I1)*P(Rc)*P(Ri) +
P(I1=X,C2,I3=X,C4,I5=X/I1)*P(I1)*P(Rc)*P(Ri) +
P(I1=X,C2,I3=X,C4,I5=Y/I1)*P(I1)*P(Rc)*P(Ri)**2 +
P(I1=X,C2,I3=X,I4=X,C5/I1)*P(I1)*P(Rc)*P(Ri) +
P(I1=X,C2,I3=X,I4=X,I5=X/I1)*P(I1)*P(Rc)*P(Ri) +
P(I1=X,C2,I3=X,I4=X,I5=Y/I1)*P(I1)*P(Rc)*P(Ri)**2 +
P(I1=X,C2,I3=X,I4=Y,C5/I1)*P(I1)*P(Rc)*P(Ri)**2 +
P(I1=X,C2,I3=X,I4=Y,I5=X/I1)*P(I1)*P(Rc)*P(Ri)**2 +
P(I1=X,C2,I3=X,I4=Y,I5=Y/I1)*P(I1)*P(Rc)*P(Ri)**2 +
P(I1=X,C2,I3=X,I4=Y,I5=Z/I1)*P(I1)*P(Rc)*P(Ri)**3 +
P(I1=X,C2,I3=Y,C4,C5/I1)*P(I1)*P(Rc)*P(Ri)**2 +
P(I1=X,C2,I3=Y,C4,I5=X/I1)*P(I1)*P(Rc)*P(Ri)**2 +
P(I1=X,C2,I3=Y,C4,I5=Y/I1)*P(I1)*P(Rc)*P(Ri)**2 +
P(I1=X,C2,I3=Y,C4,I5=Z/I1)*P(I1)*P(Rc)*P(Ri)**3 +
P(I1=X,C2,I3=Y,I4=X,C5/I1)*P(I1)*P(Rc)*P(Ri)**2 +
P(I1=X,C2,I3=Y,I4=X,I5=X/I1)*P(I1)*P(Rc)*P(Ri)**2 +
P(I1=X,C2,I3=Y,I4=X,I5=Y/I1)*P(I1)*P(Rc)*P(Ri)**2 +
P(I1=X,C2,I3=Y,I4=X,I5=Z/I1)*P(I1)*P(Rc)*P(Ri)**3 +
P(I1=X,C2,I3=Y,I4=Y,C5/I1)*P(I1)*P(Rc)*P(Ri)**2 +
P(I1=X,C2,I3=Y,I4=Y,I5=X/I1)*P(I1)*P(Rc)*P(Ri)**2 +
P(I1=X,C2,I3=Y,I4=Y,I5=Y/I1)*P(I1)*P(Rc)*P(Ri)**2 +
```

```
P(I1=X,C2,I3=Y,I4=Y,I5=Z/I1)*P(I1)*P(Rc)*P(Ri)**3 +
P(I1=X,C2,I3=Y,I4=Z,C5/I1)*P(I1)*P(Rc)*P(Ri)**3 +
P(I1=X,C2,I3=Y,I4=Z,I5=X/I1)*P(I1)*P(Rc)*P(Ri)**3 +
P(I1=X,C2,I3=Y,I4=Z,I5=Y/I1)*P(I1)*P(Rc)*P(Ri)**3 +
P(I1=X,C2,I3=Y,I4=Z,I5=Z/I1)*P(I1)*P(Rc)*P(Ri)**3 +
P(I1=X,C2,I3=Y,I4=Z,I5=W/I1)*P(I1)*P(Rc)*P(Ri)**4 +
P(I1=X,I2=X,C3,C4,C5/I1)*P(I1)*P(Rc)*P(Ri) +
P(I1=X,I2=X,C3,C4,I5=X/I1)*P(I1)*P(Rc)*P(Ri) +
P(I1=X,I2=X,C3,C4,I5=Y/I1)*P(I1)*P(Rc)*P(Ri)**2 +
P(I1=X,I2=X,C3,I4=X,C5/I1)*P(I1)*P(Rc)*P(Ri) +
P(I1=X,I2=X,C3,I4=X,I5=X/I1)*P(I1)*P(Rc)*P(Ri) +
P(I1=X,I2=X,C3,I4=X,I5=Y/I1)*P(I1)*P(Rc)*P(Ri)**2 +
P(I1=X,I2=X,C3,I4=Y,C5/I1)*P(I1)*P(Rc)*P(Ri)**2 +
P(I1=X,I2=X,C3,I4=Y,I5=X/I1)*P(I1)*P(Rc)*P(Ri)**2 +
P(I1=X,I2=X,C3,I4=Y,I5=Y/I1)*P(I1)*P(Rc)*P(Ri)**2 +
P(I1=X,I2=X,C3,I4=Y,I5=Z/I1)*P(I1)*P(Rc)*P(Ri)**3 +
P(I1=X,I2=X,I3=X,C4,C5/I1)*P(I1)*P(Rc)*P(Ri) +
P(I1=X,I2=X,I3=X,C4,I5=X/I1)*P(I1)*P(Rc)*P(Ri) +
P(I1=X,I2=X,I3=X,C4,I5=Y/I1)*P(I1)*P(Rc)*P(Ri)**2 +
P(I1=X,I2=X,I3=X,I4=X,C5/I1)*P(I1)*P(Rc)*P(Ri) +
P(I1=X,I2=X,I3=X,I4=X,I5=X/I1)*P(I1)*P(Ri) +
P(I1=X,I2=X,I3=X,I4=X,I5=Y/I1)*P(I1)*P(Ri)**2 +
P(I1=X,I2=X,I3=X,I4=Y,C5/I1)*P(I1)*P(Rc)*P(Ri)**2 +
P(I1=X,I2=X,I3=X,I4=Y,I5=X/I1)*P(I1)*P(Ri)**2 +
P(I1=X,I2=X,I3=X,I4=Y,I5=Y/I1)*P(I1)*P(Ri)**2 +
P(I1=X,I2=X,I3=X,I4=Y,I5=Z/I1)*P(I1)*P(Ri)**3 +
P(I1=X,I2=X,I3=Y,C4,C5/I1)*P(I1)*P(Rc)*P(Ri)**2 +
P(I1=X,I2=X,I3=Y,C4,I5=X/I1)*P(I1)*P(Rc)*P(Ri)**2 +
P(I1=X,I2=X,I3=Y,C4,I5=Y/I1)*P(I1)*P(Rc)*P(Ri)**2 +
P(I1=X,I2=X,I3=Y,C4,I5=Z/I1)*P(I1)*P(Rc)*P(Ri)**3 +
P(I1=X,I2=X,I3=Y,I4=X,C5/I1)*P(I1)*P(Rc)*P(Ri)**2 +
P(I1=X,I2=X,I3=Y,I4=X,I5=X/I1)*P(I1)*P(Ri)**2 +
P(I1=X,I2=X,I3=Y,I4=X,I5=Y/I1)*P(I1)*P(Ri)**2 +
P(I1=X,I2=X,I3=Y,I4=X,I5=Z/I1)*P(I1)*P(Ri)**3 +
P(I1=X,I2=X,I3=Y,I4=Y,C5/I1)*P(I1)*P(Rc)*P(Ri)**2 +
P(I1=X,I2=X,I3=Y,I4=Y,I5=X/I1)*P(I1)*P(Ri)**2 +
P(I1=X,I2=X,I3=Y,I4=Y,I5=Y/I1)*P(I1)*P(Ri)**2 +
P(I1=X,I2=X,I3=Y,I4=Y,I5=Z/I1)*P(I1)*P(Ri)**3 +
P(I1=X,I2=X,I3=Y,I4=Z,C5/I1)*P(I1)*P(Rc)*P(Ri)**3 +
P(I1=X,I2=X,I3=Y,I4=Z,I5=X/I1)*P(I1)*P(Ri)**3 +
P(I1=X,I2=X,I3=Y,I4=Z,I5=Y/I1)*P(I1)*P(Ri)**3 +
P(I1=X,I2=X,I3=Y,I4=Z,I5=Z/I1)*P(I1)*P(Ri)**3 +
P(I1=X,I2=X,I3=Y,I4=Z,I5=W/I1)*P(I1)*P(Ri)**4 +
P(I1=X,I2=Y,C3,C4,C5/I1)*P(I1)*P(Rc)*P(Ri)**2 +
P(I1=X,I2=Y,C3,C4,I5=X/I1)*P(I1)*P(Rc)*P(Ri)**2 +
P(I1=X,I2=Y,C3,C4,I5=Y/I1)*P(I1)*P(Rc)*P(Ri)**2 +
P(I1=X,I2=Y,C3,C4,I5=Z/I1)*P(I1)*P(Rc)*P(Ri)**3 +
P(I1=X,I2=Y,C3,I4=X,C5/I1)*P(I1)*P(Rc)*P(Ri)**2 +
P(I1=X,I2=Y,C3,I4=X,I5=X/I1)*P(I1)*P(Rc)*P(Ri)**2 +
P(I1=X,I2=Y,C3,I4=X,I5=Y/I1)*P(I1)*P(Rc)*P(Ri)**2 +
P(I1=X,I2=Y,C3,I4=X,I5=Z/I1)*P(I1)*P(Rc)*P(Ri)**3 +
P(I1=X,I2=Y,C3,I4=Y,C5/I1)*P(I1)*P(Rc)*P(Ri)**2 +
P(I1=X,I2=Y,C3,I4=Y,I5=X/I1)*P(I1)*P(Rc)*P(Ri)**2 +
P(I1=X,I2=Y,C3,I4=Y,I5=Y/I1)*P(I1)*P(Rc)*P(Ri)**2 +
P(I1=X,I2=Y,C3,I4=Y,I5=Z/I1)*P(I1)*P(Rc)*P(Ri)**3 +
P(I1=X,I2=Y,C3,I4=Z,C5/I1)*P(I1)*P(Rc)*P(Ri)**3 +
P(I1=X,I2=Y,C3,I4=Z,I5=X/I1)*P(I1)*P(Rc)*P(Ri)**3 +
P(I1=X,I2=Y,C3,I4=Z,I5=Y/I1)*P(I1)*P(Rc)*P(Ri)**3 +
P(I1=X,I2=Y,C3,I4=Z,I5=Z/I1)*P(I1)*P(Rc)*P(Ri)**3 +
P(I1=X,I2=Y,C3,I4=Z,I5=W/I1)*P(I1)*P(Rc)*P(Ri)**4 +
```

```
P(I1=X,I2=Y,I3=X,C4,C5/I1)*P(I1)*P(Rc)*P(Ri)**2 +
P(I1=X,I2=Y,I3=X,C4,I5=X/I1)*P(I1)*P(Rc)*P(Ri)**2 +
P(I1=X,I2=Y,I3=X,C4,I5=Y/I1)*P(I1)*P(Rc)*P(Ri)**2 +
P(I1=X,I2=Y,I3=X,C4,I5=Z/I1)*P(I1)*P(Rc)*P(Ri)**3 +
P(I1=X,I2=Y,I3=X,I4=X,C5/I1)*P(I1)*P(Rc)*P(Ri)**2 +
P(I1=X,I2=Y,I3=X,I4=X,I5=X/I1)*P(I1)*P(Ri)**2 +
P(I1=X,I2=Y,I3=X,I4=X,I5=Y/I1)*P(I1)*P(Ri)**2 +
P(I1=X,I2=Y,I3=X,I4=X,I5=Z/I1)*P(I1)*P(Ri)**3 +
P(I1=X,I2=Y,I3=X,I4=Y,C5/I1)*P(I1)*P(Rc)*P(Ri)**2 +
P(I1=X,I2=Y,I3=X,I4=Y,I5=X/I1)*P(I1)*P(Ri)**2 +
P(I1=X,I2=Y,I3=X,I4=Y,I5=Y/I1)*P(I1)*P(Ri)**2 +
P(I1=X,I2=Y,I3=X,I4=Y,I5=Z/I1)*P(I1)*P(Ri)**3 +
P(I1=X,I2=Y,I3=X,I4=Z,C5/I1)*P(I1)*P(Rc)*P(Ri)**3 +
P(I1=X,I2=Y,I3=X,I4=Z,I5=X/I1)*P(I1)*P(Ri)**3 +
P(I1=X,I2=Y,I3=X,I4=Z,I5=Y/I1)*P(I1)*P(Ri)**3 +
P(I1=X,I2=Y,I3=X,I4=Z,I5=Z/I1)*P(I1)*P(Ri)**3 +
P(I1=X,I2=Y,I3=X,I4=Z,I5=W/I1)*P(I1)*P(Ri)**4 +
P(I1=X,I2=Y,I3=Y,C4,C5/I1)*P(I1)*P(Rc)*P(Ri)**2 +
P(I1=X,I2=Y,I3=Y,C4,I5=X/I1)*P(I1)*P(Rc)*P(Ri)**2 +
P(I1=X,I2=Y,I3=Y,C4,I5=Y/I1)*P(I1)*P(Rc)*P(Ri)**2 +
P(I1=X,I2=Y,I3=Y,C4,I5=Z/I1)*P(I1)*P(Rc)*P(Ri)**3 +
P(I1=X,I2=Y,I3=Y,I4=X,C5/I1)*P(I1)*P(Rc)*P(Ri)**2 +
P(I1=X,I2=Y,I3=Y,I4=X,I5=X/I1)*P(I1)*P(Ri)**2 +
P(I1=X,I2=Y,I3=Y,I4=X,I5=Y/I1)*P(I1)*P(Ri)**2 +
P(I1=X,I2=Y,I3=Y,I4=X,I5=Z/I1)*P(I1)*P(Ri)**3 +
P(I1=X,I2=Y,I3=Y,I4=Y,C5/I1)*P(I1)*P(Rc)*P(Ri)**2 +
P(I1=X,I2=Y,I3=Y,I4=Y,I5=X/I1)*P(I1)*P(Ri)**2 +
P(I1=X,I2=Y,I3=Y,I4=Y,I5=Y/I1)*P(I1)*P(Ri)**2 +
P(I1=X,I2=Y,I3=Y,I4=Y,I5=Z/I1)*P(I1)*P(Ri)**3 +
P(I1=X,I2=Y,I3=Y,I4=Z,C5/I1)*P(I1)*P(Rc)*P(Ri)**3 +
P(I1=X,I2=Y,I3=Y,I4=Z,I5=X/I1)*P(I1)*P(Ri)**3 +
P(I1=X,I2=Y,I3=Y,I4=Z,I5=Y/I1)*P(I1)*P(Ri)**3 +
P(I1=X,I2=Y,I3=Y,I4=Z,I5=Z/I1)*P(I1)*P(Ri)**3 +
P(I1=X,I2=Y,I3=Y,I4=Z,I5=W/I1)*P(I1)*P(Ri)**4 +
P(I1=X,I2=Y,I3=Z,C4,C5/I1)*P(I1)*P(Rc)*P(Ri)**3 +
P(I1=X,I2=Y,I3=Z,C4,I5=X/I1)*P(I1)*P(Rc)*P(Ri)**3 +
P(I1=X,I2=Y,I3=Z,C4,I5=Y/I1)*P(I1)*P(Rc)*P(Ri)**3 +
P(I1=X,I2=Y,I3=Z,C4,I5=Z/I1)*P(I1)*P(Rc)*P(Ri)**3 +
P(I1=X,I2=Y,I3=Z,C4,I5=W/I1)*P(I1)*P(Rc)*P(Ri)**4 +
P(I1=X,I2=Y,I3=Z,I4=X,C5/I1)*P(I1)*P(Rc)*P(Ri)**3 +
P(I1=X,I2=Y,I3=Z,I4=X,I5=X/I1)*P(I1)*P(Ri)**3 +
P(I1=X,I2=Y,I3=Z,I4=X,I5=Y/I1)*P(I1)*P(Ri)**3 +
P(I1=X,I2=Y,I3=Z,I4=X,I5=Z/I1)*P(I1)*P(Ri)**3 +
P(I1=X,I2=Y,I3=Z,I4=X,I5=W/I1)*P(I1)*P(Ri)**4 +
P(I1=X,I2=Y,I3=Z,I4=Y,C5/I1)*P(I1)*P(Rc)*P(Ri)**3 +
P(I1=X,I2=Y,I3=Z,I4=Y,I5=X/I1)*P(I1)*P(Ri)**3 +
P(I1=X,I2=Y,I3=Z,I4=Y,I5=Y/I1)*P(I1)*P(Ri)**3 +
P(I1=X,I2=Y,I3=Z,I4=Y,I5=Z/I1)*P(I1)*P(Ri)**3 +
P(I1=X,I2=Y,I3=Z,I4=Y,I5=W/I1)*P(I1)*P(Ri)**4 +
P(I1=X,I2=Y,I3=Z,I4=Z,C5/I1)*P(I1)*P(Rc)*P(Ri)**3 +
P(I1=X,I2=Y,I3=Z,I4=Z,I5=X/I1)*P(I1)*P(Ri)**3 +
P(I1=X,I2=Y,I3=Z,I4=Z,I5=Y/I1)*P(I1)*P(Ri)**3 +
P(I1=X,I2=Y,I3=Z,I4=Z,I5=Z/I1)*P(I1)*P(Ri)**3 +
P(I1=X,I2=Y,I3=Z,I4=Z,I5=W/I1)*P(I1)*P(Ri)**4 +
P(I1=X,I2=Y,I3=Z,I4=W,C5/I1)*P(I1)*P(Rc)*P(Ri)**4 +
P(I1=X,I2=Y,I3=Z,I4=W,I5=X/I1)*P(I1)*P(Ri)**4 +
P(I1=X,I2=Y,I3=Z,I4=W,I5=Y/I1)*P(I1)*P(Ri)**4 +
P(I1=X,I2=Y,I3=Z,I4=W,I5=Z/I1)*P(I1)*P(Ri)**4 +
P(I1=X,I2=Y,I3=Z,I4=W,I5=W/I1)*P(I1)*P(Ri)**4 +
P(I1=X,I2=Y,I3=Z,I4=W,I5=H/I1)*P(I1)*P(Ri)**5.
```

Chapter 11

The Impact of Voter Granularity
in Fault-Tolerant Software
on System Reliability and Availability

Francesca Saglietti

11.1 Definition of System States

A fault-tolerant software system composed of a number of diverse versions as well as of a voting system determined by a predefined majority algorithm is characterized at each output evaluation by one of the following three states:

a) The system is in a *reliable* state R, if it produces a correct output (adjudicated from a majority of correct results).

b) The system is in an *incorrect* state I, if part of the output adjudicated is incorrect, due to a majority of (partly) wrong results.

c) The system is in a *stop* state S, if there is no output majority and therefore each diverse result has to be rejected. This implies an interruption of the operational phase.

On the basis of the previous definitions, we consider the following state unions:

d) The system is in an *available* state $A = R \cup I$ if there is no interruption due to lack of majority, i.e. the system is able to perform further operations.

e) The system is in an *undangerous* state $U = R \cup S$ if it does not produce an incorrect output.

f) The system is in an *error* state $E = S \cup I$ if it does not produce a correct output.

On the whole, the six definitions a)-f) are summarized in Table 11.1 and can be represented as subsets of the state space as illustrated by Fig. 11.1.

While state R obviously represents the only desirable event, both states I and S present different disadvantages differing in their effects according to the application considered.

In case of systems allowing an interruption of the operational time, this stop state may represent the best opportunity to avoid dangerous failures due to incorrect outputs and also to re-establish the reliable state during a correction phase.

Table 11.1. System states and operational characteristics

Def.	State	Operation
a)	R: reliable	yes: correct
b)	I: incorrect	yes: (partly) incorrect
c)	S: stop	no
d)	A: available	yes
e)	U: undangerous	correct or no
f)	E: error	(partly) incorrect or no

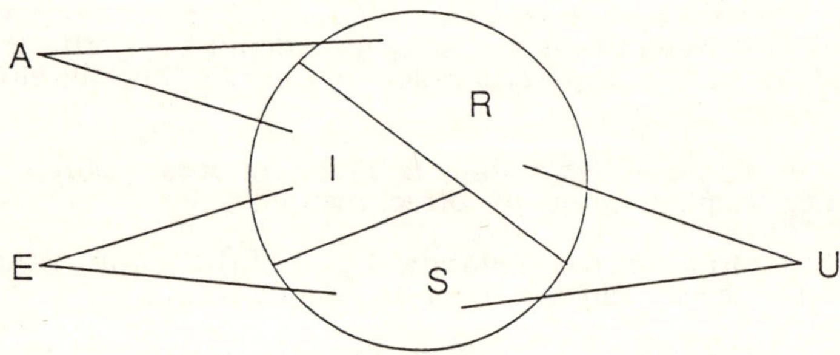

Fig. 11.1. Defined subsets of state space

On the other hand, we may think of realistic applications not wishing such a fail-safe solution, as an interruption of the system operation might cause damage costs C_S hardly differing from the costs C_I due to unreliable results. Moreover, the output accepted in an incorrect state may be wrong only in some identifiable components, allowing nonetheless to perform a correct degraded service. Nonetheless, we will assume in the following the ordinary situation $C_S < C_I$.

Thus, the relation between both error states has to be evaluated from case to case by estimating for each application the quotient $Q = C_S/C_I < 1$ of their expected costs. Even with respect to the same system this factor Q may change throughout the operational phase together with the varying required availability.

According to this estimation of the expected losses, it will be preferable to choose a voter capable of increasing resp. reducing favourably the probability of each system state, in order to minimize the total costs expected during mission time.

The intention of this chapter is to propose such a strategy capable of determining the suitable voter granularity on the basis of the cost quotient Q.

11.2 Effect of Voter Granularity on System States

In order to study the effect of different voting strategies on the single error state probabilities, we have to identify the input set partition inducing the corresponding state space partition analyzed in the previous section.

In the following we will denote (similarly as in [TSO87]) by:

G: the set of "*good inputs*" resulting in a reliable state,

B: the set of "*bad inputs*" resulting in an incorrect state,

N: the set of "*no majority inputs*" resulting in a stop state.

The unique correspondence between input subsets and states is thus summarized in Fig. 11.2.

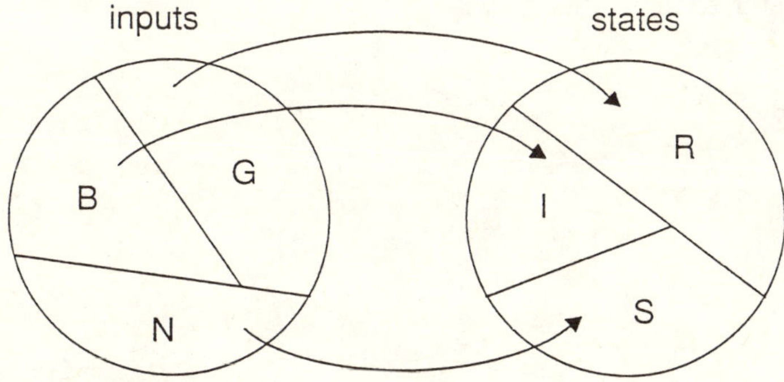

Fig. 11.2. Input Partition Mapped on Corresponding State Partition

The loss expected for each execution can now be simply determined by the probability P of selecting inputs out of the corresponding subset, in other words we have to expect amounts of

$$P\,(N){\cdot}C_S \text{ for costs due to system unavailability as well as}$$

$$P\,(B){\cdot}C_I \text{ for costs due to unreliable outputs,}$$

resulting in a total expenditure C with

$$C = P(N){\cdot}C_S + P(B){\cdot}C_I.$$

This general expression will vary according to the voting system defined in each particular case.

The voter characteristic we will analyze within this chapter is its granularity; we remind that this is defined to be "coarse", if consensus is determined at the level of complex types, and to be "fine", if adjudication is performed at the basic type level.

In case of multilevel complexities, these terms may be used for both extreme interpretations of the concepts "basic" and "complex", as well as for any other intermediate possibility.

Denoting with the sub-index "C" input subsets related to the coarse granularity and with the subindex "F" those determined by the fine one, we can easily observe that both good and bad points w.r.t. the first strategy will keep their property also in the second case, i.e.

$$G_C \subseteq G_F$$

and

$$B_C \subset B_F$$

whereas the fine granularity permits to reach consensus values among partially incorrect versions, which are not achievable by the coarse voter, that is

$$N_F \subset N_C$$

This means that the input partitions related to both voting strategies may be sketched as in Fig. 11.3.

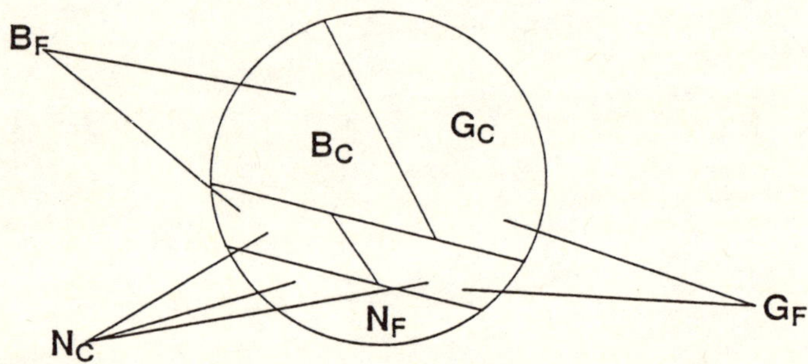

Fig. 11.3. Input partitions induced by different granularities

In particular, this implies that basic type voting decreases system unavailability, whereas complex type voting reduces the probability of incorrect outputs.

An exact comparison of both expected costs

$$C_C = P(N_C) \cdot C_S + P(B_C) \cdot C_I$$

and

$$C_F = P(N_F) \cdot C_S + P(B_F) \cdot C_I$$

yields the following difference:

$$C_F - C_C =$$

$$= [P(N_F) - P(N_C)] \cdot C_S + [P(B_F) - P(B_C)] \cdot C_I =$$

$$= C_I \cdot [P(B_F) - P(B_C) - Q \cdot (P(N_C) - P(N_F))]$$

with the cost quotient Q defined in the first section.

Equivalently,

$$C_F > C_C \quad \Leftrightarrow \quad \frac{P(B_F) - P(B_C)}{P(N_C) - P(N_F)} > Q$$

Thus, in order to develop a decision-making mechanism assisting in optimal granularity choice, we have to evaluate the ratio

$$Z := [P(B_F) - P(B_C)] / [P(N_C) - P(N_F)]$$

($Z \leq 1$, due to $B_F \backslash B_C \subseteq N_C \backslash N_F$) and to compare it with the cost quotient Q.

This will be done in detail in section 11.4, after having examined some examples in the following section.

Indirectly, a decision on the suitable granularity may also affect the question on the best location of checkpoints. In fact, in case of a sequential computation of output variables x_1 and x_2, determined in the same order by all diverse versions and resulting in the output pair (x_1, x_2), a fine final voter could be replaced by two checkpoints voting separately on x_1 first and then on x_2.

The advantage of such a separation of voting points is the possibility of recovery if the second variable x_2 depends on the value of x_1. In this case a good majority of x_1 could be injected in time into each program, preventing the further calculation of x_2 to be biased by previous errors.

This consideration already points out the essential role of dependence factors in this problem: beside the usual question about behaviour dependence among parallel versions, we have also to take into account commonalities in the computation of components, resulting unavoidably in their failure dependence.

11.3 Examples

In the following real-world examples as well as in the subsequent theoretical evaluations we will consider the realistic case of a 2-out-of-3 majority.

11.3.1. The UCLA Versions from the NASA Four-University-Experiment

The first data concern the work done at UCLA within the NASA Four-University-Experiment developing and certifying five Pascal versions (s.[TSO87]).

The experimental results reported concern all ten possible triplets subjected to 200.000 test cases and have thus to be considered as average values out of two million decisions.

The application represented a part of an integrated avionics system intended to evaluate sensor inputs, identify faulty ones and finally compute a statistical estimate of vehicle acceleration.

Fault-Tolerance was achieved by introducing five cross-checkpoints with recovery comparing eleven variables with a total of 64 elements (e.g. an array of eight Booleans for sensor status and a structure of three real numbers for acceleration components).

Comparison of the values computed by the versions could be done at three different levels of granularity:

1)   individual elements
2)   variables of complex types
3)   vectors of variables given at each checkpoint.

While no difference in the system state was found in a comparison between the second and the third granularity type, it was observed that the first and finest voter could yield majority values at ten decision points more than the other strategies (eight of them gave correct, two gave wrong majorities). In our notation these results read

$$P(N_C) - P(N_F) = 10/(2 \cdot 10^6),$$

$$P(B_F) - P(B_C) = 2/(2 \cdot 10^6),$$

so that we obtain a mean value

$$Z = 1/5$$

to be compared with the cost quotient Q.

11.3.2. The PODS Experiment

The concept of the Project on Diverse Software (PODS,s.[BAR85]) was to independently produce three programs based on a specification for a reactor protection channel required to derive a main output DL used to determine the status of trip and alarm outputs.

The failures for each of the eleven output variables detected by 65.000 test cases during a post-acceptance back-to-back testing phase are shown in table 11.2, where C, H and V represent the three versions and their combinations stand for the corresponding multiple failures.

In this case we can treat the real value DL similarly as the remaining binary variables, as the only common failure affecting it was caused by a typographical error in the look-up table having the same effect on the final results.

On the basis of some identities implied by the figures in this table (see Appendix) we can easily derive the following values for the granularity C treating the output vector as a whole and the voter F adjudicating each variable separately:

$$P(B_C) = 40/65000$$
$$P(B_F) = 78/65000$$

$$\Rightarrow \quad P(B_F) - P(B_C) = 38/65000$$

$$P(N_C) = 1202/65000$$
$$P(N_F) = 0$$

$$\Rightarrow \quad P(N_C) - P(N_F) = 1202/65000$$

On the whole, we obtain a factor

$$Z = 38/1202 \cong 0.032$$

leading to the optimal voting strategy after comparison with the cost ratio Q.

Table 11.2. Post-acceptance failures in PODS (from [BAR87])

GOLDEN VS. TEST	C	H	V	CH	CV	HV	CHV	ANY
ANY	1152	32428	388	1134	0	108	0	32726
DL <	0	0	33	0	0	0	0	33
DL >	0	50	87	0	0	50	0	87
OS 0 1	0	0	0	0	0	0	0	0
OS 1 0	0	0	0	0	0	0	0	0
LS 0 1	0	28	28	0	0	28	0	28
LS 1 0	0	0	0	0	0	0	0	0
CB 0 1	0	0	0	0	0	0	0	0
CB 1 0	32	0	0	0	0	0	0	32
AL 0 1	0	0	0	0	0	0	0	0
AL 1 0	26	0	0	0	0	0	0	26
ST 0 1	0	0	0	0	0	0	0	0
ST 1 0	17	0	0	0	0	0	0	17
TA 0 1	0	0	0	0	0	0	0	0
TA 1 0	0	0	0	0	0	0	0	0
TF0 0 1	0	0	0	0	0	0	0	0
TF0 1 0	0	0	0	0	0	0	0	0
TF2 0 1	1115	0	0	0	0	0	0	1115
TF2 1 0	0	0	0	0	0	0	0	0
TF4 0 1	0	0	0	0	0	0	0	0
TF4 1 0	0	0	0	0	0	0	0	0
TF5 0 1	0	0	240	0	0	0	0	240
TF5 1 0	0	32388	0	0	0	0	0	32388

11.4 Strategic Choice of Optimal Granularity

In this paragraph we suggest a theoretical approach to the problem of choosing the optimal granularity with respect to the expected losses.

To simplify the problem representation we will treat here only the case of two binary output variables, proposing to extend analogous considerations to a more general situation.

In case of componentwise comparison, availability does not represent a problem because w.r.t. a 2-out-of-3 majority value binarity always yields:

$$N_F = \varnothing$$

The ratio

$$Z = P(B_F \backslash B_C) \, / \, P(N_C \backslash N_F)$$

can then be simply expressed as a conditional probability

$$Z = P\,(B_F \backslash B_C \,|\, N_C \backslash N_F) = P\,(B_F \,|\, N_C) = P\,(B_F \cap N_C)/P(N_C)$$

Denoting by a symbol "r" a right binary value and by a symbol "w" a wrong one, we can uniquely represent the state of each version by

$$s_i \in \{rr,\ rw,\ wr,\ ww\}\,,\ i \in \{1,2,3\},$$

where the order of the symbols is dictated by a predefined sequence of the output variables.

We define a state set S consisting of version states to represent the corresponding state event. As a set, S is not characterized by any order of its elements.

Thus

$$S = \{s_i\} \qquad\qquad i \in \{1,2,3\}$$

will merely represent the situation with one version (no matter which) in state s_i,

$$S = \{s_i,\ s_j\}, \qquad\qquad \{i,j\} \subset \{1,2,3\}$$

will additionally require that another one is in state s_j,

$$S = \{s_i, s_j, s_k\}, \qquad\qquad \{i,j,k\} = \{1,2,3\}$$

moreover indicates that the remaining program is in state s_k, regardless of the sequence in which the states have been enumerated.

Under this notation we can easily see that the event of no coarse majority appearing in the denominator of the ratio above will exactly occur in the case of one of the following four state sets:

$$S_1 = \{rr\ ,wr,\ ww\},$$

$$S_2 = \{rr,\ rw,\ ww\},$$

$$S_3 = \{rw,\ wr,\ ww\},$$

$$S_4 = \{rr,\ rw,\ wr\},$$

whereas the numerator given by the additional condition of a bad fine result is only possible in case of the first three state sets S_1, S_2, S_3.

Therefore, the factor Z can be expressed as

$$Z = \sum_{i=1}^{3} P(S_i) \ /\ \sum_{i=1}^{4} P(S_i) =$$

$$= 1\,/\,(1 + P(S_4)\,/\sum_{i=1}^{3} P(S_i)) =$$

$$= 1\,/\,(1 + 1/\sum_{i=1}^{3} (P(S_i)/P(S_4))) =$$

$$= \quad 1 / (1 + 1 / \sum_{i=1}^{3} q_i)$$

with $\qquad q_i := P(S_i)/P(S_4) \qquad\qquad i \in \{1,2,3\}.$

The factors q_i can now be interpreted as the following quotients of conditional probabilities:

$$q_1 = P(S_1)/P(S_4) =$$

$$= P(\{rr, wr, ww\})/P(\{rr, rw, wr\}) =$$

$$= P(\{ww\}|\{rr, wr\})/P(\{rw\}|\{rr, wr\})$$

$$q_2 = P(S_2)/P(S_4) =$$

$$= P(\{rr, rw, ww\})/P(\{rr, rw, wr\}) =$$

$$= P(\{ww\}|\{rr, rw\})/P(\{wr\}|\{rr, rw\})$$

$$q_3 = P(S_3)/P(S_4) =$$

$$= P(\{rw, wr, ww\})/P(\{rr, rw, wr\}) =$$

$$= P(\{ww\}|\{rw, wr\})/P(\{rr\}|\{rw, wr\})$$

Of course, all these transformations are only valid in case of non-zero denominators resulting in well-defined conditional probabilities.

Although the resulting expression may appear complicated at a first sight, it presents nonetheless some considerable advantages.

First of all, the previous calculations did not assume any dependence resp. independence property whatsoever, neither concerning diverse programs nor with respect to the determination of the output components within each program.

Therefore, the final formula may be evaluated from case to case by observing the dependence behaviour affecting programs and output variables for the particular application considered.

Moreover, the proposed description of Z in terms of the quotients q_i presents a further advantage; each of the three ratios, namely, considers both in its numerator and in its denominator the same condition. Thus the evaluation of each q_i does not require an absolute estimation of conditional probabilities, but merely a relative comparison of probabilities of two different events occurring under a common condition.

In the following we will analyze some special cases resulting from extremely particular conditions.

Complete Dependence among Output Variables

This situation occurs when one component is correct if and only if the other is, as may be the case of output elements strongly connected by a simple operation as a scalar multiplication.

The obvious conclusion of such an assumption is that the choice of granularity does not vary the voting process at all.

In our model Z is not defined (the denominator is zero) being restricted to non-degenerate situations based on a non-trivial problem.

One-Side Dependence among Output Variables

Full dependence among output bits possibly only occurs in one direction, i.e. incorrectness of one variable implies also a failure of the other one, without assuming also the opposite as done in the previous passage.

This may for example be the case of two variables to be determined in a pre-established order and where the calculation of the second one uses, among other parameters, also the computation already performed to obtain the first output element. Here we have

$$P(S_1) = P(S_3) = P(S_4) = O,$$

so that

$$Z = 1.$$

This means that the gain in system availability expected to be achieved by fine granularity is balanced by the expected increase in the probability of incorrect output. Assuming, as usual, $Q < 1$, this extreme situation will be better handled by a coarse voter.

Independence among Versions and Output Variables

Both the assumptions about independence in the failure behaviour of diverse versions and of output elements are very idealistic and usually unrealistic.

Nonetheless, in case of multilevel forced diversity and of binary values based on completely different computations it might be possible to accept this restriction, in order to make use of the following considerations to obtain a simplified rule of granularity choice.

In this case we may look at each program as consisting of two parts, each determining one of both output components. Assuming diverse version parts to be equally reliable with probabilities R_1 resp. R_2 of correct response and ignoring conditions because of independence, we obtain for the parameters q_i, $i \in \{1,2,3\}$, the following simplified expressions:

$$q_1 = (1-R_1)/R_1$$

$$q_2 = (1-R_2)/R_2$$

$$q_3 = (1-R_1)(1-R_2)/R_1R_2$$

Their sum amounts to

$$q_1+q_2+q_3 = (1-R_1R_2)/R_1R_2,$$

resulting in a factor

$$Z = 1-R_1R_2 = 1-R,$$

where R represents the reliability of each diverse version.

Though being well-conscious of the restrictions implicit in the underlying assumptions and limiting their general applicability, in case of low dependence estimations we may nonetheless regard this very particular result as a simple rule of thumb for decision-making to be interpreted as follows:

"If the failure probability of each single version is lower than the cost quotient Q, then choose the fine granularity, otherwise the coarse one."

11.5 Mixed Solutions

Apart from both extreme cases just examined, where voting is uniformly performed with respect to the same (fine or coarse) granularity, under particular conditions the output might be more suitably treated by intermediate decision mechanisms varying according to the adjudicated variable or to past observations, as the ones described in the following.

Component-Specific Granularity

We may think of applications requiring output components x and y with considerably different levels of reliability resp. availability.

Variable x may represent a parameter without impact on system safety, or its incorrectness may be easily identifiable by means of a suitable check; its availability, however, may improve or simplify decisively system performance (e.g. the result of a sort procedure).

In this case, costs due to unavailability of x overcome those due to its incorrectness, resulting in a relatively high cost quotient $Q(x)$.

On the other hand, the output value y may be responsible for safety-relevant operations, requiring an ultrahigh reliability level. In case of undetected failure the damage caused may be extremely high, whereas an alarm signal putting the system into a safe state would merely result in an undangerous non-operational situation. Thus the cost quotient $Q(y)$ will amount to a quite low figure.

In case of such a decisive discrepancy between both cost quotients $Q(x)$ and $Q(y)$, it may be misleading to unify both distinct informations into a unique cost quotient Q, as done so far, without discriminating them. Under these particular circumstances it might be preferable to come to separate decisions with respect to the voting of the different variables. This will probably result in a fine voter for the value x and in a coarse one for y.

Degraded Operation

Component-specific decisions may be carried out not only between both the possibilities of fine or coarse granularity, but also within the elementwise comparison of a fine voter.

In fact, the considerations about fine granularity presented in section 11.4 assumed a system transition to the safe state as soon as one of the output values did not achieve a majority consensus. This, however, might not be necessary.

We can imagine a situation where the variable x out of the output pair (x,y) is required to perform the essential service to be achieved by the system, whereas the value y may be intended as a supplementary function, necessary indeed to complete the task specified, but possibly superfluous

for a degraded service fundamentally based on the operation resulting from
x.

Of course, such an interrelation between x and y may also be symmetrical, in case that both single values complete each other, but do not absolutely need each other to fulfill degraded services.

In both cases we should define voter such as to ensure as often as possible a majority value for an essential function, allowing at least partial system availability in case of an unavailable, not strictly necessary component.

Self-Adjusting Granularity

Beside varying with respect to the single output components, a voting system may change its granularity also with respect to time, taking into account the information available from past voter executions.

The decision on fine granularity is clearly based on the expectation that failures will occur in different output elements for different versions, so that they can be masked by a separate voting, as shown in the following example:

$$
\begin{array}{lll}
\text{1. Version:} & (a,b) & \text{correct} \\
\text{2. Version:} & (x,b) & x \ne a \text{ incorrect} \\
\text{3. Version:} & (a,y) & y \ne b \text{ incorrect} \\
\hline
\text{fine voter:} & (a,b) & \text{correct}
\end{array}
$$

Therefore, each time a consensus value is reached for a variable as the result of a majority of two versions against a minority of one version, this value will be accepted as the correct one and the only program with a diverging result will be considered as the only incorrect version with respect to that particular variable.

This information about the minority version can be objectively observed and easily memorized for each output element.

Once the voter identifies for the same output variable during more voting processes two different minority versions, the 2-against-1 decisions performed so far should become suspect.

In fact, the varying minority version implies that we successively trusted different majority pairs, decreasing the confidence we had until then in the ones we considered as correct.

At such a critical point, the granularity of the element in question should be better coarsened.

11.6 Conclusion

The considerations presented so far are intended to provide guidelines and rules capable of supporting the decision activity during the development of fault-tolerant software by permitting to define the optimal adjudicator for any particular application class.

In each specific case to be considered, a comparison of the underlying reliability and availability requirements will allow to determine the best voter to be chosen in order to minimize the expected loss.

References

[BAR85] M. Barnes, P.G. Bishop, B. Bjarland, G. Dahll, D. Esp P. Humphreys, J. Lahti, L. Yoshimura, A. Ball, O. Hatlevold: PODS (The Project on Diverse Software). OECD Halden Reactor Project, HPR-323, June 1985

[BAR87] M. Barnes, P. Bishop, B. Bjarland, G. Dahll, D. Esp, J. Lahti, H. Välisuo, P. Humphreys: Software Testing and Evaluation Methods (The STEM Project). OECD Halden Reactor Project, HWR-210, May 1987

[TSO87] K.S. Tso, A. Avizienis: Community Error Recovery in N-Version Software: A Design Study with Experimentation. FTCS-17, July 1987, IEEE Computer Society Press

Appendix

Derivation of figures in 11.3.2

Let I denote the input set of the diverse versions. For each program or program pair $P \in \{C,H,V,CH,CV,HV\}$ and for each output variable $Y \in \{DL, OS, LS, CB, AL, ST, TA, TF0, TF2, TF4, TF5\}$ we define the subsets

$$F_P \quad = \quad \{X \in I \mid P \text{ applied on } X \text{ produces incorrect output}\}$$

and

$$F_P(Y) = \quad \{X \in I \mid P \text{ applied on } X \text{ produces incorrect } Y\}$$

consisting of all inputs X causing a failure in the outputs, resp. in the output variable Y.

With this notation, we can stepwise observe:

1) $|F_V| = 388 = 33 + 87 + 28 + 240 =$

$$= |F_V(DL)| + |F_V(LS)| + |F_V(TF5)|$$

$$\Rightarrow \quad \left\{ \begin{array}{l} F_V(DL) \cap F_V(LS) = \varnothing \\ F_V(DL) \cap F_V(TF5) = \varnothing \\ F_V(LS) \cap F_V(TF5) = \varnothing \end{array} \right.$$

2) $|F_{CV}| = 0 \Rightarrow F_C \cap (F_V(DL) \cup F_V(LS) \cup F_V(TF5)) = \varnothing$

3) $|F_{HV}(DL)| = |F_H(DL)| < |F_V(DL)| \Rightarrow F_H(DL) \subset F_V(DL)$

4) $|F_{HV}(LS)| = |F_H(LS)| = |F_V(LS)| \Rightarrow F_H(LS) = F_V(LS)$

5)   Statements 1), 3), and 4) imply $F_H(DL) \cap F_H(LS) = \varnothing$

6)   Statements 2), 3), and 4) imply $F_C \cap F_H(TF5) = F_{CH}$

7)   We infer from the table immediately: $F_H(TF5) \cap F_V(TF5) = \varnothing$

8)   Statements 1), 3), 4) and 7) imply

$$|F_H(TF5) \cap (F_V(DL) \setminus F_H(DL))| =$$

$$|F_{HV}| - |F_{HV}(DL)| - |F_{HV}(LS)| = 30$$

9)   Statements 1), 3), and 4) imply

$$|F_H(TF5) \cap (F_H(DL) \cup F_H(LS))| =$$

$$= - |F_H| + |F_H(TF5)| + |F_H(DL)| + |F_H(LS)| =$$

$$= -32428 + 32388 + 50 + 28 = 38$$

10) $|(F_H(DL) \cup F_H(LS)) \setminus F_H(TF5)| = 78 - 38 = 40$

Chapter 12

A Theoretical Evaluation
of the Acceptance Test
in Recovery Block Programming

Francesca Saglietti

12.1 Introduction

This chapter is intended to propose a theoretical evaluation of Recovery Block systems considering, in particular, the extent to which the degree of reliability achieved depends upon the choice of the underlying acceptance test program.

The existing definitions of the term "acceptance test" and some examples clearly show the high comprehensiveness of this term as well as the need for a more accurate and formal definition. In particular, in order to estimate reliability parameters, acceptance tests should be classified with respect to those attributes having a main impact on the fault-tolerance achieved.

Generally the acceptance test program is intended to act as a sieve on the results, filtering the correct ones (possibly multiple correct answers for each input) as well as the outputs which, though not being exact, still deviate from the correct solution within an acceptable range.

As the perfect construction of such a sieve often presents serious difficulties and may lead to a considerable increase of program complexity, development cost and execution time, in the general case it must be expected that, besides the points mentioned above, also some incorrect and unacceptable outputs can be let through; a well-designed test should not, however, reject admissible results. Thus, with respect to the reasons of its wrong behaviour - the rejection of reasonable outputs and the admission of unacceptable ones - the acceptance test can be compared with a map intended to represent bad outputs. Therefore, as a map may fail to reflect reality due to some design error (incorrectness) or due to its high scale (coarseness), these both attributes have been chosen as drivers for the following analysis of unsafe events.

12.2 General Features and Examples of Acceptance Tests

Some of the following existing definitions and explanations about the expression "Acceptance Test" clearly give evidence on the generality of this term as well as on the need for a more specific distinction within it:

"...a condition that is expected to be met by successful execution of the routines" [HEC79],

"...a sequence of statements which will raise an exception if the state of the system is not acceptable" [AND81],

"...a programmer-provided error detection measure and can therefore be as cursory or as comprehensive as the programmer wishes" [AND81],

"...not intended to guarantee complete correctness, ... a check on the acceptability of the results produced by a module" [AND81].

"...it is for the designer to decide on the appropriate level of rigour of the test" [HOR74].

A first rough distinction is given in [HEC79]: the test program can be designed to detect deviations from expected program execution, or to prevent unsafe output.

In fact, the term "acceptability" may not necessarily mean "correctness", but includes a wider range of values, which though actually representing wrong outputs, still may be used for the service requested as correct ones without incurring to a dangerous system state.

A first approach towards a systematic study of the design of acceptance tests was proposed by Hecht, where the techniques used were classified according to the following subdivision:

Satisfaction of Requirements

This technique tests conditions which must be met at the completion of program execution using primarily logical or mathematical relationships.

For example, the well-known "Eight Queens-problem" requiring eight queens to be located on a chessboard without threatening each other, can be suitably treated by an acceptance test which just verifies that each horizontal, vertical and diagonal does not contain more than one queen.

Also the sort problem can be tested for satisfaction of requirements checking that after execution the elements of a sequence are in a predefined order. One could also require the additional verification that the number of elements in the sorted set is equal to the number of elements in the original set. This would not yet yield a completely exhaustive test, since both sets need not be identical. Only the further proof that the sorted output sequence is obtained by a permutation of the elements of the input sequence would imply the program correctness, but it would also cause a considerable increase of program complexity and execution time.

A problem class particularly suitable to be tested by verifying the requirements is the case where the inverse of the function given by the specification exists and is simpler than the forward operation, as for the calculation of the square root.

Reasonableness Tests

Acceptance tests belonging to this class verify relationships that are expected to prevail for the controlled system on the basis of physical constraints.

For example, in the case of airspeed calculation the aerodynamic and structural capabilities of the airframe dictate a range for the admissible results; moreover, the maximum allowable acceleration could also be used to test the limited speed changes.

Accounting Checks

These methods are restricted in their applicability, being suitable only for transaction-oriented routines and covering only elementary mathematical operations. Nonetheless, they can be very useful in data processing.

A special case is represented by the checksum, which consists of a comparison of the total amount in the records before and after a transmission among processing stations.

Besides, a possibility of detecting errors due to incorrect transcriptions or due to lost or misrouted documents is given by the double-entry bookkeeping system where the total credits for all accounts must always equal the total debits for all accounts.

Computer Run Time Checks

This class of acceptance tests is the most cursory one, testing only for anomalous states in the program without special regard to the logical problem given by the underlying specification.

Unacceptable states are entered for example by division by zero, overflow, underflow or writing into write-protected memory-areas.

As clearly shown by the different types examined, the acceptance test can be cursory or comprehensive: this fact represents both a strength and a weakness, because the desirable comprehensiveness may lead to a large and complex acceptance test and therefore to high costs and proneness to design faults.

On the other hand, keeping the acceptance test simple, so that its run-time overheads are reasonable and the test itself is reliable will probably cause cursoriness. This situation is illustrated in table 12.1.

Table 12.1. Characteristics of cursory and comprehensive tests

cursory test	comprehensive test		characteristic
low degree of exhaustiveness	high degree of exhaustiveness	error detection capability	coarseness
low test coverage	high test coverage		
low design complexity	high design complexity		correctness
low design fault proneness	high design fault proneness		
low development costs	high development costs	cost	
short run time	long run time		
low storage requirements	high storage requirements		

For this reason, a further and more detailed classification of acceptance tests characterizing their behaviour by modelling their error detection capability and costs required, could be helpful for a rational selection of the suitable test for a given application. This is the intention of the following subsections.

12.3 Formal Definition of Acceptance Test Characteristics

In order to simplify the formal definition and modelling of the acceptance test, we introduce the following assumptions:

1) The number of distinct exact answers will be assumed to be equal for each input x belonging to the input set A. An estimation n of this number is supposed to be known. Thus we can expect for each input $x \in A$ n possible correct outputs $C_1(x),...,C_n(x)$ belonging to the output set B.

2) For each $x \in A$, the actual acceptability range $S_x \subset B$ dictated by the safety requirements will be identified with the set $\{C_1(x),..., C_n(x)\} \subset B$ consisting of correct answers with respect to the underlying computer precision.

This is not a very hard restriction, because the case of an arbitrary inaccuracy allowed by the given safety constraints may be modelled according to this assumption by simulating the calculations on a computer with a corresponding lower precision.

The function of the acceptance test is to give for each input $x \in A$ and each output $y \in B$ a decision rule, whether y can be accepted as a correct result for x or not.

Thus the test may be mathematically viewed as a mapping

$$T : A \times B \rightarrow \{0,1\}$$

with

$T(x,y) = 0$ implies that y is rejected as output to the input x

$T(x,y) = 1$ implies that y is accepted as output to the input x.

This is equivalent to saying that the mapping T defines for each input $x \in A$ a subset T_x of B:

$$T_x := \{y \in B \mid T(x,y) = 1\},$$

consisting of exactly all elements which are admitted by T as correct outputs of the input x.

As the fault-tolerant strategy represented by the Recovery Block system will admit outputs from these subsets T_x, whereas a safe execution is only granted by results belonging to S_x, the goodness of an acceptance test, i.e. its error detection capability, can be estimated by comparing both subsets for all inputs.

Of course, in particular the size and the location of each T_x with respect to the corresponding S_x will prove to be fundamental for the effectiveness of the acceptance test. They reflect the two characteristics - coarseness and correctness - which have been identified in the previous subsection and which will be now formally defined.

Definition 1

The *coarseness* K of the acceptance test T is given by dividing the mean number of elements in the test subsets T_x by the number of elements in the output set B, i.e.

$$K := \frac{E_x\,[\,|\,T_x\,|\,]}{b} \quad \text{with} \quad b := |B|$$

The coarseness of an arbitrary acceptance test has thus to lie between the two allowable extreme values given by the following special cases:

a) If $T_x = B$ for each $x \in A$, then T is an empty acceptance test, which accepts every output. In this case the coarseness K has a maximal value 1.

b) If $|T_x| = n$ for each $x \in A$, then T is a complete acceptance test, which accepts exactly n elements, considering them as the correct ones. In this case the coarseness K has a minimal value n/b.

Examples

The varying coarseness of acceptance tests to the same program speci-fication can be illustrated by the following examples based on a sort problem.

We consider the set of sequences of maximal length 3 with binary values as elements, sorted according to 0<1 (see table 12.2). Thus the input and output set A = B consists of 14 possible sequences (of length 1, 2 or 3). Among them there are 9 sorted ones.

Table 12.2. Sequences of maximal length 3

length	1	2	3	TOTAL
sequences + sorted – unsorted	0 + 1 +	00 + 01 + 10 – 11 +	000 + 001 + 010 – 011 + 100 – 101 – 110 – 111 +	
number of sequences	2	4	8	14
number of sorted sequences	2	3	4	9

A cursory test T_1 verifying only that the output sequence is sorted would therefore have the coarseness

$$K_1 = 9/14 = 0.64.$$

This does not guarantee that the length of the output sequence is equal to that of the input sequence, i.e. that no digit has been lost.

A more comprehensive test T_2, which further verifies that the output has the same length as the input, yields:

$|T_x| = 2$ for each of the 2 sequences with length 1,

$|T_x| = 3$ for each of the 4 sequences with length 2,

$|T_x| = 4$ for each of the 8 sequences with length 3.

With the mean value $E_x[|T_x|] = 48/14$ the coarseness of T_2 is then

$$K_2 = (1/14) \cdot (48/14) = 0.25.$$

Now it is ensured that the output sequence is ordered and is of the same length as the input sequence, but it is not guaranteed that it consists of the same elements as the original sequence.

The complete acceptance test T_3 is obtained by the additional requirement that the output sequence results by permutation of the input sequence. In this case we obviously get

$$|T_x| = 1 \quad \text{for each input sequence x,}$$

so that the completeness of this test is reflected by its minimal coarseness

$$K_3 = 1/14 = 0.07.$$

Definition 2

The acceptance test T is defined to be *correct*, if it accepts each correct output, i.e. if

$$T(x, C_j(x)) = 1 \quad \forall\, x \in A,\ \forall j \in \{1,...,n\}$$

or equivalently

$$C_j(x) \in T_x \quad \forall x \in A,\ \forall\, j \in \{1,...,n\}$$

As already mentioned, the coarseness and the correctness of a test are responsible for the occurrence of the two events leading to its wrong behaviour, i.e.:

the acceptance A_i of incorrect results,

the rejection R_c of correct results.

Their occurrence probabilities are connected in the following way:

The correctness of a test clearly implies $P(R_c) = O$.

The high coarseness of a simple test will probably yield a high value for $P(A_i)$ due to its cursoriness and a low value for $P(R_c)$ due to its design simplicity.

The low coarseness of a complicated test will probably cause a high $P(R_c)$ due to design errors and a low $P(A_i)$ due to its comprehensiveness.

Thus starting with an empty test, where we always have $P(A_j) = 1$ and $P(R_c) = O$, we expect with decreasing coarseness K a decreasing $P(A_j)$ and an increasing $P(R_c)$.

The problem considered in the next subsection is the choice of K in order to ensure a minimization of the dangerous error probability in a Recovery Block system.

12.4 An Error Model for the Acceptance Test Behaviour

An undetected failure of a system consisting of two alternates and an acceptance test program can be caused by one of the following three error sources:

the acceptance of an incorrect result of the first versions,

the rejection of a correct result of the first version, followed by the acceptance of an incorrect result of the second version,

the rejection of an incorrect result of the first version, followed by the acceptance of an incorrect result of the second version.

With the notation

C_j =   correctness of version j

I_j =   incorrectness of version j

A_j =   acceptance of version j

R_j =   rejection of version j

A_{ij} =   acceptance of incorrect result of version j

R_{ij} =   rejection of incorrect result of version j

R_{cj} =   rejection of correct result of version j

and $j \in \{1,2\}$, we can thus express the dangerous error E and its probability as follows

$$E = I_1 A_1 \cup C_1 R_1 I_2 A_2 \cup I_1 R_1 I_2 A_2$$

$$P_K(E) \quad = P(I_1) \cdot P(A_1 | I_1) + P(C_1 I_2) \cdot P(R_1 A_2 | C_1 I_2) + P(I_1 I_2) \cdot P(R_1 A_2 | I_1 I_2) =$$

$$= P(I_1) \cdot P(A_{i1}) + P(C_1 I_2) \cdot P(R_{c1} A_{i2}) + P(I_1 I_2) \cdot P(R_{i1} A_{i2})$$

In order to be able to evaluate the probabilities of joint events occurring in this formula, we have to examine the different classes of possible dependencies by which they are linked together. We can distinguish the following three categories:

Dependence among Parallel Versions (Type 1)

This is the classical concept of failure dependence, already analyzed in previous chapters. Due to the problem complexity and to human factors, we must expect some inputs to be more difficult to be treated than other ones and thus to be particularly prone to cause common failures in the versions of a Recovery Block system.

Dependence between the Acceptance Test and Each Version (Type 2)

Similarly to the previous case we must consider the possibility of common errors in the design of a program and of its test. The probability of such a double failure occurrence will obviously depend to a great extent on the similarity in the construction of both components. In general, failure dependence between alternate and acceptance program need not be as high as for parallel versions; in the latter case the programmers' diverse reasoning during the development has to start at a common point S given by the problem specification and to move in parallel directions towards the same goal G, as shown in fig. 12.1.

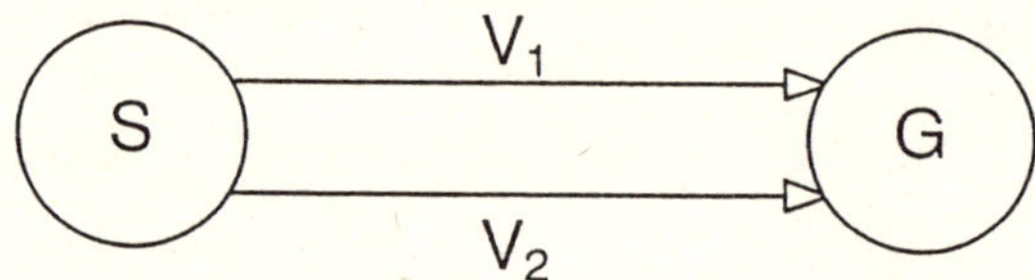

Fig. 12.1.   Diversity achieved by parallel versions V_1 and V_2

Of course, this schema can also be applied to an acceptance test, but in general the verification achieved by a Recovery Block strategy offers more flexibility, allowing to use an actual result to check its reasonableness, according to fig. 12.2.

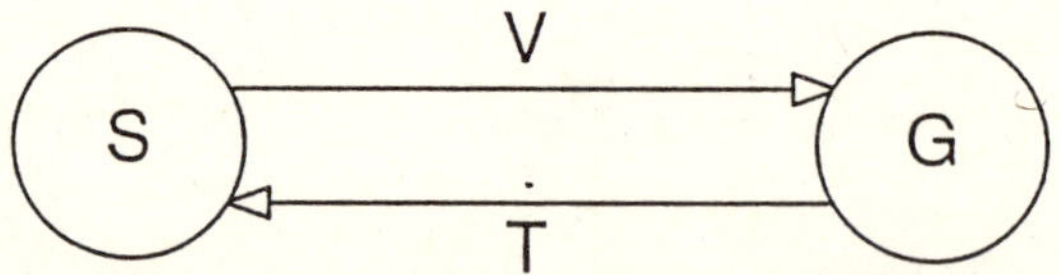

Fig. 12.2.   Diversity achieved by acceptance test T for Version V

Due to the inverse directions of reasoning one should expect a lower probability of common errors. Nonetheless, in each particular case one has also to estimate the extent of commonalities in the implementations of program and test, enforcing dissimilarity as often as possible. For example, for the case of the aforementioned "Eight Queens-problem", a check for satisfaction of requirements implemented in the same way as done in the routine to be tested would certainly increase our expectation of double failures, in spite of the opposite directions of the two approaches shown in fig. 12.2.

On the other hand, the inverse way of thinking illustrated there will give confidence in an independent failure behaviour in case that the calculation of the inverse function implemented by the acceptance test T is particularly simple and does not require any subprogram common to the original version. This is for example the case of the square function to test the correctness of a program for calculating the square root.

Dependence of Successive Executions of the Acceptance Test (Type 3)

A third class of dependence is represented by the correlation between successive applications of the test to the diverse alternatives. In fact, if the acceptance test rejects the result of the first version, it will be applied to the second variant with respect to the same input, but due to the version dependence described under point 1) the rejection of the first result will clearly have a considerable impact on the subsequent test behaviour. If we consider, for example, the case of three parallel versions which have been correctly developed on the basis of a problem specification with a unique solution for each input, then we easily see that, as the three programs always compute identical outputs, the rejection of the first of them will automatically imply the rejection of the second and of the third. This consideration extends some of the existing models, as the one presented in [SCO83], which does not take this possibility into account.

Of course, there is a direct relation between the type-1-dependence and the type-3-dependence. In fig. 12.3 all the dependence classes described are summarized for the case of two versions V_1 and V_2 and the corresponding applications T_1 and T_2 of the test T on them:

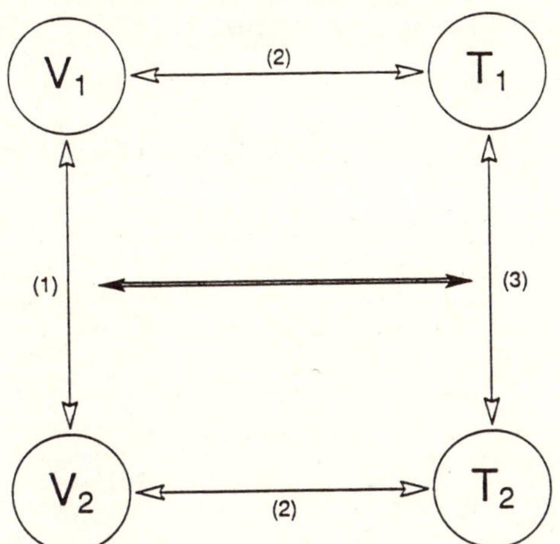

Fig. 12.3. Dependence classes

If we now look again at the expression for the dangerous error probability, we can distinguish and indicate the different correlation types which affect the single terms:

$$P_K(E) = P(I_1) \cdot P(A_{i1}) + P(C_1 I_2) \cdot P(R_{c1} A_{i2}) + P(I_1 I_2) \cdot P(R_{i1} A_{i2})$$

$$\quad (2) \qquad\quad (1) \qquad\quad (2)\ (2) \qquad\quad (1) \qquad\quad (2)\ (2)$$

$$\qquad\qquad\qquad\qquad\qquad\qquad (3) \qquad\qquad\qquad\qquad (3)$$

With respect to different coarseness measures, the probabilities of joint events may be estimated in order to choose an optimal acceptance test minimizing $P_K(E)$.

These considerations can be easily extended to more general optimization procedures, which, apart from the mere evaluation of the dangerous error probability, also take into account both the cost of the acceptance test and the loss to be expected.

The total costs involved by construction and execution of an acceptance test with coarseness K will be indicated by C(K). They include the development of the test, its run-time and its storage.

On the other hand, the expected loss L(K) during mission time can be expressed as

$$L(K) = P_k(E) \cdot N \cdot L,$$

where L represents the mean loss caused by a dangerous error occurrence and N indicates the number of (independent) program executions during mission time.

A comparison of both costs C(K) and L(K) can lead - dependent on the safety constraints of the specific application - to one of the following three strategies:

1. To limit the expected loss L(K)

   This yields an upper bound for the coarseness of the acceptance test to be chosen (and thus a lower bound for its costs).

2. To limit the test costs C(K)

   This yields a lower bound for the coarseness of the acceptance test to be chosen (and thus a lower bound for the expected loss).

3. To minimize the total costs C(K) + L(K)

   This yields an optimal value for the coarseness of the acceptance test to be chosen.

12.5 Conclusion

This chapter proposed a study about the role of acceptance tests in achieving fault-tolerance by means of Recovery Blocks.

Existing definitions and classifications of testing programs show a large variety of possible requirement levels with different consequences on the error detection capability of the test as well as on its complexity in terms of design correctness, development cost and execution overhead.

After having formally defined the correctness and the coarseness of an acceptance test and illustrated their expected relationship, the impact of both characteristics on the dangerous error probability of a Recovery Block system has been analyzed.

To do this, different types of event dependencies were considered together with their influence on particular critical situations.

The resulting error model can be useful in order to optimize the choice of testing coarseness with respect to safety or cost aspects.

References

[HOR74] J. J. Horning, H. C. Lauer, P. M. Melliar-Smith, B. Randell: A Program Structure for Error Detection and Recovery. Proc. Conf. on Operating Systems: Theoretical and Practical Aspects, IRIA, pp. 172-187, 1974

[AND81] T. Anderson, P.A. Lee: Fault-Tolerance - Principles and Practice. Prentice/Hall International, 1981

[HEC79] H. Hecht: Fault-tolerant Software. IEEE Transactions on Reliability, Vol. R-28, No. 3, August 1979

[SCO83] R.K. Scott, J.W.Gault, D.F. McAllister: Modelling Fault-Tolerant Software Reliability. Proc. Third Symposium on Reliability in Distributed Software and Database Systems, 15-27, Silver Spring, MD, U.S.A, IEEE Comput. Soc. Press, 1983

Chapter 13

Location of Checkpoints
by Considering Information Reduction

Francesca Saglietti

13.1 Introduction

All the fault-tolerant approaches proposed in the previous chapters are
essentially concerned with a fundamental question, which has long been
neglected: where to locate the checkpoints, i.e. which intermediate results
(beside the final output) should be diversely checked in order to optimize the
achievement of fault-tolerance.

The solution of this problem is highly affected by an underlying trade-off:
of course, the more checkpoints are inserted into a software product, the
less is the probability of undetected errors in the output or in internal
variables; on the other hand, each check implies an overhead in time,
testing effort and possibly creates synchronization problems; moreover, the
degree of similarity in the diverse approaches may radically increase if too
many parameters have to be commonly specified.

This chapter is intended to present a study on this topic, analyzing in
particular the impact of the reduction of information throughout a program
on the effectiveness of checkpoints.

13.2 Failure Masking

Investigations about software failure probability usually focus on identifying
possible critical intermediate steps within a program, where so far correct
information x may be wrongly handled by some function f resulting in an
incorrect parameter f(x), as shown in fig. 13.1.

Most testing strategies based on structural or functional properties are
meant to discover such erroneous data-handling by checking as
exhaustively as possible the intermediate results f(x) or the final outputs,
generally assuming that their correctness will automatically imply the
validity of all the previous calculations involved.

This implicit assumption is the main reason why the opposite situation is
hardly taken into account, i.e. the possibility of incorrect variables x being
transformed by some correct mapping f into exact values f(x), as illustrated
by fig. 13.2.

It may be objected that this case is a non-critical one, supposing the
automatic re-establishment of a correct state after an intermediate failure
and that, therefore, it should not need any particular attention.

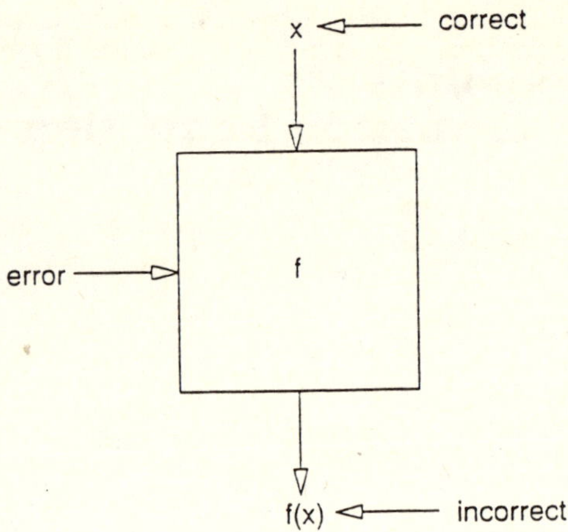

Fig. 13.1. Situation usually considered by reliability approaches

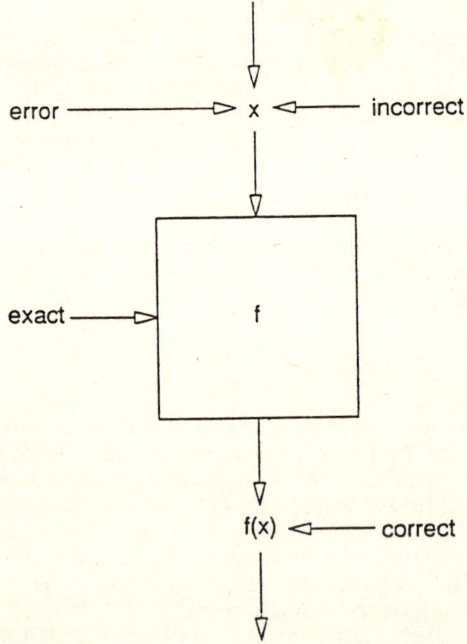

Fig. 13.2. Situation hardly considered by reliability approaches

Unfortunately, it cannot be generally excluded that the erroneous contents of x may be used for further operations during the same or future executions, as can be easily imagined in case of internal variables.

Therefore, this possibility should be generally taken into account when applying any testing strategy and in particular when locating checkpoints into a program, as their efficiency will mainly depend on their capability of intermediate failure detection.

A further objection might be that the particular situation described in fig. 13.2 is highly improbable to occur. This is true for particular functions f, but not necessarily for any mapping, as we will recognize by means of some examples in the following section.

13.3 Function Classes Reducing Information

In general, for an arbitrary function f, we can represent the probability of occurrence of the conditional event A to be considered by

$$P_f(A) := P\{f(x) \text{ correct} \mid x \text{ incorrect}\} .$$

This expression may not be generally quantifiable, as the conditional probability also depends on different possible types of incorrectness in x. For special cases this formula will be evaluated in a later section.

Anyway, we immediately realize that this probability factor $P_f(A)$ highly depends on the *loss of information* caused by applying f on x.

In fact, in case of a 1-to-1 mapping the event A cannot occur at all, i.e. $P_f(A) = 0$, because the correct $f(x)$ of a bijection f results as the functional value of one x only, and this must then obviously be the exact one.

As soon as the function f is not supposed to be injective anymore, i.e. if more different variables $x_1 \neq x_2$ are mapped on the same element $f(x_1) = f(x_2)$, however, the event A becomes possible, sometimes even with realistically high occurrence probabilities.

Of course, the underlying reduction of information is mainly responsible for these probability measures.

In case of addition of real numbers:

$$+ : \mathbf{R} \times \mathbf{R} \rightarrow \mathbf{R}$$

a correct sum of incorrect terms is highly improbable, whereas its restriction on integers

$$+ : \mathbf{Z} \times \mathbf{Z} \rightarrow \mathbf{Z}$$

would increase the occurrence probability $P_f(A)$, as compensation of two errors due to integer deviations might be regarded as a little more frequent.

Also distance metrics in a euclidean space as

$$d : \mathbf{R}^3 \times \mathbf{R}^3 \rightarrow \mathbf{R}_0^+$$

$$d(a,b) := \mid a\text{-}b \mid$$

will imply a reduction of information, as points b belonging to the same sphere around a will be mapped on the same radius value.

The previous examples were representative in that information contained in a pair (a,b) of variables is reduced by combining both of them in one figure by means of a more or less non-injective mapping.

The more reduction of information will be expected from functions mapping a pair (a,b) on one of both pair components a or b, determining which one from case to case according to their relationship.

Typical examples for this special type of information reduction are the maximum and minimum functions on real values given by:

$$\text{max: } \mathbf{R} \times \mathbf{R} \to \mathbf{R}$$

$$\max(a,b) \; := \begin{cases} a & \text{if } b \le a \\ b & \text{if } a \le b \end{cases}$$

$$\text{min: } \mathbf{R} \times \mathbf{R} \to \mathbf{R}$$

$$\min(a,b) \; := \begin{cases} a & \text{if } a \le b \\ b & \text{if } b \le a \end{cases}$$

A particular loss of information is achieved when the pair (a,b) is not mapped by turns on one of both components a or b as just seen, but rather always on a given one of them or on a constant, whereas the other one can be regarded as being exclusively responsible to monitor the correct value choice.

This may be illustrated by restricting the previous mappings max and min on boolean values $\mathbf{B} := \{0,1\}$ obtaining the logical disjunction and conjunction:

$$\vee : \quad \mathbf{B} \times \mathbf{B} \to \mathbf{B}$$

$$a \vee b \; := \max(a,b) = \begin{cases} b & \text{if } a = 0 \\ 1 & \text{if } a = 1 \end{cases} \quad = \quad \begin{cases} a & \text{if } b = 0 \\ 1 & \text{if } b = 1 \end{cases}$$

$$\wedge : \quad \mathbf{B} \times \mathbf{B} \to \mathbf{B}$$

$$a \wedge b \; := \min(a,b) = \begin{cases} 0 & \text{if } a = 0 \\ b & \text{if } a = 1 \end{cases} \quad = \quad \begin{cases} 0 & \text{if } b = 0 \\ a & \text{if } b = 1 \end{cases}$$

Here we may separately regard each variable as monitoring either the control flow or the data flow, so that a failure in one component, i.e. a data flow error, can only be observed if the alternate parameter driving control flow will allow it.

This effect is even increased in case of functions mapping the variables on constants determined by given properties of the argument.

One of them is the sign function transforming real numbers in their sign:

$$\text{sign: } \mathbf{R} \to \{-1,0,1\}$$

$$\text{sign}(x) \quad := \begin{cases} -1 & \text{if } x < 0 \\ 0 & \text{if } x = 0 \\ 1 & \text{if } x > 0 \end{cases}$$

Another one maps x on $\mathbf{B}$ depending on whether it belongs to a pre-defined set S or not:

$$\text{ind}_S: \mathbf{R} \to \mathbf{B}$$

$$\text{ind}_S(x) := \begin{cases} 0 & \text{if } x \notin S \\ 1 & \text{if } x \in S \end{cases}$$

Finally, the degenerate case opposite to the first one, i.e. with $P_f(A)=1$, is represented by a constant mapping $f \equiv \text{const}$, where const is the only correct value of $f(x)$ for any variable x.

On the whole we can summarize the different types of information reduction just identified in the following table 13.1.

Table 13.1. Identified function classes reducing information

FUNCTION CLASS	EXAMPLE
f injective, $P_f(A) = 0$	$\text{sqrt} : R_0^+ \times R_0^+ \to R_0^+$
f non–injective on "larger" domain	$+ \ : R \times R \to R$ $d \ : R^3 \times R^3 \to R_0^+$
f non–injective on "smaller" domain	$+ \ : Z \times Z \to Z$
input variables alternatively driving control or data flow	$\max : R \times R \to R$ $\min \ : R \times R \to R$
input variables separately driving control or data flow	$\text{or} \quad : B \times B \to B$ $\text{and} \ : B \times B \to B$
input variables driving only control flow	$\text{sign} : R \to \{-1, 0, 1\}$ $\text{ind}_S : R \to B$
f constant, $P_f(A) = 1$	$f \ : R \to \{\text{const}\}$

13.4 Impact of Information Reduction on Failure Dependence

Beside playing an important role in the question of locating suitable checkpoints, capable of detecting errors in internal variables, information reduction can also have an impact on the failure dependence of diverse versions. To study this effect, we may consider the situation shown in fig. 13.3, where the same parameter x has been diversely programmed as the value of variable x_1 resp. x_2:

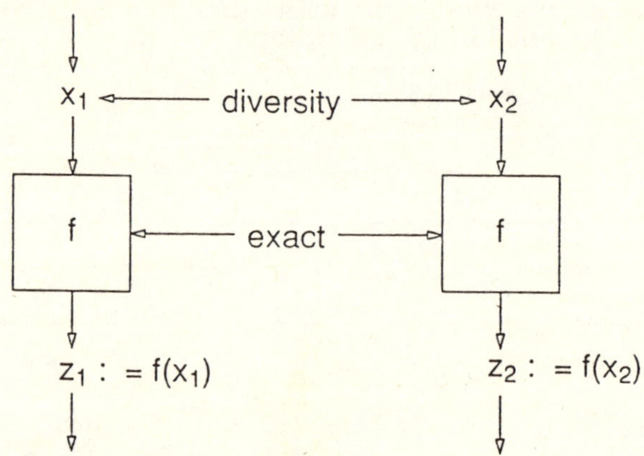

Fig. 13.3. Information reduction in diverse versions

In particular, in the following we will assume f to be such a simple operation as to be exactly implemented (e.g. s.table 13.1) and to cause an information reduction given by $P_f(A)$; in this case we obtain for the failure probability $P(z_i)$ of z_i, $i \in \{1,2\}$:

$$P(z_i)= P(x_i)\cdot P\{z_i \text{ incorrect} \mid x_i \text{ incorrect}\}=$$

$$= P(x_i)\,(1-P_f(A)) = P(x_i)\cdot c_f, \quad i\in\{1,2\},$$

where $P(x_i)$ represents the error probability in variable x_i and c_f denotes the complement of the reduction factor.

An analogous notation for the common failure probability yields:

$$P(z_1z_2) = P(x_1x_2)\cdot P\{z_1 \text{ and } z_2 \text{ incorrect} \mid x_1 \text{ and } x_2 \text{ incorrect}\}$$

Due to the expected failure dependence among diverse versions, in general this conditional probability will decisively overcome the value $(c_f)^2$ given by assuming independence and in particular cases of extremely high dependence it may even amount to the same factor c_f related to the single probabilities. Anyway, on the basis of

$$P\{z_1 \text{ and } z_2 \text{ incorrect} \mid x_1 \text{ and } x_2 \text{ incorrect}\} \geq (c_f)^2,$$

we obtain for the dependence factors of x and z:

$$P(z_1z_2)/P(z_1)P(z_2) \geq P(x_1x_2)/P(x_1)P(x_2)$$

In other words, after a reducing function we should generally expect an increasing failure dependence. In particular, even in case of valid arguments for an independent failure behaviour at the level of value x (as forcing as much as possible dissimilarity in the calculations), we cannot extend this assumption on the variable z resulting from x by information reduction.

This may be one of the reasons for some surprisingly high, experimentally observed failure dependence factors, as pointed out in [BIS88a] with regard to the experiences gained in [BAR85] and in [KNI86]. More about this topic after having analyzed in detail the case of binary logic.

13.5 Information Reduction for Binary Values

As already noted, binary operations represent a very particular case of information reduction, as their discreteness combines the boolean data deleting part of it according to a predefined algorithm.

In this section we will look in detail at the reduction induced by the binary disjunction "OR". More precisely, we will consider here the vector x consisting of two binary components a and b, x=(a,b), which will be mapped on z by OR, i.e. $z=OR(x)=a \vee b$, according to fig. 13.4.

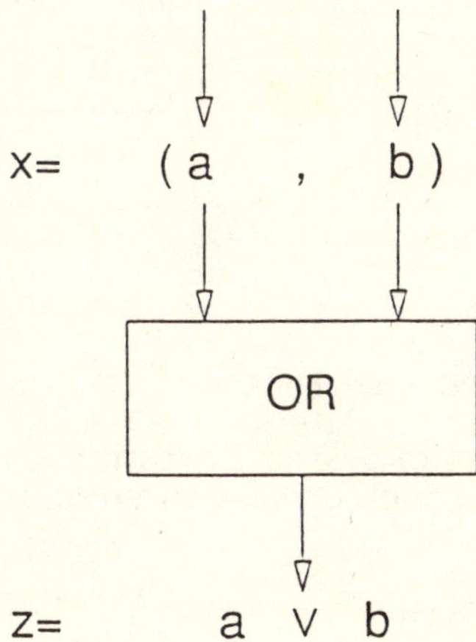

Fig. 13.4. Information reduction by binary disjunction

In the following we will estimate the reduction factor:

$$P_\vee(A) = P\{ a \vee b \text{ correct} \mid (a,b) \text{ incorrect}\}$$

$$= P\{ a \vee b \text{ correct} \mid a \text{ incorrect} \vee b \text{ incorrect}\}$$

from the following implications

$$(a \vee b = 0) \Rightarrow ((a = 0) \wedge (b = 0))$$

$$(a \vee b = 0 \text{ correct}) \Rightarrow ((a=0 \text{ correct}) \wedge (b=0 \text{ correct}))$$

$$(a \vee b = 1) \Rightarrow ((a = 1) \vee (b = 1))$$

$$(a \vee b = 1 \text{ correct}) \Rightarrow$$

$$(a=1 \text{ correct}) \vee (b=1 \text{ correct}) \vee (a \text{ incorrect} \wedge b \text{ incorrect} \wedge a \neq b)$$

Assuming independent variables a,b with negligible common failure probability, this yields:

$$P_\vee(A) = \frac{P\,(a \text{ incorrect} \wedge b = 1 \text{ correct}) + P\,(b \text{ incorrect} \wedge a = 1 \text{ correct})}{P\,(a \text{ incorrect}) + P\,(b \text{ incorrect})}$$

Analogous arguments apply on the diverse system shown in fig. 13.5.

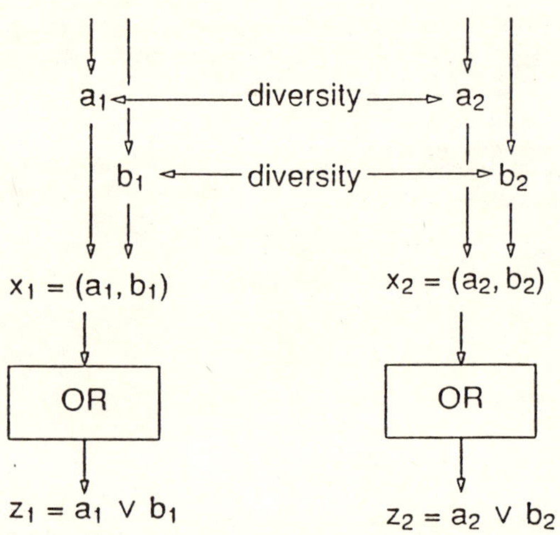

Fig. 13.5. Binary disjunction of diverse conditions

In case of common failures of z_1 and z_2 resulting from uncommon errors affecting different variables in each diverse version, e.g. a_1 and b_2, we obtain in the notation of chapter 13.4:

$$P(z_1) = P(a_1) \cdot P(z_1 \text{ incorrect} \mid a_1 \text{ incorrect}) = P(a_1) \cdot P(b_1 = 0)$$

$$P(z_2) = P(b_2) \cdot P(z_2 \text{ incorrect} \mid b_2 \text{ incorrect}) = P(b_2) \cdot P(a_2 = 0)$$

$$\Rightarrow \; P(z_1 z_2) \,/\, P(z_1)P(z_2) = (P(x_1 x_2)/P(x_1)P(x_2)) \,/\, P(0)$$

where P(0) denotes the probability of zero as the correct final output for variable z.

This was the main result reported in [BIS88a] and verified in [BIS88] by means of the following table 13.2 related to experimental data obtained in the PODS/STEM projects. They validate the theory just presented with respect to two different operational profiles resulting in different probabilities P(0).

It has to be pointed out that the above statements only hold under the restrictions mentioned before and assumed in the original paper [BIS88a]. This obviously limits the applicability of this method on particular cases. In general, estimations of information reduction will require more complex calculations taking into account possible dependencies due to common errors.

Table 13.2. Change of dependency with varying P(0) (from [Bis88])

P(0) = 0.0257		
Bug Pair	Dependency Factor	
	Measured	Predicted
V06,C16	38.2 ± 0.4	38.9
V13,C16	37.8 ± 0.4	38.9

P(0) = 0.591		
Bug Pair	Dependency Factor	
	Measured	Predicted
V06,C16	1.65 ± 0.02	1.692
V13,C16	1.41 ± 0.02	1.692

13.6 Location of Checkpoints

The aim of the present work is to make use of the theory on information reduction just proposed to support the decision phase on suitably locating checkpoints into fault-tolerant software.

The previous considerations on the loss of information along a control flow path have implied that sometimes the additional insertion of intermediate checkpoints may be more adequate than the mere verification of the final result. On the other hand, checking an internal variable implies an overhead in time and testing effort. Moreover, in case that a variable is checked by comparing it with a diverse alternative, each superfluous recovery point possibly causes an unnecessary effort due to synchronization problems as well as an undesired reduction of version dissimilarity, which may reveal as crucial with respect to common failures.

Bearing well in mind this trade-off, we intend to establish a rule to determine the optimal number and location of checkpoints.

To do this, we have to evaluate the reliability improvement expected to be achieved by each intermediate checking and to decide whether it is sufficiently promising by comparing it with the possible draw-backs resulting from cost and failure dependence.

To clarify the concept, let us apply this strategy on a particularly simple situation consisting of the evaluation of a function h combining three variables a, b and c; h may be the result of the composition of two mappings f and g on pairs of inputs:

$$h(a,b,c) = g(f(a,b,),c)$$

In this case, the question would be whether to insert an additional checkpoint CP for the intermediate value $y = f(a,b)$. Both alternatives without and with the insertion of CP are shown in fig. 13.6.

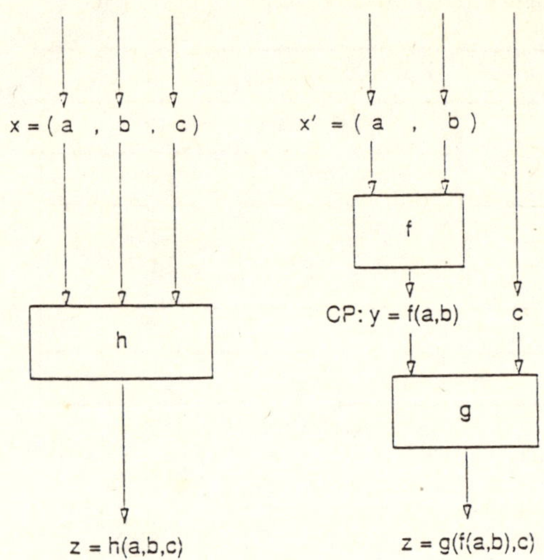

Fig. 13.6. Insertion of the intermediate checkpoint CP

Assuming perfect checks of correctness by means of correct and exhaustive acceptance tests, we may compare for both cases the error detection incapability $P(x')$ with respect to the incorrect internal variable $x' = (a,b)$. In the first situation we obtain by the only verification of the final result z:

$$P_I(x') = P\{z \text{ correct} \mid x' \text{ incorrect}\}$$

In the second situation we suppose having passed the test of correctness of z as well as the one concerning the intermediate result y:

$$P_{II}(x') = P\{z \text{ correct} \wedge y \text{ correct} \mid x' \text{ incorrect}\}$$

To evaluate the difference of both conditional probabilities, we introduce the following information reduction factors induced by the functions f and g:

$$P_f \quad := P\{y \text{ correct} \mid x' \text{ incorrect}\}$$

$$P_g(y) \quad := P\{z \text{ correct} \mid y \text{ incorrect}\}$$

Then the improvement of error detectability achieved by inserting the additional check CP can be expressed as:

$$P_I(x') - P_{II}(x') = P\{z \text{ correct} \wedge y \text{ incorrect} \mid x' \text{ incorrect}\}$$

$$= P_g(y) \cdot (1 - P_f)$$

Thus, by estimating the amount of information reduced by each mapping, we easily obtain the impact of checkpoint CP on the overall fault-tolerance achievement. By comparing this value with the costs expected to be additionally required by CP, we obtain a simple decision rule, which can be applied during the testing phase of conventional software as well as during the definition phase of fault-tolerant architectures.

13.7 Example

In this section we apply the strategy just suggested on the exemplifying case given by the disjunction of three binary values:

$$h(a,b,c) = a \vee b \vee c.$$

This may be interpreted as the repeated application of the usual disjunction, i.e.

$$h(a,b,c) = g(f(a,b),c)$$

with

$$g \equiv f \equiv OR.$$

Assuming, as before, a,b,c to be independent with negligible common failure probability, we may evaluate the information reduction of f and g by

$$1-P_f \quad = P\{a \vee b \text{ incorrect} \mid (a,b) \text{ incorrect}\} \cong$$

$$\cong P\{a \text{ incorrect} \mid (a,b) \text{ incorrect}\} \cdot P\{b=0\} +$$

$$+ P\{b \text{ incorrect} \mid (a,b) \text{ incorrect}\} \cdot P\{a=0\}$$

Supposing further that a and b are equally failure-prone, this yields:

$$1-P_f \cong [P\{a=0\} + P\{b=0\}]/2$$

Similarly, we obtain for g

$$P_g(a \vee b) \qquad = P\{ (a \vee b) \vee c \text{ correct} \mid a \vee b \text{ incorrect} \}$$

$$= P\{ c=1 \}$$

On the whole, this results in the positive impact Imp(a∨b) of the intermediate (a∨b)-checking on internal reliability:

$$Imp(a \vee b) = [P\{a=0\}+P\{b=0\}] \cdot P\{c=1\}/2$$

The right-hand side relating to correct values should be easily estimated by simulating the operational profile. The order of magnitude of the resulting figure gives a simple rule of thumb for deciding in favour of an additional checkpoint or against it.

In case, as for this example, of an associative and commutative mapping h allowing different decompositions:

$$a \vee b \vee c = (a \vee b) \vee c = a \vee (b \vee c) = (c \vee a) \vee b,$$

the above expression for Imp(a∨b) may be also evaluated for the remaining pairs of binary values, i.e. Imp(b∨c) and Imp(c∨a), in order to find the most suitable order allowing to maximize the effectiveness of checking.

13.8 Conclusion

This chapter proposed a study on information reduction throughout a program, identifying its impact on the effectiveness of checkpoints. Functions inducing a loss of information were identified and classified according to the expected probability of failure masking.

The impact of information reduction on failure dependence was studied in general and analyzed by means of a particular example.

The efficiency of a specific checkpoint was then evaluated by comparing failure masking effects occurring with and without the additional checking of intermediate values.

The conclusions reported and the strategy suggested are intended to support decision-making during the development of fault-tolerant software by identifying which internal variables or intermediate results should be checked by means of diversity in order to optimize fault-tolerance.

References

[BAR85] M. Barnes, P. Bishop, B. Bjarland, G. Dahll, D. Esp, P. Humphreys, J. Lahti, L. Yoshimura, A. Ball, O. Hatlevold: PODS (The Project on Diverse Software). OECD Halden Reactor Project, HWR-323, June 1985

[BIS88] P. G. Bishop: A Study of Software Failure Dependency Characteristics. IFAC Symposium SAFECOMP '88, Fulda, November 1988

[BIS88a] P. G. Bishop, F. D. Pullen: PODS Revisited - A Study of Software Failure Behaviour. Proc. of FTCS-18, IEEE 1988

[KNI86] J. C. Knight, N. G. Leveson: An Experimental Evaluation of the Assumption of Independence in Multiversion Programming. IEEE Transactions on Software Engineering, Vol. SE-12, No. 1, 1986

Chapter 14

Conclusions

Manfred Kersken

The efforts to put into operation software which is reliable, safe and available include a variety of constructive and analytical measures. Constructive measures comprise activities like top-down design, stepwise refinement etc., that means all the methods and rules to specify, design, code and maintain reliable software. The constructive measures are accompanied by analytical ones which are introduced in the various steps of the software life cycle to find faults and inefficient constructs and also to give an increasing confidence in the reliability of the software.

These analytical measures range from rigorous proofs of correctness, static and dynamic analysis to more informal procedures like desk inspections, walk-throughs, peer audits etc.

However, experience teaches that in spite of all these efforts software may fail due to remaining faults. The only way to cope with these residual faults is to mask them, and this is achieved by fault-tolerance techniques.

It should be stated that fault-tolerance is not the cure-all for the development and operation of reliable software. In most cases fault-tolerance is introduced to systems where a failure may cause great damage in terms of life and limb or financial terms. For such systems a combination of the available techniques to establish error-poor software (constructive approach) and to remove faults (analytical approach) should be applied, using fault-tolerance as a "last barrier" to mask the effects of residual faults.

14.1 Hardware Failure vs. Software Failure

Fault-tolerance in hardware is achieved by redundancy, i.e. by multiplication of the components which may fail. After detection of a failure the faulty component is switched off and the system is reconfigured according to the philosophy of the system architecture, as e.g. (hot or cold) standby, n-modular or hybrid n-modular redundancy. This approach is adequate for failures which occur due to changes of the physical features of components during aging (wear out), i.e. the failure arises from a fault which entered the component after some time of operation. It is not likely that multiple components are influenced by the same fault at the same time (exception: common cause faults), thus the system remains in operation and the faulty component may be replaced.

The replication of components is not a suitable means to overcome faults which are introduced from the very beginning, i.e. design faults. This type of fault may not become visible during some time of operation, but may later cause failure under specific circumstances of operation. The errors made during software development go into the product as such design faults, and due to the high logical complexity of software they are often hidden during a long time of operation.

Design faults will be the same in all versions of a merely replicated system. Therefore, if such a fault is encountered in multiple versions, it will result in exactly the same failure. In this case one of the advantages of multiple version software, the easy detection of failures by comparison of the results of the versions, does not apply. This problem can be solved to a great extent by designing each version dissimilar from the other ones, i.e. by introduction of diversity into the software system.

14.2 Diversity and the Design of Fault-tolerant Software Systems

The three main activities necessary to design fault-tolerant software are to establish

- diverse multiple versions,
- fault detection mechanisms,
- possibilities to recover from failure of a version.

As already mentioned, it is necessary to develop dissimilar versions of software to avoid common failures. There are two general possibilities to achieve this goal. One of them is the strictly independent development of the versions by different and totally separated persons. Independence is required because a common interpretation (or misinterpretation) of the problem to be solved may lead to common errors in the design. Within this approach it is assumed that independence automatically provides dissimilar versions of software. However, the kind of problem to be solved may suggest a specific algorithm, the educational background of the designers (universities, books) may be similar, a language may lead to specific solutions of a problem due to its features, etc. There is a lot of causes which might lead to similar software - and as a consequence to a higher probability of common failure - in spite of an independent development.

The other possibility is to force dissimilarity. The same team which has developed the primary version is also developing the other version(s) in a way which avoids common faults. General measures to force diversity are e.g. the use of different languages or of different development tools. More specific measures depend heavily on the actual application. The implementation of different algorithms for solving the same problem is a most powerful method to force diversity, e.g. solving a differential equation by analytical means in one version and by numerical approximations in the other one. However, the risk of common misinterpretation or "common wrong thinking" of a problem which the previous approach intended to avoid, may appear here.

Of course, there is a variety of approaches between those two. An example is the development by two independent teams with a person supervising the teams in order to avoid similar implementations.

14.3 Assessment of Software Fault-tolerance

Single Versions versus Multiple Versions

In the light of the discussion of the recent years about common failures in diverse software, it was felt necessary to investigate the question whether it is still worth to apply diversity in software systems. On the basis of theoretical and experimental results it is shown in chapter 3 that the probability of common failure is expected to be smaller as compared to the single failure probability of a twofold diverse system.

It is also interesting to provide assistance for the decision whether diversity should be applied to a system or whether the reliability of a single version should be enhanced by additional verification effort. Some cost considerations lead to a comparison between single and twofold diverse systems with respect to the effort required in each case. In particular, the probability of correct performance of at least one version of a diverse system consisting of two equally reliable programs can be bounded by a quadratic expression of the single reliabilities. Dependent upon this formula as well as upon the expected failure rate after a testing phase of a given length, one can thus decide on using diversity or on investing more effort in testing a single version. Some final observations about different failure effects allow to extend the previous considerations taking into account failure severity. The frequency of initiating events leading to undesired situations has to be estimated. Based on this estimation, upper values of the probability of dangerous failure can be calculated for a predefined risk vector.

Forced Diversity

The independent development of program versions does not necessarily guarantee the independence of failures of such a system. Therefore, an additional measure is to force potential residual faults in multiple versions to affect, in a different way, the final outputs. This in turn increases the error detectability. Forced diversity may be introduced via a dissimilar development process including different specification languages, algorithms, data structures, development tools, testing strategies, implementation languages, a.o.

In chapter 4 the improvement in failure behaviour due to forced diversity is investigated. The work started from published theoretical results which show that the increase in reliability which can be gained by forcing diversity in the development process is dependent on the choice of voter majority: a benefit may be obtained for 1-out-of-n systems, but not necessarily for (n+1)-out-of-(2n+1) systems. Published experimental data were used to confirm these results.

An extension of the existing theory is proposed, which does not only take into account the majority of the voter, but also its granularity.

Functional Diversity

Diversity, as it was interpreted up until now, starts from a specification which is common to the diverse versions. Faults within this specification, of course, cannot be tolerated by such a system. In many cases a problem can be specified in different ways, thus allowing to detect and tolerate failures due to specification faults. For assessment it is important to analyze the impact of functional diversity on the reliability of a software system. Doing this quantitatively implies that metrics characterizing the level of functional diversity must be determined. Efficient and meaningful metrics can only be found via appropriate modelling of the diverse specifications.

In chapter 5 a semantic modelling technique is described allowing the identification of crucial entities which are able to encapsulate the semantics of the different versions. These entities are called semantic functions and semantic domains. It can be said intuitively that many common semantic entities in the versions imply a low degree of diversity, and this leads to a higher amount of common faults in the diverse specifications. In order to quantify this intuitive concept.

-   an abstract definition of the degree of functional diversity was developed,

- a set of metrics allowing its measurement was derived,

- a method to evaluate the reliability of functionally diverse systems was devised through a fault analysis which is based on the architectural characteristics of the system and the complexity as well as the commonalities of the diverse versions.

To make these theoretical results useful, methods are proposed to identify the semantic entities inside the specifications, to outline their common parts and to evaluate their correctness. A specification language is proposed which provides support by means of particular constructs emphasizing the functional semantic aspects of the specifications.

Quantitative Assessment

In practice it is often very difficult, if not impossible, to compute the reliability of a diverse software system with dependent components. Therefore, in chapter 6, a study is performed which looks for an upper bound of the error involved in computations assuming independence among versions. This error bound depends on a factor which correlates the failure probabilities of single versions. The correlation factor is determined for the cases where a sufficient number of failure observations is available and where not. In the former case statistical inference methods are applied to estimate the correlation factor. The latter case uses path complexity measures obtained by static analysis to identify control flow structures being either common or dissimilar.

Dissimilarity in the Partition of the Input Space

The diversity achieved among versions may also be measured in terms of their input space subdivisions (chapter 7). According to a predefined equivalence relation, the paths through the control flow graph of a program define a partition of the input space. Similar partitions reflect a similar programming reasoning which may be measured by the deviation of the testing coverage curves.

Two metrics are proposed which provide information on the expected failure behaviour of the system and its testability.

Comparison of Mnemonics

A method has been developed which compares the dissimilarity of versions by matching their mnemonic patterns (chapter 8). It calculates the correlation between the codes by matching groups of mnemonics and looks for symmetry in the resulting histogram. It was assumed that similar programs would render symmetrical histograms "mirrored" around a central vertical line, whereas dissimilar programs would render rather asymmetrical histograms. This assumption, however, could not be verified.

A better way of measuring dissimilarity between versions would presumably be to compare the size and distribution of identical blocks of mnemonics. It was not possible, however, to develop such an approach within the time limits of the project.

FRIL Model Approach for Software Diversity Assessment

The information available about the dissimilarity/similarity of diverse versions may appear in form of measurable items as e.g. complexity measures of the control flow graph, test coverage, or number and size of commonly treated input subsets. But there is also subjective information available, e.g. from experts who judge algorithmic complexity, influence of different languages on diversity and many others. It would be desirable to combine both types of informations in order to support the judgement on the degree of diversity achieved in a software system from multiple points of view.

For this task a conceptual model was developed (chapter 9) which determines the diversity of versions by comparing whatever evidence is available with respect to these factors which are deemed to have an influence on diversity. To formulate this information in a consistent way the model was implemented as a prototype knowledge based system in FRIL language (Fuzzy Relational Inference Language). FRIL is capable of representing knowledge bases containing uncertainties of a probabilistic, fuzzy and evidential nature.

Fault Tolerance Model

The ultimate goal when trying to determine the degree of diversity among versions is to get insight in their dependent failure behaviour and to be able to obtain accurate reliability figures of fault-tolerant software systems. In chapter 10 an approach to model fault-tolerant software systems is described. The main innovative feature of this model is its ability to deal with correlated failure behaviour of the diverse versions. The modeling approach is generic, in the sense that it incorporates every kind of N-version-programming and recovery-block architecture. A computerized algorithm has been implemented which allows to automatically generate the (lengthy) formulae for the specific configurations considered.

Voter Granularity

The term granularity with respect to a voter denotes the size of the subsets of the outputs which are adjudicated (compared). The voter granularity is said to be "coarse" if consensus/discrepancy are determined at the level of complex types, respectively "fine" if adjudication is performed at a basic type level.

In practice the level of adjudication (complex or basic) is mostly given by the application, and a voter of suitable granularity must be designed. In chapter 11, it is shown that the granularity of the voter has an impact on the system reliability and availability, and guidelines are given which permit to define optimal adjudicators for different classes of application.

Acceptance Test Coarseness

The bottleneck with respect to redundancy and failure detection capability in recovery-block systems is the acceptance test. In chapter 12, the impact of the type of acceptance test on the safety of a recovery block system is investigated. The design of an acceptance test may lead to a considerable increase of the software system complexity, performance, and development costs. As a result, some incorrect results may pass this test, or some correct results may be rejected. In principle, an acceptance test may stretch out from a simple check of some syntactical features to a complete proof of correctness. The former one will most likely perform correctly, but will not detect many faulty results, whereas the latter would probably find all faults, but is too complex to be itself implemented in a fault-free manner. Chapter 12 describes a model of this trade-off which supports the choice of an acceptance test design optimizing between the extremes of a cursory and a comprehensive test.

Location of Checkpoints

During the design of fault-tolerant software the question arises at which level of execution the results should be adjudicated. This could be done after each action (calculation) performed by the versions or on the basis of the final results.

Assuming as an extreme case that the final result is only a binary yes/no decision which is resulting from complex computations, it can be easily seen that there is a loss of information between these computations and the final result. There is little information on which the adjudication could be based, thus failures may not be detected by the adjudicator.

On the other hand, if intermediate results are adjudicated very frequently, this implies a heavy constraint on design decisions towards diversity. In addition there is an overhead in execution time.

Bearing this in mind, a model is proposed in chapter 13 for the location of suitable intermediate checkpoints taking into account the loss of information during program execution.

14.4 Prospect

During our work on software fault-tolerance we have been often asked why we were concentrating on software only, not taking the view of the whole computer system. The good reason behind this question is of course that software per se cannot fulfill any task without a hardware environment. We think, however, that as long as there is a lack of understanding and describing the failure behaviour of software, the attempts to model computer systems are bound to be inaccurate, as a major component, i.e. software, is modelled inaccurately.

Concerning fault-tolerant software, models should allow to take into account the dependent failures of alternate versions of the software system. This has been done in the fault-tolerance model (chapter 10) of this book. However, dependency has to be determined, and the methods for this determination as well as the model itself have to be validated. Unfortunately, there is a lack of data from industrial fault-tolerant software systems, and also only few experimental data are available for validation. Within the REQUEST project we have used what was available in the open literature, but these data are clearly not sufficient for a sound validation approach.

Time and effort within the project did not allow to conduct experiments of its own. Fortunately, however, some projects are evolving in the ESPRIT Programme, whose results can be used complementary to the work performed in REQUEST. In the DARTS project (Demonstration of Advanced Reliability Techniques for Safety related computer systems) an experimental system comprising four diverse channels is developed. The objectives of DARTS (as taken from the project proposal) are:

1. To evaluate currently available methods and tools for creating and assessing computer based systems used in safety related applications by conducting a number of controlled experimental industrial trials to provide cost benefit indications.

2. To collect well founded sets of data on the creation of diverse versions for use by groups of researchers in Europe, both within ESPRIT and elsewhere, against which to validate proposed models and metrics of software diversity.

3. To carry out further research activity on diversity.

From these objectives it is obvious that the data collected during the experiment can be used for validation purposes.

Another related project in the ESPRIT Programme is SCOPE (Software Certification Of Programmes in Europe) whose data base on verification techniques may be exploited in order to identify relationships between safety parameters and measurable product attributes.

The PDCS project (Predictably Dependable Computing Systems) of the Basic Research Actions of the ESPRIT Programme addresses in one of its topics the provision of dependability through fault-tolerance. Clearly dependability models also need to be validated, and as far as this is done by experimental (or even real-world) data, the REQUEST work may benefit from these. Vice versa PDCS may take on board some of the REQUEST results of the kind described in the previous chapters.

This coincides with one of the objectives of this book: to present the work of the REQUEST fault-tolerance group at a level where researchers may take advantage of the results of further research and development towards achieving and assessing fault-tolerant computer systems.